COPTIC

A GRAMMAR OF ITS SIX MAJOR DIALECTS

LANGUAGES OF THE ANCIENT NEAR EAST DIDACTICA

COPTIC

A GRAMMAR OF ITS
SIX MAJOR DIALECTS

JAMES P. ALLEN

EISENBRAUNS | UNIVERSITY PARK, PA

Library of Congress Cataloging-in-Publication Data

Names: Allen, James P., 1945– author.
Title: Coptic : a grammar of its six major dialects / James P. Allen.
Description: University Park, Pennsylvania : Eisenbrauns, [2020] | Series: Languages of the
    ancient Near East didactica series | Includes bibliographical references and index.
Summary: "A current grammar of Coptic (the last stage of the ancient Egyptian language) that
    includes material from all six of its major dialects. Includes a chrestomathy of readings in the
    six dialects as well as a dictionary"—Provided by publisher.
Identifiers: LCCN 2020017979 | ISBN 9781646020645 (hardback)
Subjects: LCSH: Coptic language—Grammar. | Coptic language—Dialects—Grammar.
Classification: LCC PJ2033.A45 2020 | DDC 493/.2—dc23
LC record available at https://lccn.loc.gov/2020017979

Eisenbrauns is an imprint of The Pennsylvania State University Press.

The Pennsylvania State University Press is a member of the
Association of University Presses.

It is the policy of The Pennsylvania State University Press to use acid-free paper. Publications
on uncoated stock satisfy the minimum requirements of the National Standard for Information
Sciences—Permanence of Paper for Printed Library Material, ANSI Z39.48—1992.

Contents

PREFACE

This book was written not to supersede any of the excellent Coptic grammars currently available but because all of them, with minor exceptions (Till 1931, Steindorff 1951), deal with either Bohairic or Saidic, only two of the six major Coptic dialects. A reference grammar of *Coptic*, as opposed to Bohairic or Saidic, ought to include the other four dialects as well. That is what I have tried to do here.

Although this was written primarily as a reference grammar, I have included short exercises at the end of each chapter for those who may want to use it for instruction or self-instruction.

I am grateful to the two anonymous reviewers who carefully vetted my manuscript before publication; the work is better for their comments. I am also grateful to Dr. Christian Casey for reading through the initial draft of this book and supplying useful comments as well as catching mistakes. Dr. Casey is as close to a native speaker of Bohairic as anyone could be nowadays, and the book is much better for his input.

Providence, December 2019

1. WRITING AND PHONOLOGY

1 History

Coptic is the name of the final stage of the ancient Egyptian language, spoken and written from the third century AD until perhaps sometime in the seventeenth century. It is still used today in the rituals of the Coptic (Egyptian Christian) Church.

Coptic existed alongside the last stage of ancient Egyptian writing, Demotic, for about two and a half centuries; the last known Demotic text is dated to AD 452. The name "Coptic" is applied to Egyptian texts written in an alphabet derived from the Greek (§ 1.4). The earliest texts, prior to the second century, are usually known collectively as Old Coptic (OC). The earliest use of the Coptic alphabet is for glosses in Demotic magical texts, to specify the correct pronunciation of certain words and phrases; the oldest such examples come from the Ptolemaic Period (after 332 BC). The use of Coptic rather than Demotic to write ancient Egyptian can perhaps be traced to the introduction of Christianity in Egypt, the alphabetic script being preferred for writing Christian scriptures because it was free of the "pagan" taint of the older writing system.

2 Dialects

Regional differences in the pronunciation, vocabulary, and grammar of ancient Egyptian undoubtedly existed through the history of the language, but they are usually obscured by the hieroglyphic writing system and its descendants, hieratic and Demotic. Coptic scribes, however, regularly wrote the language as they were accustomed to speaking it. As a result, there is no uniform "Coptic" language, but a number of different dialects (Fig. 1). The six most important of these are named after the region of the country they were associated with: Akhmimic (abbreviated A), Bohairic (B), Fayumic (F), Lycopolitan (L, originally called Subakhmimic, A₂; also called Lyco-Diospolitan), Oxyrhynchite (M, for Mesokemic or Middle Egyptian), and Saidic (S, also called Sahidic).[1]

The dominant dialects were Saidic and Bohairic. Saidic, centered in Thebes, is attested from the third to fourteenth centuries AD and was the dominant dialect until the ninth to eleventh centuries, when it was increasingly overshadowed and eventually supplanted by Bohairic. Bohairic, a northern dialect, is first attested in the fourth century AD but is primarily represented by texts from the ninth century and later; it is also the dialect used in the modern Coptic Church. Fayumic is the name of the dialect spoken in the Fayum; it is attested from the third to tenth century AD. The other major dialects are mostly known from texts of the

---

1   See Funk 1988. In this book, if no dialect letter is given before a Coptic term, the term is the same all dialects.

fourth and fifth centuries and are Upper Egyptian in origin, from Oxyrhynchus, Asyut (Lycopolitan), and Akhmim.

A number of minor dialects are also known, often from a single manuscript, including P, ancestral to Saidic, from a Theban manuscript; H, associated with Hermopolis; and G, related to Bohairic. Some texts also display a mixture of dialects, such as Saidic with an Akhmimic influence (Sᴬ).

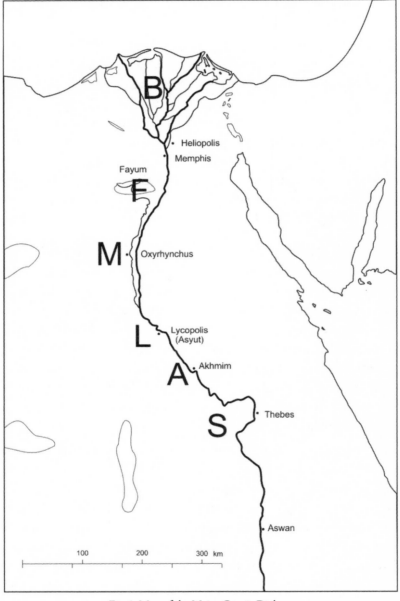

Fig. 1. Map of the Major Coptic Dialects

1.3   Sources

Most Coptic grammars concentrate on Saidic, because that was the primary literary dialect for much of the language's history. Steindorff 1951 (see the Bibliography), in German, is a good outline of Saidic grammar, which often notes major dialectal differences. Layton 2000 is a recent comprehensive grammar of Saidic; its basic points are summarized in Layton 2007, also available online. Lambdin 1983 can also be recommended. For Bohairic, the standard grammar is Mallon 1926 (reprinted often). The only grammar specifically devoted to dialectal differences is Till 1931, in German.

The basic dictionaries of Coptic are Crum 1939 and Westendorf 2008, complemented by Kasser 1966, which includes dialects M, P, H, and G, identified and systematized after Crum's dictionary was published. These dictionaries are ordered after the Coptic alphabet (§ 1.4), but primarily based on consonantal roots, with vowels considered secondarily, so that ⲕⲱⲛⲥ "pierce," for example, precedes ⲕⲣⲟ "far side." [2]

Coptic texts are primarily Christian scripture and the writings of Coptic monks. A number of the grammars contain reading selections (chrestomathies).

1.4   The Alphabet

The Coptic alphabet is derived from the Greek alphabet, with eight additional signs, derived from Demotic, primarily for sounds not present in Greek. Some of the signs are peculiar to a single dialect, some have different values in one dialect than in others, and some are pronounced differently in the rituals of the Coptic Church than they were in antiquity, due to the influence of Arabic and reforms during the nineteenth century that aligned the pronunciation of Coptic more closely with that of modern Greek. The probable phonetic value of the signs is derived from variant spellings; some have a value similar to that of their Greek ancestors in the Classical Period (third century BC), when the alphabet was first used to write Egyptian, rather than that which evolved in the centuries when Coptic texts are first attested (κοινή "common"). The order of the Coptic alphabet, and the names of its letters, follow that of its Greek ancestor.

ⲁ	ⲁⲗⲫⲁ	/a/; probably [a],[3] as in Italian *gatta*, perhaps also [æ], as in *hat*, and [ɑ], as in *father*, in some words or dialects
ⲃ	ⲃⲏⲧⲁ	/b/; [β], a bilabial fricative (the *b* of Spanish *cabo*, a [b] sound with the lips not completely closed); name also ⲃⲓⲇⲁ
ⲅ	ⲅⲁⲙⲙⲁ	/g/; in Greek loanwords and as a variant of ⲕ in some words; probably pronounced [k]

---

2   In this book, ordering is strictly alphabetical: thus, for example, ⲕⲣⲟ before ⲕⲱⲛⲥ, and ⲟⲩⲛⲟⲩ "hour" before ⲟϩⲉ "yard."

3   Slanted lines mark phonemes. Square brackets indicate probable pronunciation, using symbols of the International Phonetic Alphabet (IPA); [˘] stands for an unknown vowel.

ⲁ	ⲀⲗⲫⲀ	/d/; in Greek loanwords; probably pronounced [t]
ⲉ	ⲈⲒ/ⲈⲒⲈ	/ε/; [ə], like the *u* in *but*, also [ε], like the *e* in *bet*, in some words and dialects; perhaps [ε] when stressed and [ə] otherwise
ⲍ	ⲌⲎⲦⲀ	/z/; [s], in Greek loanwords and as a variant of ⲥ in some words
ⲏ	ⲎⲦⲀ	/e/; [ε], like the *e* in *bet*, also perhaps [e], like the *a* in *bate*, in some words and dialects; also ⲀⲎⲦⲀ
ⲑ	ⲐⲎⲦⲀ	/tḥ/ and /tʰ/; in most dialects, this is a monogram for ⲦⲀ; in Bohairic, it represents an aspirated *t*, as in *tea*; also ⲐⲒⲦⲀ
ⲓ	ⲒⲰⲦⲀ	/i/; like the *i*'s in *cuisine*, both the [ɪ] of *cui-*, and the [i] of *-sine*, and [j] like the *y* in *yet*; often spelled ⲉⲓ in many dialects, and ï after a vowel; ⲉï for /εj/, distinguished from ⲉⲓ for /i/; also ⲒⲀⲨⲆⲀ
ⲕ	ⲔⲀⲡⲡⲀ	/k/; unaspirated [k], similar to the *g* in *go*, and aspirated [kʰ], like the *k* in *key*; in Bohairic, this letter represents [k]; in the other dialects, it may have represented both [kʰ] and [k]
ⲗ	ⲗⲀⲨⲆⲀ	/l/; [l], like the *l* in *lay*
ⲙ	ⲘⲒ/ⲘⲎ/ⲘⲈ	/m/; [m], like the *m* in *may*
ⲛ	ⲚⲈ	/n/; [n], like the *n* in *nay*
ⲝ	ⲜⲒ	/ks/; a monogram for ⲔⲤ
ⲟ	ⲟ	/ɔ/; [ɔ], like the *o* in *not*
ⲡ	ⲠⲒ	/p/; unaspirated [p], similar to the *b* in *bought*, and aspirated [pʰ], like the *p* in *pot*; in Bohairic, this letter represents [p]; in the other dialects, it may have represented both [pʰ] and [p]
ⲣ	ⲣⲟ	/r/; probably like the [ɾ] of Spanish *pero* (pronounced with the tip of the tongue against the roof of the mouth); also ⲣⲱ/Ⲁⲣⲱ
ⲥ	ⲤⲎⲘⲘⲀ	/s/; [s], like the *s* in *see*; also ⲤⲨⲘⲘⲀ
ⲧ	ⲦⲀⲨ	/t/; unaspirated [t], like the *t* in the American pronunciation of *batter*, and aspirated [tʰ], like the *t* in *tap*; in Bohairic, this letter is [t]; in the other dialects, it may have represented both [tʰ] and [t]
ⲩ	ⲀⲈ	/u/; used by itself primarily in Greek words, where it was pronounced [i] or [ε]; in Coptic words, this letter is almost always combined with a preceding vowel, where it was pronounced either [u], like the *u* of *gnu*, or [w], as in *woo* (e.g., ⲚⲀⲨ "see" [na-u] or [naw]); ⲟⲨ represents /u/; ⲟⲟⲨ represents /ɔu/ or /ɔw/
ⲫ	ⲪⲒ	/pḥ/ and /pʰ/; a monogram for ⲠⲀ except in Bohairic, where it represents an aspirated [pʰ] (as in *pot*)
ⲭ	ⲬⲒ	/kḥ/ and /kʰ/; a monogram for ⲔⲀ except in Bohairic, where it represents an aspirated [kʰ], as in *key*
ⲯ	ⲮⲒ	/ps/; a monogram for ⲠⲤ

ⲱ	ⲱ	/o/; [o], as in *note*
ⳡ	ϣⲁⲓ	/š/; [ʃ], like the *sh* in *she*; also ϣⲉⲓ
ϥ	ϥⲁⲓ/	/f/; [ɸ], a bilabial fricative, like *f* pronounced with the two lips rather than the teeth and lower lip; also ϥⲉⲓ
ϩ	ϩⲟⲡⲓ	/ḥ/; [ħ], harsher than English *h*, pronounced with an audible "rasp"; equivalent to Arabic ح
ϩ	[ϩⲁⲓ]	/x/; in Akhmimic, [x], like the *ch* in German *ach* or Scottish *loch* (name not attested)
ⳉ	ⳉⲁⲓ	/x/; in Bohairic, equivalent to Akhmimic ϩ; also ⳉⲉⲓ
ⲝ	ⲝⲁⲛⲝⲓⲁ	/d̠/; in Bohairic, this sound was unaspirated [tʲ], somewhat like the *d* in *procedure*; in the other dialects it may have represented both [tʲ] and an aspirated [tʰʲ], somewhat like the *t* in *nature*
ϭ	ϭⲓⲙⲁ	/k̠/ and /t̠/; in most dialects, a [kʰʲ] or [kʲ], somewhat like the *c* in *cute* or the *g* in *argue*; in Bohairic, this letter represented [tʰʲ], the aspirated counterpart of ⲝ (like the *t* in *nature*)
†	†	/ti/; a monogram for ⲧⲓ

Additional letters occur in Old Coptic and Dialect P: OC ϭ and P ⳋ for /x/ ([xʲ]) and OC ˂ and P ⳑ for vowel length or for [ə]. In the major Coptic dialects, the first has disappeared (> ϩ/ϣ). For the second, most dialects use a doubled vowel, representing [V:]: for example, S ⲙⲁⲁⲩ, FL ⲙⲉⲉⲩ "mother" /ˈmaːu/, /ˈmɛːu/; Bohairic and Oxyrhynchite do not use doubled vowels: B ⲙⲁⲩ, M ⲙⲉⲩ "mother."

In Bohairic and Oxyrhynchite, a supraliteral dot or tick (ⲝⲓⲛⲕⲓⲙ "movement") is sometimes used to identify a letter that serves as a syllable by itself: for instance, ⲁ́ⲛⲟⲕ or ⲁ̀ⲛⲟⲕ "I" for /a-ˈnɔk/. This is also the case when the letter is a consonant, as in ⲛ́ⲑⲟϥ or ⲛ̀ⲑⲟϥ "he" for /n̠-ˈtʰɔf/.[4] Other dialects use a supraliteral stroke over consonants: e.g., ⲛ̄ⲧⲟϥ "he." This can also span two consonants, as in S ϣⲟⲙⲛ̄ⲧ "three" for /ˈšɔm-n̠t/. A longer supraliteral stroke indicates abbreviations, such as ASF ⲭⲥ̄ for ⲭⲟⲉⲓⲥ/ⲭⲁⲉⲓⲥ "lord."

The phonetic values of ⲉ and ⲏ are uncertain. Variants such as F ⲥⲱⲧⲙ ~ ⲥⲱⲧⲉⲙ "hear" suggest that ⲉ was [ə] — i.e, [ˈso-tm̠] ~ [ˈso-təm] — but variants such as A ⲡⲉ ~ ⲡⲏ "sky" also suggest that it was [ɛ] when stressed, and that ⲏ was either [ɛ] or [e]: thus, ⲡⲉ ~ ⲡⲏ represents either variant spellings of [pɛ], or [pɛ] ~ [pe]. When (ⲉ)ⲓ and (ⲟ)ⲩ follow a vowel, they may have been diphthongal rather than independent vowels: ⲛⲁⲓ "to me" either [ˈna-i] or [nai̯], and ⲛⲁⲩ "see" either [ˈna-u] or [nau̯].

4   In this book, an underscored consonant signifies a syllabic consonant: e.g., /n̠/ for IPA [n̩]. English has such syllabic consonants in certain words, such as *isn't*, pronounced [ˈɪz-n̠t]. In Coptic, any consonant is capable of syllabic function.

The six major Coptic dialects have several phonological subgroupings. The most important is that of Bohairic and Saidic versus the other dialects: BS have o and ⲁ in many words where AFLM have ⲁ and ⲉ, respectively. The /x/ of Akhmimic and Bohairic, represented by ϩ and ⳉ, has become ϩ or ϣ in the other dialects. Oxyrhynchite has o in many words where the other dialects have ⲱ. Fayumic usually has ⲗ for the ⲣ of other dialects, and Bohairic distinguishes aspirated consonants from unaspirated ones, where the other dialects do not (or have lost aspiration). Phonologically, Lycopolitan is the most neutral of the dialects, with no unique features.

1.5   Aspiration

Most dialects do not distinguish consonants on the basis of aspiration, just as English *latter* is pronounced ['læt-r̩] in America (unaspirated *t*) but ['lætʰ-r̩] in England (aspirated *t*). Thus, S ⲧⲱⲣⲉ means both "willow" and "handle," perhaps distinguished by aspiration: ['tʰo-rə] "willow" and ['to-rə] "handle." Bohairic is the exception: ⲑⲱⲣⲓ "willow" versus ⲧⲱⲣⲓ "handle." In Bohairic, aspiration generally occurs before a stressed vowel or before the consonants ⲃ ⲗ ⲙ ⲛ ⲣ (called "sonants") or ⲉⲓ/ⲓ or ⲟⲩ preceding a stressed vowel: for example, B ϣⲑⲟⲣⲧⲉⲣ "become disturbed" /'štʰɔr-ter/ and ϣⲧⲉⲣⲑⲱⲣ "disturbed" /šter-'tʰor/, B ⲑⲛⲁⲭϩⲓ /'tʰnad̲-ḥi/ "the tooth" and ⲫⲓⲟⲙ "the sea" /pʰi-'ɔm/.

This feature always applies to ⲫ/ⲡ: e.g., B ⲫⲁⲓ "this" /pʰaj/ (like English *pie*) and ⲡⲁⲓⲣⲱⲙⲓ "this man" /paj-'ro-mi/. It also applies to ⲭ/ⲕ, ⲑ/ⲧ, and ϭ/ϫ, as in ϣⲑⲟⲣⲧⲉⲣ/ ϣⲧⲉⲣⲑⲱⲣ, above, but for those three pairs the distinction is also phonemic, as in aspirated ⲑⲱⲣⲓ "willow" /'tʰo-ri/ versus unaspirated ⲧⲱⲣⲓ "handle" /'to-ri/. In such cases, the aspirated consonant is usually preserved in unstressed syllables: e.g., ϭⲓⲥⲓ "exalt" /'t̲i-si/ and ϭⲉⲥⲫⲛⲟⲩϯ "exalt God" /t̲ɛs-'pʰnu-ti/.

Since most dialects do not mark aspirated consonants in writing, it is often necessary to look for the Bohairic version of a word, or for its Egyptian ancestor, to determine aspiration.[5] Thus, for example, FLMS ⲕⲱ "throw" is [kʰo] because of Bohairic ⲭⲱ, but AFS ⲕⲱⲧ "build" is [kot] in view of Bohairic ⲕⲱⲧ and Egyptian *qd*.

1.6   Syllables and Stress

In Coptic, a syllable can consist of a single vowel or consonant, as in the first syllable of ⲁⲛⲟⲕ "I" and ⲛⲧⲟⲕ "you." Words can also be monosyllabic: BS ⲟ "big" [ɔ], AS ϥⲛⲧ "worm" [ɸn̩t]. Syllables can begin or end with consonant clusters: e.g., S ϥⲥϭⲣⲁϩⲧ "he is at rest," theoretically [ɸsk̑jraḥt], more probably [ɸ-'sk̑jraḥ-t̩]. Individual words have one primary syllable that is stressed, usually last or second-last: for example, AS ⲙⲛⲧⲣⲙⲛⲕⲏⲙⲉ "Egyptian" [mn̩t-rm̩-n̩-'ke-mə], B ⲙⲉⲧⲟⲩⲣⲟ "kingdom" [mət-u-'rɔ]. In native words, the vowels ⲏ, ⲟ, and ⲱ generally mark the stressed syllable in most dialects: e.g., ABFS ⲃⲁⲣⲱⲧ "bronze" [βa-'rot]. The other

---

5   In general, Egyptian *k/t/t̲* > aspirated [kʰ/tʰ/tʰʲ] and *q/d/d̲* > unaspirated [k/t/tʲ].

vowels can be stressed or unstressed: AFM ⲀⲚⲀⲔ "I" [a-'nak]; ALS ⲃⲉⲕⲉ "wage" [βə-'kɛ]; BF ⲓⲛⲓ "get" ['i-ni]; ABFLMS ⲟⲩⲛⲟⲩ "hour" [u-'nu]. It is not always possible to determine where the stress lay, although dialectal variants can provide a clue: for example, ALS ⲙⲛⲧⲣⲉ "witness" was [mn̠-'trɛ] because of B ⲙⲉⲑⲣⲉ [mə-'tʰrɛ].

Because of the single dominant stress, Coptic nouns and verbs can appear in three variant forms, called absolute, construct, and pronominal. In grammars and dictionaries, the construct and pronominal forms are marked by a final - and ⸗, respectively: e.g., S ⲥⲱⲧⲙ/ⲥⲉⲧⲙ-/ⲥⲟⲧⲙ⸗ "hear." Absolute forms appear either as words by themselves or as the final element of a compound: ⲥⲱⲧⲙ "hear," ⲕⲛⲁⲥⲱⲧⲙ "he will hear." Constructs are used as non-final elements of a compound and are usually reduced from the absolute form as much as possible: AS ⲣⲱⲙⲉ "person" ['ro-mə] and ⲣⲙ̅ⲛ̅ϯⲙⲉ "villager" ("person-of-town") [rm̠-n̠-'ti-mə]. Pronominal forms have a final suffix pronoun: S ⲣⲁⲛ "name" and ⲣⲓⲛⲥ "her name."

Spelling

Within dialects, Coptic spelling is fairly uniform: the word for "sky," for example, always appears as ⲡⲉ in Saidic and as ⲫⲉ in Bohairic. Variation, however, also occurs, as in Akhmimic ⲡⲉ ~ ⲡⲏ, both spellings of the word for "sky." Variation is common between ⲉⲓ and ⲓ: e.g., FLS ⲥⲉⲓ and ⲥⲓ "enjoy." Other variants, within and across dialects, are ⲃ ~ ⳝ, ⲃ ~ ⲡ, ⲓ ~ ⲏ, ⲕ ~ ϭ, ⲣ ~ ⲗ, ⲥ ~ ϣ, and ⲟⲩ ~ ⲃ: e.g., F ⲛⲁⳝⲡⲓ ~ ⲛⲁϭⲁⲓ "good," S ⲥⲓⲃ ~ B ⲥⲓⲡ "tick," B ⲛⲏⲃⲓ ~ ⲛⲓⲃⲓ "swim," F ⲕⲉ ~ ϭⲏ "other," S ⲥⲱϣⲉ ~ F ϣⲱϣⲓ "field." In general, scribes seem to have written the language as they heard it.

Variation between ⲣ and ⲗ is primarily a feature of the Fayumic dialect. Most words that have ⲣ in the other dialects have ⲗ in Fayumic: e.g., ALS ⲣⲱⲙⲉ, B ⲣⲱⲙⲓ, M ⲣⲟⲙⲉ versus F ⲗⲱⲙⲓ "person." When Fayumic uses ⲣ, therefore, as in the variant ⲣⲱⲙⲓ, it may reflect the influence of other dialects, such as Bohairic, rather than a variant pronunciation: i.e., ⲗⲱⲙⲓ and ⲣⲱⲙⲓ both pronounced ['lo-mi]. This may also have been true for words consistently spelled with ⲣ, such as ⲉⲣⲱϯ/ⲗⲣⲱϯ "milk" (AS ⲉⲣⲱⲧⲉ, B ⲉⲣⲱϯ, M ⲉⲣⲟⲧⲉ), perhaps regularly pronounced [ə-'lo-ti / a-'lo-ti] in Fayumic.

Most Coptic manuscripts do not separate individual words by spaces or other means (see the Chrestomathy). Some use a dot or other device such as > to mark the ends of clauses or sentences. In this book, words and compounds with a single main stress are separated from other such words by a space (except in the Chrestomathy): thus, for example, in Exercise 1, ⲡⲉⲛⲟⲉⲓⲕ ⲉⲧⲛⲏⲩ ⲧⲁⲁⳝ ⲛⲁⲛ ⲙ̅ⲡⲟⲟⲩ rather than undivided ⲡⲉⲛⲟⲉⲓⲕⲉⲧⲛⲏⲩⲧⲁⲁⳝⲛⲁⲛⲙ̅ⲡⲟⲟⲩ.

Morphemic Integrity

Consonants can be affected by neighboring ones: for example, S ⲥⲟⲩⲥⲟⲟⲩϣⲉ "sacrifice" [su-'sow-ʃə], B ϣⲟⲩϣⲱⲟⲩϣⲉ [ʃu-'ʃow-ʃə]. Morphemic boundaries, however, are generally respected. For example, although S ⲡⲱⲛⲕ "bail" is B ⲫⲱⲛⲕ ['pʰo-nk̠] because of the Bohairic rule of aspiration (§ 1.5), S ⲡⲱⲛⲉ "the stone," consisting of the morphemes, ⲡ "the" and ⲱⲛⲉ "stone," is B ⲡⲱⲛⲓ, suggesting the pronunciation [p-'o-ni] rather than *['po-ni]. Where other morphemes are part of a word, the same tendency may have applied: for example, B ϭⲓ "carry" is [ɸi] but ϭⲓ "he comes" may have been [ɸ̱-'i] rather than [ɸi]. This applies to the morpheme boundary between a consonant and a vowel, not two consonants: B ⲫⲛⲟⲩϯ ['pʰnu-ti] "the God" (ⲡ + ⲛⲟⲩϯ) and ⲭⲣⲓⲙⲓ ['kʰr̥i-mi] "you weep" (ⲕ + ⲣⲓⲙⲓ). It is possible, therefore, that words such as B ⲡⲱⲛⲓ and ϭⲓ "he comes" contained an unwritten (and therefore non-phonemic) glottal stop: [p-'ʔo -ni] and [ɸ̱-'ʔi].

1.9   Vocalic Alternants and Variants

The vowel ⲱ is usually replaced by ⲟⲩ after ⲙ or ⲛ: e.g., B ms ⲫⲱⲕ and fs ⲑⲱⲕ but pl ⲛⲟⲩⲕ "yours." Word-final ⲱ is usually also replaced by ⲟⲩ in Akhmimic: BFLMS ⲭⲱ vs. A ⲭⲟⲩ "say." Oxyrhynchite regularly has medial ⲟ for the ⲱ of other dialects: M ⲥⲟⲛⲉ vs. ALS ⲥⲱⲛⲉ, BF ⲥⲱⲛⲓ "sister."

The stressed vowel pairs ⲓ vs. ⲁ/ⲉ and (except in Oxyrhynchite) ⲱ vs. ⲁ/ⲟ often appear as alternants in open and closed syllables, respectively: e.g., ALMS ⲭⲓⲥⲉ ['tʲi-sə], F ⲭⲓⲥⲓ ['tʲi-si] "exalt" vs. AFLM ⲭⲉⲥⲧϥ ['tʲɛs-tf̱], S ⲭⲁⲥⲧϥ ['tʲas-tf̱] "exalt him"; ABLS ⲥⲱⲧⲡ ['so-tp̱], F ⲥⲱⲡⲧ ['so-pṯ] "choose" vs. ALM ⲥⲁⲧⲡⲥ ['sat-ps̱], BS ⲥⲟⲧⲡⲥ ['sɔt-ps̱], F ⲥⲁⲡⲧⲥ ['sap-ts̱] "choose it."

Bohairic has ⲉ before a sonant where the consonant is syllabic in other dialects: e.g., FLS ⲥⲱⲧⲙ̄, M ⲥⲟⲧⲙ̄ ['so-tm̩, 'sɔ-tm̩] vs. B ⲥⲱⲧⲉⲙ ['so-təm] "hear." In Akhmimic, a final syllabic sonant is regularly replaced by the sonant plus ⲉ: A ⲥⲱⲧⲙⲉ ['so-tmə].

1.10   Greek Words

Many Coptic texts contain Greek words in Coptic transcription. Some are used for concepts for which the Egyptian language had no precise lexical counterpart, such as ⲡⲟⲛⲏⲣⲟⲥ "evil" (πονηρός) and ⲡⲓⲥⲧⲉⲩⲉ "believe" (πίστευε). Others are more common words, such as the particle ⲇⲉ (δὲ) "and, but." When transcribing Greek words, Coptic scribes often adopted the contemporary Greek pronunciation rather than the Classical one represented by Greek spelling: for example, S ⲇⲓⲕⲉⲟⲥ "just" (Prov. 12:10; Greek δίκαιος) and B ϧⲁⲣⲁⲕⲧⲏⲣ "mark, sign" (Girgis 1967–68, 61; Greek χαρακτήρ), reflecting the κοινή pronunciations ['ði-kɛ-ɔs] and [xa-rak-'tir] rather than the Classical ['di-kaj-ɔs] (with voiced [d]) and [kʰa-rak-'tɛːr]. This suggests that the pronunciation of Greek loanwords was most likely that of contemporary (κοινή) Greek: i.e., ⲁⲓ [ɛ], ⲏ/ⲉⲓ/ⲟⲓ/ⲩ [i], ⲫ [f], and ⲭ [x]: thus, Coptic ⲏⲓ "house" [ɛj] but Greek ⲏ (ἤ) "and, or" [i].

Exercise 1

Below is the Coptic text of the "Lord's Prayer" (Matt. 6:9–13) in Saidic, Bohairic, and Oxyrhynchite with phonemic transcription below the Coptic, divided into syllables, with stress indicated. Practice pronouncing the text.

Saidic

ⲡⲉⲛⲉⲓⲱⲧ ⲉⲧϨⲚⲘⲡⲏⲩⲉ ⲙⲁⲣⲉⲡⲉⲕⲣⲁⲛ ⲟⲩⲟⲡ
/pɛn-i-ot' ɛt-ḥn-m-pe'-uɛ ma-rɛ-pɛk-ran' u-ɔp'/
our-father who-in-the-skies may-your-name be-holy

ⲧⲉⲕⲘⲚⲧⲣⲣⲟ ⲙⲁⲣⲉⲥⲉⲓ ⲡⲉⲕⲟⲩⲱϣ ⲙⲁⲣⲉϥϣⲱⲡⲉ
/tɛk-mnt-r-rɔ' ma-rɛs-i' pɛk-uoš' ma-rɛf-šo'-pɛ/
your-kingdom may-it-come your-will may-it-happen

Ⲛ̄ⲑⲉ ⲉⲧϥϨⲚ̄ⲧⲡⲉ ⲙⲁⲣⲉϥϣⲱⲡⲉ ⲟⲛ ϨⲓϪⲘ̄ⲡⲕⲁϨ
/n-tḥɛ' ɛt-f-ḥn-tpɛ' ma-rɛf-šo'-pɛ ɔn ḥi-dm-pkaḥ'/
in-the-way that-it-in-the-sky may-it-happen also on-the-earth

ⲡⲉⲛⲟⲉⲓⲕ ⲉⲧⲛⲏⲩ ⲧⲁⲁϥ ⲛⲁⲛ Ⲙ̄ⲡⲟⲟⲩ
/pɛn-ɔ'-ik ɛt-neu' ta:f nan m-pɔw'/
our-bread that-is-coming give-it to-us today

ⲕⲱ ⲛⲁⲛ ⲉⲃⲟⲗ Ⲛ̄ⲛⲉⲧⲉⲣⲟⲛ
/ko nan ɛ-bɔl' n-nɛt-ɛ-rɔn'/
throw out the-which-against-us

Ⲛ̄ⲑⲉ Ϩⲱⲱⲛ ⲟⲛ ⲉⲧⲉⲛⲕⲱ ⲉⲃⲟⲗ Ⲛ̄ⲛⲉⲧⲉⲟⲩⲚ̄ⲧⲁⲛ ⲉⲣⲟⲟⲩ
/n-tḥɛ' ḥo:n ɔn ɛt-ɛn-ko' ɛ-bɔl' n-nɛ-tɛ-un'-tan ɛ-rɔu'/ (ⲟⲩⲚ̄ for ['wn̠])
in-the-way ourselves also that-we-throw out the-which-we-have against-them

Ⲛ̄Ⲅ̄Ⲧ̄ⲘⲭⲓⲧⲚ̄ ⲉϨⲟⲩⲛ ⲉⲡⲓⲣⲁⲥⲙⲟⲥ
/ng-tm-di'-tn ɛ-ḥun' ɛ-pi-ras-mɔs' (Greek πειρασμός)/
and-you-not-take-us in to-temptation

ⲁⲗⲗⲁ Ⲛ̄Ⲅ̄ⲛⲁϨⲙⲉⲛ ⲉⲃⲟⲗ ϨⲓⲦⲘ̄ⲡⲡⲟⲛⲏⲣⲟⲥ
/al-la' (Greek ἀλλά) ng-naḥ'-mɛn ɛ-bɔl' ḥi-tm-ppɔ-ne-rɔs' (Greek πονηρός)/
but and-you-save-us out from-the-evil

Bohairic

ⲡⲉⲛⲓⲱⲧ ⲉⲧϧⲉⲛⲛⲓⲫⲏⲟⲩⲓ ⲙⲁⲣⲉϥⲧⲟⲩⲃⲟ Ⲛ̄ϫⲉⲡⲉⲕⲣⲁⲛ
/pɛn-i-ot' ɛt-xɛn-ni-pʰe'-ui ma-rɛf-tu-bɔ' n-dɛ-pɛk-ran'/
our-father who-in-the-skies may-it-be-made-holy namely-your-name

ⲙⲁⲣⲉⲥⲓ Ⲛ̄ϫⲉⲧⲉⲕⲙⲉⲧⲟⲩⲣⲟ ⲡⲉⲧⲉϨⲛⲁⲕ ⲙⲁⲣⲉϥϣⲱⲡⲓ
/ma-rɛs-i' n-dɛ-tɛk-mɛt-u-rɔ' pɛ-tɛḥ-nak' ma-rɛf-šo'-pi/
may-it-come namely-your-kingdom the-which-you-want may-it-happen

Ⲙ̀ⲪⲢⲎϮ ⲂⲉⲚⲦⲪⲉ ⲚⲉⲘⲂⲒⲬⲉⲚⲠⲔⲀⲂⲒ
/m-pʰre'-ti xɛn-pʰɛ' nɛm-hi-dɛn-pkah'-i/
In-the-manner in-the-sky and-on-the-earth

ⲠⲉⲚⲰⲒⲔ Ⲛ̀ⲦⲉⲢⲀⲤϮ ⲘⲎⲒϥ ⲚⲀⲚ Ⲙ̀ⲪⲞⲞⲨ
/pɛn-o'-ik n-tɛ-ras'-ti me'-if nan m-pʰɔu'/
our-bread of-the-morrow give-it to-us today

ⲞⲨⲞⲂ ⲬⲀ ⲚⲉⲦⲉⲢⲞⲚ ⲚⲀⲚ ⲉⲂⲞⲖ
/uɔh kʰa nɛt-ɛ-rɔn' nan ɛ-bɔl'/
and throw those-which-against-us for-us out

Ⲙ̀ⲪⲢⲎϮ ⲂⲰⲚ ⲉⲦⲉⲚⲬⲰ ⲉⲂⲞⲖ Ⲛ̀ⲚⲎ ⲉⲦⲉⲞⲨⲞⲚ Ⲛ̀ⲦⲀⲚ ⲉⲢⲰⲞⲨ
/m-pʰre'-ti hon ɛt-ɛn-ko' ɛ-bɔl' n-ne' ɛt-ɛ-uɔn' n-tan' ɛ-ro'-u/
In-the-manner ourselves that-we-throw out those that-are with-us against-them

ⲞⲨⲞⲂ Ⲙ̀ⲠⲉⲢⲉⲚⲦⲉⲚ ⲉⲂⲞⲨⲚ ⲉⲠⲒⲢⲀⲤⲘⲞⲤ
/uɔh m-pɛr-ɛn'-tɛn ɛ-xun' ɛ-pi-ras-mɔs' (Greek πειρασμός)/
and don't-bring-us in to-temptation

ⲀⲖⲖⲀ ⲚⲀⲂⲘⲉⲚ ⲉⲂⲞⲖ ⲂⲀⲠⲒⲠⲉⲦⲂⲰⲞⲨ
/al-la' (Greek ἀλλά) nah'-mɛn ɛ-bɔl' ha-pi-pɛt-ho'-u/
but save-us out with-that-which-wicked

OXYRHYNCHITE

ⲠⲉⲚⲒⲞⲦ ⲉⲦⲂ̄Ⲛ̄Ⲙ̄ⲠⲎ ⲠⲉⲔⲢⲉⲚ ⲘⲀⲢⲉϥⲦⲞⲨⲂⲀ
/pɛn-i-ɔt' ɛt-hn-m-pe' pɛk-rɛn' ma-rɛf-tu-ba'/
our-father who-in-the-skies your-name may-it-be-made-holy

ⲦⲉⲔⲘ̄ⲚⲦⲉⲢⲀ ⲘⲀⲢⲉⲤⲉⲒ ⲠⲉⲦⲉⲂⲚⲉⲔ ⲘⲀⲢⲉϥϢⲰⲠⲉ
/tɛk-mnt-ɛ-ra' ma-rɛs-i' pɛt-ɛh-nɛk' ma-rɛf-šɔ'-pɛ/
your-kingdom may-it-come the-which-you-want may-it-happen

Ⲛ̀Ⲑⲉ ⲉⲦϢⲀⲠ Ⲃ̄ⲚⲦⲠⲎ ⲘⲀⲢⲉⲤϢⲰⲠⲉ ⲂⲒⲬ̄Ⲛ̄ⲠⲔⲉⲂⲉ
/n-tʰɛ' ɛt-šap' hn-tpe' ma-rɛs-šɔ'-pɛ hi-dn-pkɛh'-ɛ/
in-the-way that-is in-the-sky may-it-happen on-the-earth

ⲠⲉⲚⲀⲉⲒⲔ Ⲛ̀ⲢⲉⲤⲦⲉ ⲘⲀⲉⲒϥ ⲚⲉⲚ Ⲙ̀ⲠⲀⲞⲨ
/pɛn-a'-ik n-rɛs'-tɛ ma'-if nɛn m-pau'/
our-bread of-morrow give-it to-us today

ⲔⲰ ⲉⲂⲀⲖ Ⲛ̀ⲚⲉⲦⲉⲢⲀⲚ
/ko' ɛ-bal' n-nɛt-ɛ-ran'/
throw out those-which-against-us

Ⲛ̀Ⲑⲉ ⲂⲰⲚ ⲉⲦϢⲀⲚⲔⲰ ⲉⲂⲀⲖ Ⲛ̀ⲚⲉⲦⲉⲞⲨⲚ̄ⲦⲚ̄ ⲉⲢⲀⲨ
/n-tʰɛ' hon ɛt-šan-ko' ɛ-bal' n-nɛ-tɛ-un'-tn ɛ-raw'/ (ⲞⲨⲚ̄ for ['wn])
in-the-way ourselves that-usually-we-throw out those-which-we-have against-them

ⲁⲅⲱ ⲘⲠⲢⲚⲦⲚ ⲈⲌⲞⲨⲚ ⲈⲠⲒⲢⲀⲤⲘⲞⲤ

/a-uo′ m-pr-n′-tn ε-ḥun′ ε-pi-ras-mɔs′ (Greek πειρασμός)/

and don't-bring-us in to-temptation

ⲀⲖⲖⲀ ⲚⲈⲌⲘⲚ ⲈⲂⲀⲖ ⲚⲦⲀⲦϤ ⲘⲠⲠⲞⲚⲎⲢⲞⲤ

/al-la′ (Greek ἀλλά) nεḥ′-mn ε-bal′ n-tat′-f m-ppɔ-ne-rɔs′ (Greek πονηρός)/

but save-us out from-his-hand of-the-evil

2. NOUNS AND ADJECTIVES

States

Nouns in Coptic can have as many as four lexical states: singular absolute, singular construct, singular pronominal, and plural. No noun has all four, and some nouns have only one (absolute). Examples are S ⲉⲓⲱⲧ "father," construct ⲉⲓⲧ-, plural ⲉⲓⲟⲧⲉ; B ⲭⲱⲝ "head," construct ⲭⲁⲝ-, pronominal ⲭⲱⸯ; and AFLS ⲥⲱⲛⲉ, BF ⲥⲱⲛⲓ, M ⲥⲟⲛⲉ "sister." These are lexical states because Coptic has no regular grammatical rules for forming the construct, pronominal, and plural form of a noun, just as English "irregular" plurals such as *children* and *mice* are lexical rather than grammatical items.

Singular Forms

Most nouns are either masculine or feminine in gender. No morphological distinctions mark either gender: for example, masculine B ⲛⲁⲩ "time," feminine ⲙⲁⲩ "mother"; masculine S ⲱⲏⲣⲉ "child," feminine ⲱⲏⲩⲉ "altar." Many feminine nouns end in –ⲉ, remnant of the older feminine ending –*at*; in Bohairic and Fayumic, this ending has become –ⲓ: e.g., *šndt* "acacia" *['šan'-tat] > ALM ⲱⲁⲛⲧⲉ, S ⲱⲟⲛⲧⲉ and B ⲱⲟⲛϯ, F ⲱⲁⲛϯ. Not all nouns with this ending, however, are feminine; AS ⲥⲁⲃⲉ "wise man" and BF ϯⲙⲓ "village" are both masculine.

Some nouns have masculine and feminine counterparts, such as AFLM ⲥⲁⲛ, BS ⲥⲟⲛ "brother" and AFLS ⲥⲱⲛⲉ, BF ⲥⲱⲛⲓ, M ⲥⲟⲛⲉ "sister," ALS ⲱⲏⲣⲉ "(male) child" and ALS ⲱⲉⲉⲣⲉ "(female) child." Gender can also be specified by a noun phrase: M ⲱⲏⲣⲉ ⲛ̄ϩⲁⲟⲩⲧ "male child" and ⲱⲏⲣⲉ ⲛ̄ⲥϩⲓⲙⲉ "female child." Some nouns are not gender-specific and can be treated as either masculine or feminine, such as AFMS ⲕⲟⲩⲓ, B ⲕⲟⲩⲭⲓ, F ⲕⲟⲩϭⲓ, L ⲕⲟⲩⲉⲓ "little one." Greek nouns are treated as masculine if they are masculine or neuter in Greek, and as feminine if they are feminine.

Construct forms are used when the noun is the first element of a compound (§ 2.5): for example, S ⲱⲏⲣⲉ "(male) child" and ⲱ̄ⲣϩⲟⲟⲩⲧ "male child," A ⲓⲟⲟⲡⲉ "channel" and ⲓⲉⲣⲟ "river" (literally, "big channel"). Nouns are unstressed in the construct state, and therefore are reduced to their consonantal skeleton: stressed vowels are lost (as in ⲱⲏⲣⲉ → ⲱ̄ⲣ-) or reduced to ⲉ or ⲁ (as in ⲓⲟⲟⲡⲉ → ⲓⲉⲣ-).

Pronominal forms are attested for a few common nouns that retained the ability to be used with suffix pronouns (§ 3.2): for example, AS ⲧⲱⲣⲉ, BF ⲧⲱⲣⲓ, M ⲧⲟⲣⲉ "handle" and ALS ⲧⲟⲟⲧϥ, B ⲧⲟⲧϥ, FM ⲧⲁⲧϥ "its handle." Some nouns exist only in pronominal form, such as ALFM ⲣⲉⲧⸯ, BS ⲣⲁⲧⸯ "foot, leg." Pronominal forms retain primary stress, although it may be different from that of the absolute form: e.g., ALFS ϩⲏⲧ "heart" and ϩⲑⲏⲥ "her heart."

2.3 Plural Forms

Unlike the singular, Coptic plurals have absolute forms only. Most plurals are lexicalized remnants of forms with the original grammatical endings *–w* *[u] (masculine) and *–wt* *[uat/wat] (feminine): e.g., *šrj* *['šu-ri] "little" > S ϣHPE "child," plural *šrjw* *[šu-'ri-u] > ϣPHY; *ḥmt* *['ḥi-a-matʰ] "woman" > S 2IME "wife," plural *ḥmwt* *[ḥi-'am-watʰ] > 2IOME. Coptic also has a "new" plural suffix, A -EOYE, B -ⲰOYI, F -AYI, LM -AYE/ AOYE, S -OOYE, which is used with some nouns and with Greek loanwords: A TBNI, BF TEBNH, S TBNH "animal," plural A TBNEOYE, B TEBNⲰOYI, F TEBNAYI, L TBNAYE, M TBNAOYE, S TBNOOYE; ⲯYXH "spirit" (Greek ψυχή), plural S ⲫYXOOYE.

A number of Coptic nouns have no distinct lexical plurals. These were pluralized by the articles 2EN- (indefinite) and N̄- (definite) (§ 2.4): for example, ALS PⲰME "person" (masculine or feminine), and 2ENPⲰME "people," N̄PⲰME "the people." Nouns that have distinct lexical plurals can also be also treated in this manner: S N̄ϣPHY or N̄ϣHPE "the children."

2.4 Articles

Coptic has a series of indefinite and definite articles, which can be prefixed to nouns in all their forms.

INDEFINITE

    sg OY-   pl ALFMS 2EN-, B 2AN-

The singular article is the construct form of ALFM OYE, B OYAI, S OYA (m), and ALS OYEIE, BF OYEI, M OYI (f) "one"; the plural is the construct form of ALM 2AINE, S 2OEINE "some." These are affixed prosodically to the noun: S OYPⲰME "a person" (Matt. 8:9), B 2ANPⲰMI "some people" (Luke 5:18). The noun in question need not be one that is normally considered countable: S OYбOM AYⲰ OYEOOY "power and glory" (Matt. 10:9), literally, "a power and a glory."

DEFINITE

    ms AFLMS ⲠΙ-, B Π/ⲫ-, often ΠI-; before a consonant cluster ΠE-

    fs AFLMS T-, B T/Θ- , often ϯ-; before a consonant cluster TE-

    pl ABFLMS N; M before M or Π; B often NI-; before a consonant cluster NE-

Examples: S ΠϣHPE "the (male) child," TϣEEPE "the (female) child," NEϣPHY and N̄ϣHPE "the children"; A M̄ΠHOYE "the skies'; B ΠOY2OP "the dog," ⲫOYⲰNϣ "the wolf." The definite article can be used with the absolute singular to specify gender as well as number: L ΠKOYEI "the little boy," TKOYEI "the little girl," N̄KOYEI "the little ones."

2.5 Compounds

Coptic compounds consisting of two or more nouns are of two kinds, which can be called direct and indirect.

Direct compounds are the descendant of the older construction called the "direct genitive", in which stress priority was generally given to the second, or final, noun. In Coptic, the first noun appears in the construct state: e.g., B ⲣⲱⲘⲓ "person" + ⲃⲁⲕⲓ "town" → ⲣ̄Ⲙⲃⲁⲕⲓ "villager."

Indirect compounds are more common, deriving from the older "indirect genitive" construction, which two nouns are linked by ⲛ (or ⲙ before ⲙ or ⲡ).[1] The first noun can be reduced to the construct state: F ⲗⲱⲘⲓ "person" + ⲛ + ⲕⲏⲘⲓ "Egypt" → ⲗⲉⲘⲛ̄ⲕⲏⲘⲓ "Egyptian." The construction is also used to link two fully-stressed nouns, as in S ⲡϣⲏⲣⲉ Ⲙⲡⲛⲟⲩⲧⲉ "the son of God" (Matt. 4:3). In Bohairic, the linking word is ⲛ̄ⲧⲉ- if the first noun is defined: ⲛⲓⲣⲱⲘⲓ ⲛ̄ⲧⲉⲡⲓⲘⲁ "the people of the place" (Matt. 14:35).

2.6 Prefixes

Coptic uses a number of construct nouns as prefixes to form derivatives of nouns, in the same way that English uses suffixes such as –er (e.g., play → player) and –dom (e.g., king → kingdom).

A common instance of this construction involves what is known as the "conjunct participle," the construct form of an old noun of agent, with with the vowel ⲁ, followed by a stressed noun: for example A ⲥⲁⲩ- "drinker" (A ⲥⲟⲩ "drink") + ⲏⲣⲡ "wine" → ⲥⲁⲩⲏⲣⲡ "wine-drinker," B ϧⲁⲧⲉⲃ- "killer" + ⲣⲱⲘⲓ "person" → ϧⲁⲧⲉⲃⲣⲱⲘⲓ "murderer," S Ⲙⲁⲥⲧⲉ- "hater" + ⲣⲱⲘⲉ → ⲘⲁⲥⲧⲉⲣⲱⲘⲉ "people-hating."

Other common prefixes include AFS ⲁⲧ-, B ⲁⲧ-/ⲁⲑ- "-less"; ABFLMS Ⲙⲁⲛ̄- "place of"; ALMS Ⲙⲛ̄ⲧ-, BF Ⲙⲉⲧ-, construct of the older noun *mdt* "matter," used to form abstracts; ABLMS ⲣⲉϥ-, F ⲗⲉϥ-, construct of ⲣⲱⲘⲉ/ⲣⲱⲘⲓ/ⲗⲱⲘⲓ/ⲣⲟⲘⲉ ⲉϥ- "person who," used with the infinitive to form nouns of agent; and BF ⲭⲓⲛ-, LMS ϭⲓⲛ- "act of," used with the infinitive to form nouns of action: for example, LS ⲁⲧⲘⲟⲩ "deathless" (Ⲙⲟⲩ "die") A Ⲙⲁⲛ̄ⲉⲗⲁⲁⲗⲉ "vineyard" ("place of vine'), B Ⲙⲉⲧⲟⲩⲣⲟ "kingdom," L ⲣⲉϥⲟⲩⲱϣⲧ "worshipper" ("person who worships"), F ⲭⲓⲛϣⲉⲭⲓ "speaking" ("act of speaking').

2.7 Adjectives

Coptic has only one word used solely as a modifier, ALFMS ⲛⲓⲘ, B ⲛⲓⲃⲉⲛ "every, each, all." This word is only used with a noun, which it follows; the noun regularly has no article: M Ⲙⲛ̄ⲧⲉⲣⲁ ⲛⲓⲘ "every kingdom." The nouns ALFM ⲟⲩⲁⲛ, BS ⲟⲩⲟⲛ "one" and ABFLS ϩⲱⲃ, M ϩⲟⲃ, or AM ⲛ̄ⲕⲉ, B ⲛ̄ⲭⲁⲓ, F ⲛ̄ⲕⲉⲓ, L ⲛ̄ⲕⲉⲉⲛ, S ⲛ̄ⲕⲁ "thing" are used before ⲛⲓⲘ/ⲛⲓⲃⲉⲛ for

---

1 ⲛ does not change to ⲙ before an ⲙ that is the plural definite article: ⲙ̄Ⲙⲉⲉⲣⲉ "of midday" but ⲛ̄ⲙ̄ⲡⲏⲩⲉ "of the skies."

non-specific referents: B ⲞⲨⲞⲚ ⲚⲒⲂⲈⲚ "everyone" (Matt. 5:15); and M ⲌⲞⲂ ⲚⲒⲘ (Matt. 8:33), S Ⲛ̄ⲔⲀ ⲚⲒⲘ (Matt. 13:44) "everything."

All other adjectives are nouns of quality, and are generally treated as such: for example, ALFM ⲠⲚⲀϬ, S ⲠⲚⲞϬ, B ⲪⲚⲒϢϮ "the big (one)." Most adjectives modify a noun through the indirect compound construction: S ⲞⲨⲚⲞϬ Ⲛ̄ⲤⲘⲎ "a loud voice" (Luke 19:37), ⲌⲈⲚⲢⲰⲘⲈ Ⲛ̄ⲚⲞϬ "big men" (Acts 15:22). The same construction allows other nouns to function as adjectives: for example, B ⲞⲨⲢⲰⲘⲒ Ⲛ̄ϢⲰⲦ "a merchant" (Matt. 13:45; literally, "a-man of-trader").

A few words can be treated like English adjectives, following directly the noun they modify, including S ⲔⲞⲨⲒ and ϢⲎⲘ "little" as well as ⲚⲞϬ "big": S Ⲛ̄ϢⲎⲢⲈ ⲔⲞⲨⲒ "the little children" (Matt. 21:16), ⲦϢⲈⲈⲢⲈ ϢⲎⲘ "the little girl" (Matt. 9:24), ⲌⲞⲞⲨ ⲚⲞϬ "great day" (John 7:37). Rarely, Coptic has a noun-adjective construction that derives from an original direct compound: *rmṯ ʿꜣ* "big man" *[ra-mat^hj-'ʿa] > ALS ⲠⲢ̄ⲘⲘⲀⲞ, B ⲢⲀⲘⲀⲞ, F ⲖⲈⲘⲈⲀ, M ⲠⲢ̄ⲘⲘⲈⲀ "rich man"; *stj nfr* *[sˇ-t^hji-'na-fir] "good smell" > AFMS ⲤⲦⲚⲞⲨϤⲈ, B ⲤⲐⲚⲞⲨϤⲒ "perfume."

Coptic has no specific comparative or superlative forms of adjectives. Degree is conveyed solely by context. Thus, S ⲠⲚⲞϬ "the big one" can also mean "the greater" (Matt. 23:17) or "the greatest" (Matt. 18:4).

EXERCISE 2

Pronounce and translate the following nouns and noun phrases. Pronunciation of individual terms can be found in the Lexicon.

1. S ⲦⲘ̄ⲚⲦⲢⲢⲞ Ⲛ̄Ⲙ̄ⲠⲎⲨⲈ
2. B ⲠϢⲎⲢⲒ Ⲙ̀ⲪⲚⲞⲨϮ
3. S ϢⲎⲢⲈ ϢⲎⲘ ⲚⲒⲘ
4. S ⲞⲨⲚⲞϬ Ⲙ̄ⲘⲎⲎϢⲈ
5. B ⲌⲀⲚⲢⲈϤⲘⲰⲞⲨⲦ
6. B ⲞⲨⲘⲀⲚ̀Ⲙ̄ⲦⲞⲚ
7. L Ⲛ̄ϢⲎⲢⲈ Ⲛ̄ⲀⲂⲢⲀⲌⲀⲘ
8. F ⲞⲨⲢⲈϤⲢ̄ⲚⲀⲂⲒ
9. M ϬⲒⲚⲤⲈϪⲈ
10. A ⲌⲰⲂ ⲚⲒⲘ Ⲙ̄ⲘⲎⲈ

VOCABULARY

ⲀⲂⲢⲀⲌⲀⲘ L "Abraham"
ⲘⲎⲈ A "truth"
ⲘⲎⲎϢⲈ S "multitude"

ⲘⲚⲦⲢⲢⲞ S "kingdom"

ⲙⲡⲏⲩⲉ S "heaven" (literally, "the-skies")

ⲘⲦⲞⲚ B "rest"

ⲘⲰⲞⲨⲦ B "die"

ⲫⲚⲞⲨϯ B "God" (literally, "the God")

ⲢⲚⲀⲂⲒ F "sin" (literally, "do-sin" (ⲚⲀⲂⲒ))

ⲥⲉⲝⲉ M "speak"

ϯⲘⲉ A "village"

ⲱⲎⲢⲉ S, ⲱⲎⲢⲒ B "son" ("male child")

3. PRONOUNS

The Relative Pronoun

Coptic has four kinds of pronouns: in order of complexity, relative, interrogative, demonstrative, and personal.

The relative pronoun usually has the form ⲉⲧ- in all dialects, descended from the older relative adjective *ntj*. It also appears as ⲉⲧⲉ- in certain constructions, and as ⲉ-, Ⲛ̄-, and Ⲛ̄ⲧ-/ⲉⲛⲧ- before certain verb forms in various dialects (§§ 10.8–9).

The relative pronoun can introduce both a clause in which it serves as subject and one in which something else is the subject: e.g, M ⲡⲟⲩⲁⲉⲓⲛ ⲉⲧⲛ̄ϩⲏⲧⲕ "the light that is in you" (Matt. 6:23; literally, "the-light which-in-you"), S ⲡⲙⲁ ⲉⲧϥⲛ̄ϩⲏⲧϥ "the place in which he was" (Mark 2:4; literally, "the-place which-he-in-it"). Introduced by the definite article, a relative clause with ⲉⲧ- can also function as a noun without expressed antecedent, as in S ⲡⲉⲧⲙ̄ⲙⲁⲩ "the one who is there" (John 16:8; literally, "the-who-there"). The relative A ⲉⲧⲙ̄ⲙⲟ, B ⲉⲧⲉⲙⲙⲁⲩ, S ⲉⲧⲙ̄ⲙⲁⲩ, FL ⲉⲧⲙ̄ⲙⲉⲩ, M ⲉⲧⲙ̄ⲙⲉ "who (is) there" often serves as a demonstrative: e.g., S ⲡⲙⲁ ⲉⲧⲙ̄ⲙⲁⲩ "that place" (literally, "the-place which-there").

Interrogative Pronouns

Coptic has three pronouns used in questions, both direct and indirect:

A ⲉϩ, BS ⲁϣ, FLM ⲉϣ "who, what" — B ⲁϣⲛⲉ "What are they?" (Luke 24:19; literally, "what-they"); also A Ⲛ̄ⲉϩ Ⲛ̄ϩⲉ, B Ⲛ̄ⲁϣ Ⲛ̄ⲑⲉ, F Ⲛ̄ⲉϣ Ⲛ̄ϩⲓ, L Ⲛ̄ⲉϣ Ⲛ̄ϩⲉ, M Ⲛ̄ⲉϣ Ⲛ̄ϩⲏ, S Ⲛ̄ⲁϣ Ⲛ̄ϩⲉ "how" (literally, "in-what of-manner") — S Ⲛ̄ⲁϣ Ⲛ̄ϩⲉ "How?" (Matt. 10:19)

A ⲟ, BMS ⲟⲩ, F ⲟⲩⲛ, L ⲉⲩ "what, who" — S ⲟⲩⲛⲉ "What are they?" (Luke 24:19; literally, "what-they")

ABFLMS ⲛⲓⲙ "who" — M ⲛⲓⲙⲧⲉ ⲧⲁⲙⲁⲩ "Who is my mother?" (Matt. 12:48; literally, "who-she my-mother"); M ϣⲓⲛⲉ ϫⲉⲛⲓⲙ ⲡⲉⲧⲙ̄ⲡϣⲉ "Ask who is worthy" (Matt. 10:11; literally, "ask that-who the-which-of-the-worth")

Demonstrative Pronouns

There are three sets of demonstrative pronouns in Coptic, which distinguish gender and number and two states, stressed and unstressed. The primary demonstrative is:

STRESSED		UNSTRESSED	
ms	AFM ⲡⲉⲓ̈, B ⲫⲁⲓ, L ⲡⲉⲉⲓ, S ⲡⲁⲓ	ms	AFMS ⲡⲉⲓ̈-, B ⲡⲁⲓ-, L ⲡⲉⲉⲓ-
fs	AFM ⲧⲉⲓ̈, B ⲑⲁⲓ, L ⲧⲉⲉⲓ, S ⲧⲁⲓ	fs	AFMS ⲧⲉⲓ̈-, B ⲧⲁⲓ-, L ⲧⲉⲉⲓ-
pl	AFM ⲛⲉⲓ̈, BS ⲛⲁⲓ, L ⲛⲉⲉⲓ	pl	AFMS ⲛⲉⲓ̈-, B ⲛⲁⲓ-, L ⲛⲉⲉⲓ-

The stressed form is used independently: B ογπε ϕⲁⲓ "What is this?" (Mark 11:3), M ⲛⲉⲓ ⲧⲏⲣⲟⲩ "all these" (Matt. 4:9; literally, "these their-limit"). The unstressed form is appended as a construct prefix to nouns: S ⲡⲉⲓⲣⲱⲙⲉ "this person" (Matt. 27:24).

The second set has the stressed form FLMS ⲡⲏ, ⲧⲏ, ⲛⲏ, B ϕⲏ, ⲑⲏ, ⲛⲏ, which is used absolutely, at the head of a relative clause: B ⲙⲁⲣⲓⲁ ⲑⲏ ⲉⲧⲁⲥⲙⲉⲥⲓ̅ⲏ̅ⲥ̅ "Mary, she who gave birth to Jesus" (Matt. 1:16).[1] Related to these is the unstressed form -ⲡⲉ, -ⲧⲉ, -ⲛⲉ, which is used only primarily as a copula between two nouns: S ⲛ̅ϫⲁϫⲉ ⲙ̅ⲡⲣⲱⲙⲉⲛⲉ ⲛⲉϥⲣⲙ̅ⲛ̅ⲏⲓ "The enemies of a man are his kinsmen" (Matt. 10:36; literally, "the-enemy of-the-man-they his-people-of-house").

The third set has construct and pronominal states: AFLMS ⲡⲁ-, ⲧⲁ-, ⲛⲁ-, B ϕⲁ-, ⲑⲁ-, ⲛⲁ-; and ALFS ⲡⲱ⸗, ⲧⲱ⸗, S ⲛⲟⲩ⸗ / ALF ⲛⲱ⸗, B ϕⲱ⸗, ⲉⲱ⸗, ⲛⲟⲩ⸗, M ⲡⲟ⸗, ⲧⲟ⸗, ⲛⲟⲩ⸗. The construct form is used with nouns to form nouns of relationship ("one of, those of"): e.g., AS ⲧϣⲉⲗⲉⲉⲧ "the bride" and ⲡⲁⲧϣⲉⲗⲉⲉⲧ "bridegroom" (literally, "the-of-the-bride"). The pronominal forms are used with suffix pronouns to express absolute possessive pronouns, such as B ϕⲱⲥ "hers" (referring to a masculine noun).

3.4   Personal Pronouns: Suffix Forms

Coptic personal pronouns have several forms, depending on their syntactic use. Suffix pronouns are appended to another word. They have variant forms, depending on the ending of the word to which they are appended. The following are common:

	V=	VV=	C=	ⲧ⸗	C+B/ⲗ/ⲙ/ⲛ/ⲣ
1s	ⲓ/ⲉⲓ/ⲓ̈	ⲧ	ⲧ		ⲉⲧ
2ms	ⲕ	ⲕ	ⲕ (–ⲛ̅ⲅ̅)	ⲕ	ⲉⲕ
2fs[2]		ⲉ	ⲉ, ⲃ ⲓ (ⲑ)	ⲉ, ⲃ ⲓ (ⲑ)	ⲉ, ⲃ ⲓ
3ms	ϥ	ϥ	ϥ	ϥ	ⲉϥ
3fs	ⲥ	ⲥ	ⲥ	ⲥ	ⲉⲥ
1pl	ⲛ, ⲃ ⲛ/ⲧⲉⲛ	ⲛ, ⲁ ⲛⲉ	ⲛ, ⲁ ⲛⲉ	ⲛ, ⲉⲛ, ⲁ ⲛⲉ	ⲉⲛ, ⲛ
2pl	ⲧ̅ⲛ̅/ⲧⲉⲛ, ⲁ ⲧⲛⲉ	{ AL ⲑⲛⲉ, B ⲑⲏⲛⲟⲩ, FM ⲑⲏⲛⲟⲩ, S ⲑⲏⲩⲧ̅ⲛ̅ }			
3pl	ⲟⲩ/ⲩ	ⲟⲩ/ⲩ, ⲁ ⲟⲩⲉ,[3] BFL (ⲧ)ⲟⲩ	ⲟⲩ	ⲟⲩ	ⲟⲩ

These pronouns are used (a) as possessive suffixes of a few nouns, (b) as object of prepositions and (c) the infinitive, and as suffixes of (d) verbal prefixes and (e) the construct possessive. Examples are: ALS ⲧⲟⲟⲧ̅ϥ, B ⲧⲟⲧ̅ϥ, F ⲧⲁⲁⲧ̅ϥ, M ⲧⲁⲧ̅ϥ "his hand"; ALFM ⲛⲉϥ, BS ⲛⲁϥ "for him"; ALFSM ϫⲓⲧ̅ϥ, B ϭⲓⲧ̅ϥ "take him"; ALMS ⲁϥⲉⲓ, BF ⲁϥⲓ "he came." The

---

1   ⲓ̅ⲏ̅ⲥ̅ is a common abbreviation for ⲓⲏⲥⲟⲩⲥ "Jesus."

2   In B, no ending after ⲩ⸗, ⲁ⸗ → ⲉ.

3   With reduction of ⲟⲩⲟⲩ to ⲟⲩ: e.g., ϩⲟⲩⲟⲩⲕ "yourself" but ϩⲟⲩⲟⲩⲉ "themselves."

construct possessive generally consists of ms ⲡⲉ⸗, fs ⲧⲉ⸗, pl ⲛⲉ⸗, in agreement with the gender and number of the noun, plus a suffix pronoun:

1s	ⲡⲁ-, ⲧⲁ-, ⲛⲁ-
2ms	ⲡⲉⲕ-, ⲧⲉⲕ-, ⲛⲉⲕ-
2fs	ABFLM ⲡⲉ-, ⲧⲉ-, ⲛⲉ-; S ⲡⲟⲩ-, ⲧⲟⲩ-, ⲛⲟⲩ-
3ms	ⲡⲉϥ-, ⲧⲉϥ-, ⲛⲉϥ-
3fs	ⲡⲉⲥ-, ⲧⲉⲥ-, ⲛⲉⲥ
1pl	ⲡⲉⲛ-, ⲧⲉⲛ-, ⲛⲉⲛ-
2pl	ALMS ⲡⲉⲧⲛ̄-, ⲧⲉⲧⲛ̄-, ⲛⲉⲧⲛ̄-; BF ⲡⲉⲧⲉⲛ-, ⲧⲉⲧⲉⲛ-, ⲛⲉⲧⲉⲛ-
3pl	ABL ⲡⲟⲩ-, ⲧⲟⲩ-, ⲛⲟⲩ-; FMS ⲡⲉⲩ-, ⲧⲉⲩ-, ⲛⲉⲩ-

The construct possessive is used as prefix to a noun: AFM ⲡⲉϩⲉⲓ̈, B ⲡⲉϩⲁⲓ, S ⲡⲟⲩϩⲁⲓ, L ⲡⲉϩⲉⲉⲓ "your (f) husband"; ALS ⲧⲉⲕⲥⲱⲛⲉ, BF ⲧⲉⲕⲥⲱⲛⲓ, M ⲧⲉⲕⲥⲟⲛⲉ "your (m) sister"; ALMS ⲛⲉⲥϣⲏⲣⲉ, BF ⲛⲉⲥϣⲏⲣⲓ "her children."

Independent Pronouns

Coptic independent pronouns have two states, absolute and construct. The absolute forms are:

1s	AFLM ⲁⲛⲁⲕ, BF ⲁⲛⲟⲕ
2ms	AFLM ⲛ̄ⲧⲁⲕ, B ⲛ̀ⲑⲟⲕ, S ⲛ̄ⲧⲟⲕ
2fs	ALS ⲛ̄ⲧⲟ, B ⲛ̀ⲑⲟ, FM ⲛ̄ⲧⲁ
3ms	AFLM ⲛ̄ⲧⲁϥ, B ⲛ̀ⲑⲟϥ, S ⲛ̄ⲧⲟϥ
3fs	AFLM ⲛ̄ⲧⲁⲥ, B ⲛ̀ⲑⲟⲥ, S ⲛ̄ⲧⲟⲥ
1pl	AFLM ⲁⲛⲁⲛ, BS ⲁⲛⲟⲛ
2pl	A ⲛ̄ⲧⲱⲧⲛⲉ, B ⲛ̀ⲑⲱⲧⲉⲛ, F ⲛ̄ⲧⲁⲧⲉⲛ, LS ⲛ̄ⲧⲱⲧⲛ̄
3pl	AFLM ⲛ̄ⲧⲁⲩ, B ⲛ̀ⲑⲱⲟⲩ, S ⲛ̄ⲧⲟⲟⲩ

These serve as pronominal predicates and as intensifiers of other pronominal forms: e.g., B ⲁⲛⲟⲕⲡⲉ "It is I" (Matt. 14:27), S ⲁⲛⲟⲕ ϯⲛⲏⲩ "(As for) me, I am coming" (Matt. 8:7; see § 3.6), S ⲉⲣⲟⲓ ⲁⲛⲟⲕ "to *me*" (Luke 8:46).

The construct state is an unstressed version of the absolute form, and is attested for the following pronouns and dialects:

1s	AFMS ⲁⲛⲕ̄-, ⲁⲛⲧ̄-	1pl	AFMS ⲁⲛⲛ̄-, ⲁⲛ-
2ms	AMS ⲛ̄ⲧⲕ̄-, F ⲛⲧⲉⲕ-	2pl	AS ⲛ̄ⲧⲉⲧⲛ̄- F ⲛ̄ⲧⲉⲧⲉⲛ-
2fs	AFS ⲛ̄ⲧⲉ-		
3ms	AS ⲛ̄ⲧϥ̄-, F ⲛ̄ⲧⲉϥ-		

These are used as subject of a nominal predicate: e.g., S ⲚⲦⲰⲦⲚ ⲚⲦⲈⲦⲚⲌⲈⲚⲈⲂⲞⲖ ⲌⲘⲠⲔⲀⲌ ⲀⲚⲞⲔ ⲀⲚⲅⲞⲨⲈⲂⲞⲖ ⲌⲚⲦⲠⲈ "You, you are earthly ones; I, I am a heavenly one" (John 8:23; literally, "you you-some-out in-the-earth I I-an-out in-the-sky").

3.6 Subject Pronouns

A third set of personal pronouns is used as subject of certain verb forms and in sentences with adverbial predicate:

1s	ABFLS ⲧ-	1pl	ALS ⲦⲚ-, BF ⲦⲈⲚ-
2ms	ⲕ-, B ⲕ-/ⲭ-	2pl	ALS ⲦⲈⲦⲚ-, BF ⲦⲈⲦⲈⲚ-
2fs	ⲦⲈ-, F ⲦⲈⲖ-		
3ms	ϥ-	3pl	ⲥⲉ-, ⲥⲟⲩ-
3fs	ⲥ-		

Examples are: A ⲦⲈⲦⲚⲚⲞ "you see" (Matt. 24:2), S ϥⲘⲘⲀⲨ "he (was) there" (John 12:9).

3.7 Pronominal Equivalents

Coptic has a few non-pronominal words that correspond to English pronominal expressions:

ⲕⲉ "other"

This is a noun with absolute and construct states, the former in two forms:

m/fs	ABL ⲕⲉ, F ⲕⲏ/ϭⲏ, M ⲕⲉ/ⲕⲏ
ms	B ⲭⲉⲧ, F ⲕⲏⲧ, S ⲕⲉⲧ
fs	B ⲭⲉ†, M ⲕⲏⲦⲈ, S ⲕⲈⲦⲈ/ⲕⲏⲦⲈ
pl	B ⲕⲉⲭⲱⲞⲨⲚⲒ, S ⲕⲞⲞⲨⲈ
construct	ABF ⲕⲉ-, L ⲕⲀⲒ-, M ⲕⲉ-/ⲕⲏ-, S ⲕⲉ-/ⲕⲞⲨ-

The construct form is used to modify nouns: M ⲠⲔⲈⲞⲨⲈ "the other one" (Matt. 6:24), B ⲌⲀⲚⲔⲈⲘⲎⲱ "many others" (Matt. 15:30; literally, "some-other-multitude"). With the definite article it can have the meaning "even, also": BS ⲦⲈϥⲔⲈⲯⲨⲭⲎ "his soul also, even his soul, his own soul" (Luke 14:26). The absolute forms are used as nouns in their own right: B ⲚⲦⲭⲉⲧ, M ⲚⲦⲈⲕⲏⲦⲈ "of the other" (Matt. 12:13), S ⲌⲈⲚⲔⲞⲞⲨⲈ, B ⲌⲀⲚⲔⲈⲕⲱⲞⲨⲚⲒ "others" (Matt. 13:5).

ⲌⲰⲰ꞊ "self, also"

This is an older noun meaning "body" (ḥʿw "limbs"), surviving as ⲌⲰ (A ⲌⲞⲨⲈ) in the absolute state and as the following in the pronominal state:

1s	A ⲌⲞⲨⲞⲨⲦ, BFLMS ⲌⲰ, S ⲌⲰⲦ
2ms	A ⲌⲞⲨⲞⲨⲔ, BM ⲌⲰⲔ, FLS ⲌⲰⲰⲔ
2fs	BF ⲌⲰⲒ, M ⲌⲰⲦⲈ, S ⲌⲰⲰⲦⲈ
3ms	A ⲌⲞⲨⲞⲨϥ, B ⲌⲞⲨⲞⲨϥ, S ⲌⲰⲰϥ

3fs   A ⲍⲟⲩⲟⲩⲥ, B ⲍⲱϥ S ⲍⲱⲱⲥ
1pl   A ⲍⲟⲩⲟⲩⲛⲉ, L ⲍⲱⲛⲉ
2pl   A ⲍⲟⲩⲧⲏⲛⲉ, BF ⲍⲱⲧⲉⲛ, F ⲍⲱⲧⲧⲏⲛⲟⲩ, S ⲍⲱⲧⲧⲏⲩⲧⲛ̄
3pl   A ⲍⲟⲩⲟⲩⲉ, BMS ⲍⲱⲟⲩ, F ⲍⲱⲱⲟⲩ

These are used as intensifiers of other pronouns: for example, S ⲛⲁⲓ ⲍⲱⲟⲩ "these also" (Mark 4:16), S ⲧⲉⲧⲛⲁⲍⲙⲟⲟⲥ ⲍⲱⲧⲧⲏⲩⲧⲛ̄ "you yourselves will sit" (Matt. 19:28; literally, "you-will-sit yourselves").

ⲧⲏⲣ⸗ "all"

This is an older noun used with suffix pronouns, originally meaning "limit": thus, for example, M ⲧⲏⲣⲟⲩ "all of them," A ⲧⲏⲣⲥ "all of it." Forms are ABLMS ⲧⲏⲣ⸗, F ⲧⲏⲗ⸗. It is used like an adjective meaning "all, entire": B ⲡⲉⲕⲥⲱⲙⲁ ⲧⲏⲣϥ "your entire body" (Matt. 5:29), L ⲛⲉⲉⲓ ⲧⲏⲣⲟⲩ "all these" (John 15:21).

EXERCISE 3

Translate the following phrases and sentences.

1. M ⲛⲁⲡⲛ̄ⲧ̄ ... ⲛⲁⲛ̄ⲣⲟⲙⲉ
2. M ⲛ̄ⲧⲁⲕ ⲍⲱⲕ
3. S ⲧⲉϥⲕⲉ ⲯⲩⲭⲏ
4. S ⲛ̄ⲧⲱⲧⲛ̄ ⲛ̄ⲧⲉⲧⲛ̄ⲍⲉⲛⲉⲃⲟⲗ ⲍ̄ⲙ̄ⲡⲕⲁⲍ
5. B ⲛⲓⲙ ⲡⲉ ⲫⲁⲓ
6. S ⲁⲛⲅ̄ⲟⲩ ⲁⲅⲁⲑⲟⲥ ⲁⲛⲟⲕ
7. B ⲛ̄ⲑⲱⲧⲉⲛ ⲍⲱⲧⲉⲛ
8. L ⲡⲉⲧⲉ ⲡⲱϥ ⲡⲉ
9. B ⲛⲏ ⲉⲧⲉⲛⲟⲩⲓ
10. S ⲧⲁⲡⲁⲣⲭⲏ ⲙ̄ⲡⲉⲡⲛ̄ⲁ̄

VOCABULARY

ⲁⲅⲁⲑⲟⲥ S "good (person)" (Greek ἀγαθός)
ⲁⲣⲭⲏ S "beginning" (Greek ἀρχή)
ⲉⲃⲟⲗ ⲍ̄ⲙ̄ S "from"
ⲉⲧⲉ- L "who"
ⲕⲁⲍ S "earth"
ⲡⲛ̄ⲁ̄ abbreviation of ⲡⲛⲉⲩⲙⲁ "spirit" (Greek πνεῦμα)
ⲡⲛ̄ⲧ̄ M abbreviation of ⲡⲛⲟⲩⲧ "God"
ⲯⲩⲭⲏ S "life" (Greek ψυχή)
ⲣⲟⲙⲉ M "people"

4. Numbers and Particles

1

Numerals

Like the Greek alphabet from which it is derived, the Coptic alphabet was used to designate numerals as well as letters. When used as numerals, the individual signs were marked with supraliteral strokes:

ⲁ̄	1	ī	10	ⲣ̄	100	ⲁ̄	1,000
ⲃ̄	2	ⲕ̄	20	ⲥ̄	200	ⲃ̄	2,000
ⲅ̄	3	ⲗ̄	30	ⲧ̄	300	ⲅ̄	3,000
ⲇ̄	4	ⲙ̄	40	ⲩ̄	400	ⲇ̄	4,000
ⲉ̄	5	ⲛ̄	50	ⲫ̄	500	ⲉ̄	5,000
ⲋ̄[1]	6	ⲝ̄	60	ⲭ̄	600	ⲋ̄	6,000
ⲍ̄	7	ⲟ̄	70	ⲯ̄	700	ⲍ̄	7,000
ⲏ̄	8	ⲡ̄	80	ⲱ̄	800	ⲏ̄	8,000
ⲑ̄	9	ϥ̄	90	ⲣ̄	900	ⲑ̄	9,000

ī is used for 10,000. These are used like, and arranged in the order of, Arabic numerals, thousands–hundreds–tens–ones:e.g., ⲇ̄ⲫ̄ⲡⲅ̄ "4,583."

2

Cardinal Numbers

Dialects of Coptic other than Fayumic and Bohairic often use the word for a cardinal number rather than its numeral. The two methods can also be combined, as in B ⲉ̄ⲛϣⲟ "five hundred" (Matt. 14:21; literally, "5-of-hundred"), for which M has ϯⲟⲩ ⲛϣⲁ "five of-hundred." Words for the ones and for the first three tens have masculine and feminine forms. Some numbers also have construct forms, and in some dialects the ones also have a combinatory form used after tens.

"one" — m AM ⲟⲩⲉ, B ⲟⲩⲁⲓ, FL ⲟⲩ(ⲉ)ⲉⲓ, S ⲟⲩⲁ; f A ⲟⲩⲓⲉ, BFM ⲟⲩⲓ; MS -ⲟⲩⲉ

"two" — m A ⲥⲛⲟ, BS ⲥⲛⲁⲩ, FLM ⲥⲛⲉⲩ; f AMS ⲥ̄ⲛⲧⲉ, B ⲥⲛⲟⲩϯ, F ⲥⲛⲏϯ; A -ⲥⲛⲁⲩⲥ, M -ⲥⲛⲁⲟⲩⲥ, S -ⲥⲛⲟⲟⲩⲥ (m) and M -ⲥⲛⲁⲟⲩⲥⲉ, S -ⲥⲛⲟⲟⲩⲥⲉ (f)

"three" — m A ϩⲁⲙⲧ̄, B ϣⲟⲙⲧ̄, LM ϣⲁⲙⲧ̄/ϣⲁⲙⲛ̄ⲧ, S ϣⲟⲙⲛ̄ⲧ; f A ϩⲁⲙⲧⲉ, B ϣⲟⲙϯ, LM ϣⲁⲙⲧⲉ, S ϣⲟⲙⲧⲉ; A ϩ̄ⲙⲧ/ϩ̄ⲙⲧⲉ-, S ϣ̄ⲙⲧ/ϣ̄ⲙⲛ̄ⲧ-; S -ϣⲟⲙⲧⲉ

"four" — m ALM ϥⲧⲁⲩ, B ϥⲧⲱⲟⲩ, BS ϥⲧⲟⲟⲩ; f AS ϥⲧⲟⲉ; AS ϥⲧⲟⲩ-, M ϥⲧⲉⲩ-; AM -ⲉϥⲧⲉ/-ⲧⲉϥⲧⲉ, S -ⲁϥⲧⲉ/-ⲧⲁϥⲧⲉ

"five" — m ABLMS ϯⲟⲩ, f ABLS ϯⲉ, M ϯ; A -ϯ, LMS -ⲧⲏ

"six" — m ALM ⲥⲁⲩ, B ⲥⲱⲟⲩ, BS ⲥⲟⲟⲩ; f ALS ⲥⲟⲉ, M ⲥⲁ; LM -ⲉⲥⲉ/-ⲧⲉⲥⲉ, -ⲁⲥⲉ/-ⲧⲁⲥⲉ

---

1   Taken from the Greek numeral.

"seven" — m A cаз̄ч, B ϣaϣ̄ч, M ceϣ̄ч, S caϣ̄ч; f A caзчe, B ϣaϣчı, LS caϣчe; A - caзвe, S -caϣчe

"eight" — m A змоγн, B ϣмнн, LMS ϣмоγн; f B ϣмнни, MS ϣмоγнe; L -ϣмнн, S - ϣмнне

"nine" — m AS фıc, BS фıт; f LMS фıтe, B фıт

"ten" — m ABLMS мнт; f MS мнтe, B мн†; AMS м̄нт-,[2] B мeт-

"twenty" — m AS χoγωт, B χωт, M χoγoт; f S χoγωтe; ALMS χoγт-,[3] M χoγ-

"thirty" — m A мааве, B мав, LS мааB, M мeв; f S мааве; S мав-

"forty" — ABLS змe, M змн

"fifty" — A тeïoγe, B тeoγı, L таeıoγ, M тeıoγ S таıoγ

"sixty" — ABS ce, M cн; also A з̄мтχoγωт ("three-twenty")

"seventy" — A c̄звe, BS ϣчe, M ϣвн

"eighty" — B ḫмeнe, S змeнe; also S чтoγχoγωт ("four-twenty")

"ninety" — B пıcтeoγı, S п̄cтаıoγ

"one-hundred" — ABLS ϣe, F ϣн, M ϣγ

"two-hundred" — FLS ϣнт; f S ϣ̄нтc̄нтe

"five-hundred" — ABLS †oγ н̄ϣe, M †oγ н̄ϣγ; also F бıcтве, S бıcтва ("half-ten-thousand")

"thousand"— A зo, BLS ϣo, FM ϣа

"ten-thousand" — AS тва, B θвo, F тве (usually an indefinite large number).

Compound numbers were formed in several ways: (1) for tens, with the tens (in the construct form for "ten," "twenty," and "thirty") followed by the combinatory form of the ones (e.g., MS м̄нтoγe "eleven," S змeтачтe "forty-four"); (2) for tens, with the preposition ALMS м̄н-, B нeм- "with" (e.g., B тeoγı нeмoγаı "fifty-one"); (3) for hundreds and thousands, (a) with the construct form of "three" and "four" followed by ϣe/ϣн/ϣγ "hundred" or зo/ϣo/ϣа "thousand" (e.g., A з̄мтϣe "three hundred"), and (b) with the absolute form of the number followed by н "of" and ϣe/ϣн/ϣγ "hundred" or зo/ϣo/ϣа "thousand" (e.g., S чтooγ н̄ϣo "four thousand"); (4) with the absolute form of the numbers (e.g., S ϣe таıoγ ϣoмтe "one-hundred fifty three" John 21:11).

When used adjectivally, most numbers precede the noun they modify, with н̄ "of"; if the number has gendered forms, it agrees in gender with the noun: e.g., S чтooγ н̄рωмe, B д̄ н̄рωмı "four men" (Acts 21:23), BMS мнтe м̄парθeнoc (Greek παρθένος) "ten virgins" (Matt. 25:1). The number "one" generally follows the same pattern: B oγаı н̄нeчϣфнр, S oγа н̄нeчϣвнр "one of his fellows" (Matt. 18:28); M oγı н̄нeïeнтoλн, S oγeı н̄нeïeнтoλн (Greek ἐντολή) "one of these commandments" (Matt. 5:19). But the construct form oγ- can also be used, specified as a number rather than the indefinite article by ABFLS н̄oγωт, M

<hr>

2   Note A мн† and MS мнтн rather than *мн†т/мнттн.
3   Note A χoγ† and LMS χoγтн rather than *χoγ†т/χoγттн

ⲚⲞⲨⲞⲦ "single" following the noun: e.g., S ⲞⲨⲂⲰ ⲚⲞⲨⲰⲦ "a single hair, one hair" (Matt. 5:36). The number "two" follows the noun it modifies, which is in the singular: M ⲤⲀⲚ ⲤⲚⲈⲨ "two brothers" (Matt. 4:18), S ⲰⲦⲎⲚ ⲤⲚⲦⲈ "two tunics" (Matt. 10:10).

The noun can be in the construct form, privileging the number: S ⲢⲘⲠⲈⲤⲚⲦⲈ vs. B ⲢⲞⲘⲠⲒ ⲤⲚⲞⲨⲦ "two years" (Matt. 2:16). This construct is common with the constructs FLMS ⲬⲠ- "hour," ABFS ⲤⲞⲨ- "day of the month" (from ALS ⲤⲎⲨ), and FS ⲦⲤⲎⲦ- or ⲦⲤⲈⲠ- "year": e.g., S ⲦⲤⲈⲠⲞⲨⲈⲒ "Year One."

4.3 Ordinal Numbers

Coptic has a specific word for "first": A ⲄⲀⲢⲠ, BS ⲰⲞⲢⲠ, FLM ⲰⲀⲢⲠ; construct A ⲄⲢⲠ-, BLMS ⲰⲈⲢⲠ-. This word is used for masculine and feminine referents; a feminine also exists, though rarely used: B ⲰⲞⲢⲠⲒ, F ⲰⲀⲢⲠⲒ, M ⲰⲀⲢⲠⲈ, S ⲰⲞⲢⲠⲈ. It is treated like other Coptic modifiers (§ 2.7): e.g., ⲦⲰⲞⲢⲠ ⲚⲈⲚⲦⲞⲖⲎ "the first commandment" (Mark 12:28). The remaining ordinals are formed with the prefix ABFL ⲘⲀⲄ-, BMS ⲘⲈⲄ- before the ordinal; the resulting compound is treated as a modifier: S ⲠⲘⲈⲄⲤⲀⲰϥ ⲚⲄⲞⲞⲨ "the seventh day" (Hebr. 4:4), B ⲦⲘⲀⲄⲤⲚⲞⲨⲦ "the second" (Mark 12:31).

4.4 Fractions

Parts of whole numbers were expressed by BS ⲢⲈ-, F ⲖⲈ-, S ⲢⲀ- prefixed to a cardinal number: e.g., B ⲪⲢⲈϤⲦⲰⲞⲨ "the quarter" (Num. 28:7). The nouns ALS ⲠⲈⲰⲈ, B ⲪⲀϢⲒ, F ⲠⲈϢⲒ, S ⲠⲀϢⲈ "half (share)" and B ⲬⲞⲤ/ⲬⲈⲤ, F ϬⲀⲤ/ϬⲒⲤ-, L ⲔⲤ-, S ϬⲞⲤ/ϬⲒⲤ-/ϬⲈⲤ- "half" were used for halves: B ⲦⲪⲀϢⲒ ⲚⲦⲀⲘⲈⲦⲞⲨⲢⲞ, S ⲦⲠⲀϢⲈ ⲚⲦⲀⲘⲚⲦⲈⲢⲞ "the half of my kingdom" (Mark 6:23), S ϬⲒⲤⲦⲂⲀ "half-ten-thousand" vs. B ⲉ̄ ⲚϢⲞ "5 thousand." For fractions in which the numerator is 1, the expression ABFLS ⲞⲨⲰⲚ Ⲛ- or AS ⲞⲨⲚ-, B ⲞⲨⲈⲚ- is also used: S ⲠⲞⲨⲚϢⲞⲘⲚⲦ ⲚⲘⲘⲞⲞⲨ "the third of the waters" (Rev. 8:11).

4.5 Initial Particles

Coptic has a number of particles that stand at the beginning of a clause or sentence, with various functions:

A ⲖⲞⲨ, B ⲞⲨⲞⲄ and ⲞⲨⲞⲄⲈ, FLMS ⲀⲨⲰ "and" — usually conjoins clauses and sentences, less often nouns and phrases, and can also introduce a sentence: B ⲞⲨⲞⲄ ⲚⲀϤⲄⲒⲰⲒϢ "And he was preaching" (Mark 1:7), M ⲀⲨⲰ ⲤⲀⲨⲦⲚ ⲚⲚⲈϤⲄⲒⲎ "and straighten his paths" (Matt. 3:3)

A ⲈⲒⲀ, BF ⲒⲀ, MS ⲈⲒⲈ, S ⲈⲈⲒⲈ "consequently, then" — with clauses: S ⲈϢⲬⲈ ⲀⲚⲞⲔ ⲈⲒⲚⲞⲨⲬⲈ ⲈⲂⲞⲖ ⲚⲚⲆⲀⲒⲘⲞⲚⲒⲞⲚ ⲄⲚⲂⲈⲈⲖⲌⲈⲂⲞⲨⲖ ⲈⲒⲈ ⲈⲢⲈⲠⲈⲦⲚϢⲎⲢⲈ ⲚⲞⲨⲬⲈ ⲈⲂⲞⲖ ⲄⲚⲚⲒⲘ "If I, for my part, by Beelzebub cast out demons, then by whom do your sons cast out?" (Luke 11:19; literally, "if I, I-do-cast out the-demons by-Beelzebub, then do-your-sons cast out by-who"); ⲈⲒⲈ … ⲈⲒⲈ "whether … or"

ALS ⲈⲒⲤ, B ⲒⲤ "behold, here is," often used with following B ⲄⲎⲎⲠⲈ/ⲄⲎⲠⲈ, LS ⲄⲎⲎⲦⲈ, F ⲄⲈⲒⲈ/ⲄⲈⲒ, M ⲄⲈⲒⲠⲈ/Ⲅ|, and reduced to AS ⲈⲒⲤⲦⲈ, A ⲈⲤⲦⲈ — introduces nouns and statements: B ⲓⲥ ⲑⲃⲱⲕⲓ ⲛ̄ⲧⲉⲡϭⲥ̄ "Behold, the maidservant of the lord" and S ⲉⲓⲥ ϩⲏⲏⲧⲉ ⲁⲛⲅⲑⲙϩⲁⲗ ⲙ̄ⲡⲭⲟⲉⲓⲥ "Behold, I am the servant of the lord" (Luke 1:38)

A ⲉⲓϩⲭⲉ/ⲉⲓϩⲡⲉ, B ⲓⲥⲭⲉ/ⲓⲥⲭⲉⲕ, FS ⲉϣⲭⲉ/ⲉϣⲭⲡⲉ, L ⲉϣⲡⲉ, M ⲉϣⲭⲉ "if" — with clauses and sentences, and admirative "how" with adjective-verbs: B ⲓⲥⲭⲉ ⲛⲑⲟⲕⲡⲉ ⲡⲭⲥ̄ ⲁⲭⲟⲥ ⲛⲁⲛ "If you are the Christ, tell us" (Luke 22:67), S ⲉϣⲭⲉ ⲛⲉⲥⲉⲛ̄ⲟⲩⲉⲣⲏⲧⲉ ⲛ̄ⲛⲉⲧⲉⲩⲁⲅⲅⲉⲗⲓⲍⲉ ⲛ̄ⲙⲡⲉⲧⲛⲁⲛⲟⲩⲩ "How beautiful are the feet of those who proclaim those that are good" (Rom. 10:15)

AFS ⲉⲛⲉ, A ⲛⲉ, S ⲉⲛ, B ⲁⲛ "is it that?" — interrogative: B ⲁⲛ ⳓϣⲉ ⲛ̄ⲣⲱⲙⲓ ⲉϩⲓⲧⲉϥϭ̄ϩⲓⲙⲓ ⲉⲃⲟⲗ "Is it fitting for a man to cast his wife out?" (Mark 10:2)

BS ⲙⲟ, S ⲙ̄ⲙⲟ; f B ⲙⲉ; pl B ⲙⲱⲓⲛⲓ, S ⲙ̄ⲙⲏⲉⲓⲧⲛ̄ "here" — used as presentative: B ⲙⲱⲓⲛⲓ ⲉⲣⲟⲩ "Here he is" (John 19:6)

ALFMS ⲛ̄ϭⲓ-, BF ⲛ̄ⲭⲉ-, M ⲛ̄ϭⲏ "namely" — used to specify the nominal referent of a personal pronoun: B ⲁⲩⲉⲓ ⲛ̄ⲭⲉⲓⲱⲁⲛⲛⲏⲥ ⲡⲓⲣⲉϥϯⲱⲙⲥ, M ⲁⲩⲉⲓ ⲛ̄ϭⲓⲓ̈ⲱⲁⲛⲛⲏⲥ ⲡⲃⲁⲡⲧⲓⲥⲧⲏⲥ "he came, John the Baptist" (Matt. 3:1) (Greek βαπτιστής)

B ⲡⲁⲓⲣⲏϯ "then, so" (literally, "this-manner"): ⲡⲁⲓⲣⲏϯ ⲙⲁⲣⲉⲧⲉⲛⲟⲩⲱⲓⲛⲓ ⲉⲣⲟⲩⲱⲓⲛⲓ "So, let your light shine" (Matt. 5:16; literally, "so may-your-light make-light")

B ϣⲁⲛ "or": ⲉⲑⲃⲏⲧϥ ϣⲁⲛ ⲉⲑⲃⲉⲕⲉⲟⲩⲁⲓ "about him(self), or about another one"

ⲭⲉ- "that, in that" — introduces (a) appositives: L ⲟⲩⲉⲉⲇⲉ ⲛ̄ϩⲏⲧⲟⲩ ⲭⲉⲕⲁⲓⲫⲁⲥ "and one of them, Caiaphas" (John 11:49), B ⲟⲩⲃⲁⲕⲓ ⲭⲉⲛⲁⲍⲁⲣⲉϯ "a town called Nazareth" (Luke 2:4); (b) the name with ⲙⲟⲩⲧⲉ ⲉⲡⲣⲁⲛ "call, name": S ⲕⲛⲁⲙⲟⲩⲧⲉ ⲉⲡⲉϥⲣⲁⲛ ⲭⲉⲓ̈ⲱϩⲁⲛⲛⲏⲥ "you will call him John" (Luke 1:13); (c) causal clauses: S ⲁⲙⲏⲓⲧⲛ̄ ⲭⲉⲁⲛ̄ⲕⲁ ⲛⲓⲙ ⲥⲟⲃⲧⲉ "Come, for everything has become ready" (Luke 14:17); (d) noun clauses: M ⲧ̄ⲛⲥⲁⲟⲩⲛ ⲭⲉⲛ̄ⲧⲕⲟⲩⲙⲉⲉ "we know that you are true" (Matt. 22:16; literally, "we-know that-you-a-true"); (e) direct quotations: S ⲡⲉⲭⲁⲩ ⲛⲁⲩ ⲭⲉⲙⲛ̄ⲧⲥⲛⲟⲟⲩⲥ "They said to him, 'Twelve'" (Mark 8:19)

F ⲭⲉ-, LMS ⲭⲛ̄- "or" — M ⲟⲩ ⲅⲁⲣ ⲡⲉⲧⲙⲁⲧⲛ̄ ⲛ̄ⲭⲁϥ ⲭⲉⲥⲉⲛⲉⲕⲉⲛⲉⲕⲛⲁⲃⲉ ⲛⲉⲕ ⲉⲃⲁⲗ ⲭⲛ̄ⲉⲭⲁⲥ ⲭⲉⲧⲟⲩⲛⲕ̄ ⲙⲁϣⲉ "For what is that which is easier to say, 'Your sins will be thrown out for you' or to say, 'Arise, walk'?" (Matt. 9:5).

ALS ⲭⲉⲕⲁⲁⲥ, B ⲭⲉⲭⲁⲥ, F ⲭⲉⲕⲉⲉⲥ/ⲕⲉⲥ, FM ⲭⲉⲕⲉⲥ, L ⲭⲉⲕⲁⲥⲉ, LS ⲭⲉⲕⲁⲥ "so that" — introduces final clauses: L ⲭⲉⲕⲁⲥⲉ ⲉⲧⲉⲧⲛ̄ⲁⲭⲓ ⲙ̄ⲡⲱⲛϩ "so that you might get life" (John 5:40)

In addition, Coptic uses a number of initial particles derived from Greek, mostly to introduce clauses and sentences, including ⲁⲗⲗⲁ (ἀλλά) "but," ⲁⲣⲁ (ἄρα) "then, so," ⲏ (ἤ) "and, or" ⲙⲏ (μή) "is it not the case that" (interrogative), ⲧⲟⲧⲉ (τότε) "then," and ϩⲓⲛⲁ (ἵνα) "so that."

4.6   Enclitic Particles

The enclitic particles of Coptic are stressed as well as unstressed, and include the following words:

AFLM ⲉⲛ, BS ⲁⲛ "not": S ⲛ̄ⲧⲟⲟⲩ ⲉⲓⲣⲉ ⲁⲛ ⲙ̄ⲡⲁⲓ "Do they themselves not do this?" (Matt. 5:47)

F ⲙ̄ⲙⲉϯ, LM ⲙ̄ⲙⲉⲧⲉ, S ⲙ̄ⲙⲁⲧⲉ/ⲉⲙⲁⲧⲉ "only": M ⲡⲣⲟⲙⲉ ⲛⲉⲟⲛ̄ϩ ⲉⲡⲁⲉⲓⲕ ⲙ̄ⲙⲉⲧⲉ ⲉⲛ "Man will not live only by bread" (Matt. 4:4)

ABFLMS ⲙ̄ⲙⲓⲛ "own, proper, self": L ⲡⲉϥⲣⲉⲛ ⲙ̄ⲙⲓⲛ ⲙ̄ⲙⲁϥ "his own name itself" (John 5:43)

AFLM ⲛ̄ⲧⲁϥ, B ⲛ̀ⲑⲟϥ, S ⲛ̄ⲧⲟϥ "but" (3ms pronoun: § 3.5): B ⲧⲉⲧⲉⲛⲥⲱⲟⲩⲛ̄ ⲙ̀ⲙⲟⲥ ⲁⲛ ⲛ̀ⲑⲟⲟϥ "But you don't know it" (Matt. 16:3; literally, "you-know it-not but")

A ϩⲟⲩⲟⲩϥ/ϩⲟⲩϥ, BFM ϩⲱϥ, LS ϩⲱⲱϥ/ϩⲱϥ "also" (literally, "itself": § 3.7): S ⲥⲉⲛⲁⲭⲱ ϩⲱⲱϥ ⲙ̄ⲡⲉⲛⲧⲁⲧⲁⲓ ⲁⲁϥ "they will also say what this one did" (Matt. 26:13)

ALS -ϭⲉ, B -ⲭⲉ, FM -ϭⲏ "thus, so": L ⲉⲩ̄ⲛⲧⲉⲕϭⲉ ⲁⲃⲁⲗ ⲧⲟ ⲙ̄ⲡⲙⲁⲩ ⲉⲧⲁⲁⲛϩ "So, from where do you have the living water?" (John 4:11; literally, "you-have-so from where of-the-water which-alive"); "again, more": B ⲛ̀ⲛⲁⲟⲩⲁϩⲧⲟⲧⲭⲉ "I will not do it any more" (Gen. 8:21; literally, "not-I-will-lay-hand again")

Coptic also makes extensive use of the Greek enclitic particles ⲅⲁⲣ (γάρ) "for" and -ⲇⲉ (δὲ) "and, but, so."

EXERCISE 4

Translate the following phrases and sentences.

1. S ⲡⲉⲭⲁⲩ ⲛⲁϥ ⲭⲉⲡϣⲟⲣⲡⲡⲉ
2. M ϣⲁⲙⲛ̄ⲧ ⲛ̄ϩⲁⲩ
3. S ⲡⲉⲭⲁⲩ ⲛⲁϥ ⲭⲉϯⲟⲩ ⲙ̄ⲛ̄ⲧⲃ̄ⲧⲥⲛⲁⲩ
4. B ⲫ̄ ⲛ̀ⲥⲁⲑⲉⲣⲓ
5. B ⲓⲃ̄ ⲛ̀ⲣⲟⲙⲡⲓ
6. M ϣⲩ ⲛ̄ⲉⲥⲁⲩ
7. M ⲡⲙⲉϩⲥⲛⲉⲩ ⲏ ⲡⲙⲉϩϣⲁⲙⲧ̄ ϣⲁⲡⲙⲉϩⲥⲉϣ̄ϥ
8. S ⲧⲙⲉϩϥ̄ⲧⲟⲇⲉ ⲛ̄ⲟⲩⲛⲣⲱϣⲉ ⲛ̄ⲧⲉⲩϣⲏ
9. B ⲉⲧⲁⲩⲥⲱⲧⲉⲙⲇⲉ ⲛ̀ⲭⲉⲡⲓⲕⲉⲓ ⲙ̄ⲙⲁⲑⲏⲧⲏⲥ ⲁⲩⲭⲣⲉⲙⲣⲉⲙ ⲉⲑⲃⲉⲡⲓⲥⲟⲛ ⲃ̄
10. L ⲭⲟⲩⲧⲏ ⲛ̄ⲥⲧⲁⲇⲓⲟⲛ ⲏ ⲙⲁⲁⲃ

VOCABULARY

ⲉⲥⲁⲩ M "sheep"
ⲉⲧⲁⲩⲥⲱⲧⲉⲙ B "when they heard"
ⲉⲑⲃⲉ B "about"
ⲭⲣⲉⲙⲣⲉⲙ B "grumble"
ⲙⲁⲑⲏⲧⲏⲥ B "disciple" (Greek μαθητής)
ⲙ̄ⲛ S "and"

ⲚⲀϤ S "to him"

Ⲛ̄ⲦⲈⲨϢⲎ S "of the night"

ⲞⲨⲎⲢϢⲈ S "watch" (f)

ⲠⲈ S "it is"

ⲠⲈϪⲀⲨ S "they said"

ⲢⲞⲘⲠⲒ B "year" (f)

ⲤⲀⲐⲈⲢⲒ B "stater" (a coin, Greek στατήρ)

ⲤⲦⲀⲖⲒⲞⲚ L "stade" (202¼ yards, 185m) (Greek στάδιον)

Ⲧ̄ⲂⲦ S "fish"

ⲌⲀⲨ M "day"

ϢⲀ M "up to"

5. PREPOSITIONS AND ADVERBS

5.1 **Simple Prepositions**

Coptic uses both native and Greek prepositions, most of which have construct and pronominal states:

AL ⲁ-/ⲁⲣⲁ⸗, BS ⲉ-/ⲉⲣⲟ⸗, F ⲉ-/ⲉⲗⲁ⸗, M ⲉ-/ⲉⲣⲁ⸗; A ⲁⲣⲱⲧⲛⲉ, B ⲉⲣⲱⲧⲉⲛ, S ⲉⲣⲱⲧⲛ "with respect to" — (a) direction: S ⲉⲕⲉⲭⲟⲟⲩϥ ⲉⲡⲏⲓ ⲙ̄ⲡⲁⲓⲱⲧ "you shall send him to the house of my father" (Luke 16:27); (b) reference: B ⲁⲩⲧⲁⲙⲟϥ ⲉϩⲱⲃ ⲛⲓⲃⲉⲛ "they informed him concerning everything (Mark 6:30), S ⲛⲉϩⲟⲃⲥ ⲉⲣⲟⲟⲩ "it was hidden from them" (Luke 9:45), S ⲁⲩⲥⲙ̄ⲙⲉ ⲉⲣⲟϥ "they appealed about him" (Acts 25:15); (c) antagonism: B ⲉⲣⲛⲟⲃⲓ ⲉⲣⲟⲓ "sin against me" (Matt. 18:21); comparison: S ⲛⲟϭ ⲉⲡⲣⲡⲉ "greater than the temple" (Matt. 12:6); (d) purpose, with the infinitive: S ⲛ̄ⲧⲁⲓⲉⲓ ⲅⲁⲣ ⲉⲡⲱⲣⲭ ⲛ̄ⲟⲩⲣⲱⲙⲉ ⲉⲡⲉϥⲉⲓⲱⲧ "For I have come to separate a man from his father" (Matt. 10:35)

AS ⲁⲭⲛ̄-/ⲁⲭⲛ̄ⲧ⸗, B ⲁ(ⲧ)ϭⲛⲉ-/ⲁ(ⲧ)ϭⲛⲟⲩ⸗, F ⲁⲭⲉⲛ-/ⲁⲭⲉⲛⲧ⸗, M ⲁⲭⲭⲛ̄- "without": B ⲁϭⲛⲉⲁⲥⲟⲩⲓ "without a sack" (Luke 22:35)

ALFM ⲙ̄ⲛ-/ⲛⲉⲙⲉ⸗, B ⲛⲉⲙ-/ⲛⲉⲙⲁ⸗, S ⲙ̄ⲛ-/ⲛ̄ⲙⲙⲁ⸗ "with" — (a) accompaniment: ⲃⲱⲕ ⲛ̄ⲙⲙⲁϥ "go with him" (Matt. 5:41); (b) conjoining two nouns or phrases: S ⲧⲉⲭⲱⲣⲁ ⲙ̄ⲛⲑⲁⲓⲃⲥ ⲙ̄ⲡⲙⲟⲩ "the region and the shadow of death" (Matt. 4:16), B ⲣⲟⲙⲡⲓ ⲥⲛⲟⲩϯ ⲛⲉⲙⲥⲁⲡⲉⲥⲏⲧ "two years and under" (Matt. 2:16)

ALFM ⲛ̄-/ⲙ̄ⲙⲁ⸗, B ⲛ̄ⲧⲉ-, BS ⲛ-/ⲙ̄ⲙⲟ⸗, F ⲉⲛ-, B ⲛ̀ⲙⲟ⸗; A ⲙ̄ⲙⲟ (2fs), ⲙ̄ⲙⲱⲧⲛⲉ, B ⲙ̀ⲙⲱⲧⲉⲛ, M ⲙ̄ⲙⲟⲧⲛ̄ "of"[1] — (a) linking two nouns in a genitival relationship: S ⲡⲏⲓ ⲙ̄ⲡⲉϣⲗⲏⲗ "the house of prayer" (Matt. 21:13); (b) introducing the object of an infinitive: L ϯⲭⲱ ⲙ̄ⲙⲁⲥ "I say it" (John 3:3)

ALFM ⲛ̄-/ⲙ̄ⲙⲁ⸗, BS ⲛ̄-/ⲙ̄ⲙⲟ⸗, F ⲉⲛ-, B ⲛ̀ⲙⲟ⸗; A ⲙ̄ⲙⲟ (2fs), ⲙ̄ⲙⲱⲧⲛⲉ, B ⲙ̀ⲙⲱⲧⲉⲛ, M ⲙ̄ⲙⲟⲧⲛ̄ "in, from, with" — (a) location (also destination and origin): B ϩⲉⲙⲥⲓ ⲙ̄ⲡⲁⲓⲙⲁ, S ϩⲙⲟⲟⲥ ⲙ̄ⲡⲉⲓⲙⲁ "Sit in this place" (Matt. 25:36), B ⲁⲩⲓ ⲛ̀ⲭⲱⲣϩ, S ⲛⲉⲛⲧⲁⲩⲉⲓ ⲛ̄ⲧⲉⲩϣⲏ "they came by night" (Matt. 28:13), B ϩⲓⲛⲁ ⲛ̀ⲧⲉϥⲥⲉⲡϩⲑⲏϥ ⲙ̄ⲡⲉϥⲧⲏⲃ ⲙ̀ⲙⲱⲟⲩ "so that might dip the tip of his finger in water" (Luke 16:24), S ⲡⲧⲱϩⲙ̄ ⲛ̄ⲧⲡⲉ "the summons from heaven" (Hebr. 3:1); (b) means: L ⲁϥϣⲱϭⲉ ⲛ̄ⲓⲏ̄ⲥ̄ ⲛ̄ⲟⲩⲕⲟⲩⲣ "he hit Jesus with a blow" (John 18:22), S ⲙ̄ⲡⲣⲱⲣⲕ̄ ⲛ̄ⲧⲡⲉ "Don't swear by heaven" (Matt. 5:34); (c) introducing a second object of a verb: L ⲁϥⲉⲉϥ ⲛ̄ϣⲏⲣⲉ ⲙ̄ⲡⲛⲟⲩⲧⲉ "he made himself son of God" (John 19:7); (e) state: B ⲁⲩⲭⲁϥ ⲉϥⲟⲓ ⲙ̀ⲫⲁϣⲙⲟⲩ "they left him half dead" (Luke 10:30; literally, "they-left-him he-being-made as-half-dead")

---

1   Pronominal forms are those of ⲛ̄- "in, with, from" (see next).

N̄-, AFLM Ne⸗, BS NA⸗; A NHTNE, BF NHI, B NⲰTEN and NⲰOY, F NH (2fs) and NHTEN, LMS NHTN̄ "to, for" — dative: L N̄CETEEϥ NEϥ "except for giving it to him" (John 6:65), L ϯⲬⲰ M̄MAC NEK "I say it to you" (John 3:3)

ABFLS OYBE-/OYBH⸗, FMS OYE-/OYH⸗ "opposite" — S ΠAI ENEϥϢOOΠ OYBHN "that which was against us" (Col. 2:14)

ABFLMS OYTE-/OYTⲰ⸗ (M OYTO⸗) "between, among" — S OYTⲰK OYTⲰϥ "between you and him" (Matt. 18:15), S OYTEⲠΡΠE MN̄ΠEΘYCIACTHΡION "between the temple and the altar" (Matt. 23:35)

ALM ϢA-/ϢAΡA⸗, BS ϢA-/ϢAΡO⸗, F ϢA-/ϢAⲖⲖA⸗, S ϢAA-/ϢAAΡO⸗ "toward (a person), up to, until" — B MAΡON ϢAΡOϥ "let us go unto him" (John 11:15), M ϢAΠEOYAEIϢ M̄ΠO2C "until the time of the harvest" (Matt. 13:30)

BS 2A-/2AΡO⸗ "at, with, by": B CEXH 2AΡON "they are set with us"

AFLS 21-/21ⲰⲰ⸗, BM 21-/21ⲰT⸗ "on" — (a) location: M 21TE21H ETM̄ME "on that road" (Matt. 8:28); (b) origin ("from on"): S EΠECHT 21ΠETOOY "down from the mountain" (Matt. 8:1); (c) time: B 21ΠIOYⲰTEB EBOⲖ N̄TEBABYⲖⲰN "at the displacement to Babylon" (Matt. 1:11); (d) addition: M 2M̄X 21CIϢE "vinegar with gall" (Matt. 27:48); (e) conjoining two undetermined nouns: B 2A2 M̄ΠΡOΦHTHC 21Ṗ̄ΡO "many a prophet and king" (Luke 10:24)

A 2A-/2AΡA⸗, B ϧA-/ϧAΡO⸗, F 2A-/2AⲖⲖA⸗, LM 2A-/2AΡA⸗, S 2A-/2AΡO⸗ "under" — (a) location: S 2AOYϢI "under a basket" (Matt. 5:15); (b) origin ("from under"): S ϢOΠN̄ EBOⲖ 2AΠCA2OY M̄ΠNOMOC "take us out from the curse of the law" (Gal. 3:13); (c) exchange: B OYBAⲖ ϧAOYBAⲖ OYO2 OYNAX21 ϧAOYNAX21 "an eye for an eye and a tooth for a tooth" (Matt. 5:38); (d) benefit: B ΦH N̄ΘOK ETEKEΡMEΘΡE ϧAΡOϥ "the one for whom you yourself bore witness" (John 3:26)

ALS 2HT⸗ "before" — spatial, with pronominal suffix anticipating, and agreeing with, a following noun introduced by M̄-: S N̄CETⲰT AN 2HTϥ M̄ΠEOOY "they do not tremble before the glorious one" (2 Pet. 2:10)

A 2N̄-/N2HT⸗, B ϧEN-/N̄ϧHT⸗, F 2E-/N̄2HT⸗, LMS 2N̄-/N̄2HT⸗ "in" — (a) location, spatial and temporal: M ETEΠEKA2A N̄2HTϥ "which your treasure is in" (Matt. 6:21), B ϧENNE2OOY N̄TE2HΡⲰAHC "in the days of Herod" (Matt. 2:1); (b) origin, after EBOⲖ "out" and E2ΡAI "up": L N̄TAΡEϥTⲰNAE ABAⲖ 2N̄NETMAOYT "And when he rose from the dead" (John 2:22), S EϥNHY E2ΡAI 2N̄TCⲰϢE "coming up from the field" (Mark 15:21); instrument: S 2N̄OYϬBOI EϥXOCE "with a raised arm" (Acts 13:17)

ALS X̄N-, B ICXEN-, FMS XIN-, F ϬHN-/XE-/XI-/N̄XIN, M N̄XIN- "from, since" — (a) spatial: B ICXEΠΠϢⲰI EΠECHT, M N̄XINΠϢⲰI EΠECHT, S XINTΠE EΠECHT "from the top to the bottom" (Matt. 27:51) ; (b) temporal: B ICXENϯOYNOY ETEM̄MAY, M N̄XINΠNEY ETM̄ME, S XINTEYNOY ETM̄MAY "from that hour" (Matt. 15:28)

Greek prepositions used in Coptic are generally treated as constructs; these include EIMHTI- (εἰμὴ τι) "except," KATA- (κατὰ) "according to," ΠAΡA-/M̄ΠAΡA- (παρὰ) "more than," XⲰΡIC-

(χωρίς) "without," and ϩⲱⲥ- (ὡς) "as." Pronominal states of some of these were formed with ⲁⲣⲁ⸗/ⲉⲣⲟ⸗/ⲉⲗⲁ⸗/ⲉⲣⲁ⸗: S ⲕⲁⲧⲁⲣⲟϥ "what pertains to it" (1Cor. 15:38).

.2   Compound Prepositions

The combination of a preposition with a noun, often one referring to a part of the body, forms a number of common Coptic prepositional expressions.

(a) with the preposition AL ⲁ-, BFMS ⲉ- "to"

AL ⲁⲣⲉⲧ⸗, BS ⲉⲣⲁⲧ⸗, FM ⲉⲣⲉⲧ⸗ (from ⲣⲁⲧ⸗/ⲣⲉⲧ⸗ "foot"): (a) mostly with ALS ⲱϩⲉ, B ⲟϩⲓ, F ⲱϩⲓ, MS ⲟϩⲉ "stand": B ⲡⲓⲙⲏϣ ⲉⲛⲁϥⲟϩⲓ ⲉⲣⲁⲧϥ ϩⲓⲙⲏⲣ ⲙ̄ⲫⲓⲟⲙ "the crowd that was standing on the shore of the sea" (John 6:22); (b) "toward": S ⲡⲙⲏⲛϣⲉ ⲡⲏⲧ ⲉⲣⲁⲧϥ "the crowd had run toward him" (Mark 9:25)

AL ⲁⲧⲛ̄-/ⲁⲧⲟⲟⲧ⸗, B ⲉⲧⲉⲛ-/ⲉⲧⲟⲧ⸗, FM ⲉⲧⲛ̄-/ⲉⲧⲁⲧ⸗, S ⲉⲧⲛ̄-/ⲉⲧⲟⲟⲧ⸗ (from ⲧⲱⲣⲉ/ⲧⲱⲣⲓ/ⲧⲟⲣⲉ "hand") "to": S ϥⲛⲁϩⲱⲛ ⲉⲧⲟⲟⲧⲟⲩ ⲛ̄ⲛⲉϥⲁⲅⲅⲉⲗⲟⲥ "he will command his angels" (Matt. 4:6; literally, "he-will-command to-their-hand of-his-angels")

AL ⲁϩⲣⲛ̄-/ⲁϩⲣⲉ⸗, B ⲉϩⲣⲉⲛ-/ⲉϩⲣⲁ⸗, F ⲉϩⲁⲉ⸗, FM ⲉϩⲣⲉ⸗, S ⲉϩⲣⲛ̄-/ⲉϩⲣⲁ⸗ (from ϩⲁ/ϩⲟ "face") "among": B ⲁⲩⲫⲱϣ ⲛ̄ⲛⲉϥϩⲃⲱⲥ ⲉϩⲣⲁⲩ "they divided his clothes among them" (Mark 15:24)

AL ⲁϫⲛ̄-/ⲁϫⲱ⸗, BF ⲉⲭ(ⲉ)ⲛ-/ⲉⲭⲱ⸗, M ⲉⲭⲛ̄-/ⲉⲭⲟ⸗, S ⲉϫⲛ̄-/ⲉϫⲱ⸗ (from ϫⲱ⸗ "head") — (a) "over, on": B ⲉⲭⲉⲛⲟⲩⲧⲱⲟⲩ, M ⲉⲭⲛⲟⲩⲧⲁⲩ "on a mountain" (Matt. 4.8); (b) "on account of" S ⲁⲓϣ̄ⲡϩⲁϩ ⲅⲁⲣ ⲛ̄ϩⲓⲥⲉ ϩ̄ⲛⲟⲩⲣⲁⲥⲟⲩ ⲉⲧⲃⲏⲏⲧϥ "for I have received many troubles in a dream because of him" (Matt. 27:19); (c) "against" M ⲛ̄ⲧⲉϩⲉⲛϣⲏⲣⲉ ⲧⲟⲩⲛⲟⲩ ⲉϩⲣⲏⲓ ⲉϫⲛⲛⲉⲩⲉⲓⲁⲧⲉ "children will rise up against their fathers" (Matt. 27:10); (d) "in addition to": S ⲡⲉⲧⲛⲁⲟⲩⲱϩ ⲉϩⲣⲁⲓ ⲉϫⲱϥ "he who will add to it" (Rev. 22:18)

ALFM ⲉⲧⲃⲉ-/ⲉⲧⲃⲏⲧ⸗, B ⲉⲑⲃⲉ-/ⲉⲑⲃⲏⲧ⸗, S ⲉⲧⲃⲉ-/ⲉⲧⲃⲏⲏⲧ⸗ (from ⲧⲟⲩⲟⲩⲃⲉ/ⲧⲱⲃ/ⲧⲱⲱⲃⲉ "repay, exchange") "because of, concerning": B ⲉⲑⲃⲉⲡⲥⲁϫⲓ ⲛ̄ⲧⲥϩⲓⲙⲓ, L ⲉⲧⲃⲉⲡⲥⲉⲭⲉ ⲛ̄ⲧⲥϩⲓⲙⲉ, S ⲉⲧⲃⲉⲡϣⲁϫⲉ ⲛ̄ⲧⲉⲥϩⲓⲙⲉ "because of the word of the woman" (John 4:39)

S ⲉⲧⲟⲩⲛ-/ⲉⲧⲟⲩⲱ⸗ (from ⲧⲟⲩⲱ⸗/ⲑⲟⲩⲱ⸗ "bosom") "beside": ⲁⲛⲥϭⲏⲣ ⲉⲧⲟⲩⲛ-ⲕⲩⲡⲣⲟⲥ "we sailed beside Cyprus" (Acts 27:4)

(b) with the preposition ⲙ̄ⲛ- "with"

A ⲙ̄ⲛ̄ⲛⲥⲉ-/ⲙ̄ⲛ̄ⲛⲥⲱ⸗, BF ⲙⲉⲛⲉⲛⲥⲁ-/ⲙⲉⲛⲉⲛⲥⲱ⸗, LS ⲙ̄ⲛ̄ⲛ̄ⲥⲁ-/ⲙ̄ⲛ̄ⲛ̄ⲥⲱ⸗ (from ⲛⲥⲉ-/ ⲛⲥⲁ-: see c) "after" (time): B ⲙⲉⲛⲉⲛⲥⲁⲡⲟⲩⲱⲧⲉⲃ ⲉⲃⲟⲗ ⲛ̄ⲧⲉⲃⲁⲃⲩⲗⲱⲛ, M ⲙ̄ⲛ̄ⲛⲥⲁⲡⲡⲟⲛⲉ ⲉⲃⲁⲗ ⲛ̄ⲧⲃⲁⲃⲩⲗⲱⲛ "after the displacement to Babylon" (Matt. 1:12)

(c) with the preposition ALFM ⲛ̄-/ⲉⲛ- "in"

ALS ⲙ̄ⲡⲉⲙⲧⲟ ⲛ-, B ⲙ̄ⲡⲉⲙⲑⲟ ⲛ̀-, FM ⲙ̄ⲡⲉⲙⲧⲁ ⲛ̄- (from ⲙ̄ⲧⲟ/ⲙ̄ⲧⲁ "presence") "in the presence of, before": M ⲕⲱ ⲙ̄ⲡⲉⲕⲇⲱⲣⲟⲛ ⲙ̄ⲡⲉⲙⲧⲁ ⲙ̄ⲡⲉⲑⲩⲥⲓⲁⲧⲏⲣⲓⲟⲛ "leave your gift before the altar" (Matt. 5:24)

AL (N̄)NAϨP̄N-/(N̄)NAϨPE⸗, B NAϨPEN-/NAϨPA⸗, F NAϨPEN-/NAϨλE⸗, M N̄NAϨP̄N-, S NAϨP̄N-/NAϨPA⸗ (from ϨA/ϨO "face") "in the presence of, before": M NAϨP̄NΠEIⲰT, S N̄NAϨP̄MΠIⲰT "before the father" (John 5:45)

A N̄CE-/N̄CⲰ⸗, BLFS N̄CA-/N̄CⲰ⸗, M N̄CA-/N̄CO⸗ (from CA "side") — (a) "behind, after": S N̄CAPACTE "after tomorrow" (Luke 13:33); (b) "except, beyond": S M̄N̄NOYTE N̄CAOYA "there is no god but one" (1Cor. 8:4); (c) "incumbent on": S ECN̄CⲰN ETM̄P̄NOBE "It is incumbent on us not to sin" (Crum 314b)

ALS N̄T̄N-/N̄TOOT⸗, B N̄TEN-/N̄TOT⸗, FM N̄T(E)N-/N̄TAT⸗ (from TⲰPE/TⲰPI/TOPE "hand") — (a) location: S OYAλABACTPON N̄COϬN N̄TOOTC "a jar of ointment in her hand" (Mark 14:3); (b) origin: B N̄TOTϤ M̄ΠETENIⲰT, M N̄T̄NΠETN̄IOT "from your father" (Matt. 6:1); (c) agency: S AYXIBAΠTICMA N̄TOOTϤ "they were baptized by him" (Mark 1:5); (d) possession: B ⲫH ETEN̄TOTϤ "the one who has" (Matt. 13:12; literally, "that who-in-his-hand")

(d) with the preposition ϨA- "at"

ABLSF ϨAΘH (from ϨH "front") "before": L ϨAΘH M̄ΠΠACXA "before the Passover" (John 11:55)

(e) with the preposition ϨI- "on"

AL ϨIPET⸗, S ϨIPAT⸗ (from PET⸗/PAT⸗ "foot") "toward": L AYEI ABAλ ϨIPETϤ "they came out toward him" (John 12:13)

ALS ϨIT̄N-/ϨITOOT⸗, B ϨITEN-/ϨITOT⸗, FM ϨIT̄N-/ϨITAT⸗ (from TⲰPE/TⲰPI/ TOPE "hand") "from, through, by," often with ABAλ/EBOλ "out": L EEINNHY ABAλ ϨI-T̄NΠNOYTE, S EÏNHY EBOλ ϨITM̄ΠNOYTE "I have come from God" (John 8:42), S EI EϨOYN ϨIT̄NTOYATϤE N̄OYϨAM̄N̄TⲰΠ "go in through the hole of a needle" (Matt. 19:24), B ETCⲫHOYT EBOλ ϨITOTϤ M̄ΠIΠPOⲫHTHC "which is written by the prophet" (Matt. 2:5)

ALF ϨITOYⲰ⸗, B ϨIΘOYⲰ⸗, M ϨITOYO⸗, S ϨITOYN̄-/ϨITOYⲰ⸗ (from TOYⲰ⸗/ ΘOYⲰ⸗/TOYO⸗ "bosom") "beside": S ΠETϨITOYⲰK "your neighbor" (Matt. 5:43; literally, "the-who-beside-you")

ALS ϨIXN̄-/ϨIXⲰ⸗, BF ϨIXEN-/ϨIXⲰ⸗, M ϨIXN̄-/ϨIXO⸗ (from XⲰ⸗ "head') "upon, over": B ϨIXENΠAITⲰOY, L ϨIXN̄ΠEEITAY, S ϨIXN̄ΠEÏTOOY "on this mountain" (John 4:20)

(f) with the preposition ϨA-/ⲭA-/ϨA- "under"

A ϨATE⸗ϨH, B ⲭATE⸗ϨH, FLMS ϨATE⸗ϨH (from ϨH "front") "before": S ϤNAMOOⲰE ϨATEϤϨH "he will go before him" (Luke 1:17)

A ϨАPAT⸗, B ⲭAPAT⸗, F ϨAλAT⸗, LS ϨAPAT⸗, M ϨAPET⸗ (from PAT⸗/PET⸗ "foot") "under": S EPEϨENMATOÏ ⲰOOΠ ϨAPAT "soldiers are under me" (Matt. 8:9)

B ⲭAPEN-/ⲭAPⲰ⸗, S ϨAP̄N-/ϨAPⲰ⸗ (from PO "mouth") "beneath, before": B AϤ-ⲰENϨHT ⲭAPⲰOY "he was heartsick before them" (Matt. 9:36)

B ϩⲁⲧⲉⲛ-/ϩⲁⲧⲟⲧ⸗, F ϩⲁⲧ(ⲉ)ⲛ-/ϩⲁⲧⲁⲧ⸗, LS ϩⲁⲧⲛ̄-/ϩⲁⲧⲟⲟⲧ⸗, M ϩⲁⲧⲛ̄-/ϩⲁⲧⲁⲧ⸗ (from ⲧⲱⲣⲉ/ⲧⲱⲣⲓ "hand") "beside, with": M ⲉϥⲙⲁϣⲉⲗⲉ ϩⲁⲧⲛ̄ⲑⲁⲗⲗⲁⲥⲥⲁ "And as he was walking by the sea" (Matt. 4:18)

A ϩⲁϩⲧⲉ-/ϩⲁϩⲧⲏ⸗, F ϩⲁⲑⲏ-/ϩⲁⲑⲏ⸗, LMS ϩⲁϩⲧⲛ̄-/ϩⲁ(ϩ)ⲧⲏ⸗ (from ϩⲏⲧ "heart") "with, beside": S ⲉⲧϩⲙⲟⲟⲥ ϩⲁϩⲧⲏϥ "who were seated beside him" (Mark 3:34)

A ϩⲁϫⲛ̄-/ϩⲁϫⲱ⸗, B ϩⲁⲝⲉⲛ-/ϩⲁⲝⲱ⸗, F ϩⲁⲝⲉⲛ-/ϩⲁⲝⲱ⸗, M ϩⲁⲝⲟ⸗, S ϩⲁϫⲛ̄-/ ϩⲁϫⲱ⸗ (from ϫⲱ⸗ "head") "before, in front of": B ⲛⲓⲉϩⲟⲟⲩ ⲉⲧϩⲁϫⲱϥ ⲙ̄ⲡⲓⲕⲁⲧⲁⲕⲁⲩⲥⲙⲟⲥ "the days that were before the Flood" (Matt. 24:38)

5.3 Adverbs and Adverbial Expressions

Some Coptic adverbs are adverbs in their own right and others are nouns or other expressions used adverbially:

ALFM ⲁⲛ, BS ⲟⲛ "again, also, still"

BM ⲁⲣⲏⲟⲩ, F ⲁⲗⲏⲟⲩ, S ⲁⲣⲏⲩ/ϩⲁⲣⲏⲩ "perhaps"

A ⲙⲉϩⲉⲕ, S ⲙⲉϣⲁⲕ "perhaps" — from *bw rḫ.k* "you don't know"

A ⲙ̄ⲙⲟ, BS ⲙ̄ⲙⲁⲩ, FL ⲙ̄ⲙⲉⲟⲩ, M ⲙ̄ⲙⲉ "there"

B ⲫⲟⲟⲩ, F ⲡⲗⲁⲟⲩ/ⲡⲁⲗⲁⲟⲩ, L ⲡⲟⲟⲩ/ⲡⲟⲟⲩⲅⲉ, S ⲡⲟⲟⲩ "today" — noun "the day"

ALFM ⲥⲁⲡ, BS ⲥⲟⲡ "sometimes" — noun "time"

BS ⲧⲁⲓ "here"; also B ⲉⲙⲛⲁⲓ

ABLSF ϯⲛⲟⲩ, FMS ⲧⲉⲛⲟⲩ "now" — from ⲧⲉⲓ/ⲧⲁⲓⲟⲩⲛⲟⲩ "this hour"

AL ⲧⲟ, B ⲑⲱⲛ, FS ⲧⲱⲛ, FM ⲧⲟⲛ "where"

A ϩⲟⲩⲛ, B ϧⲟⲩⲛ, FLMS ϩⲟⲩⲛ "inside" — noun "interior"

AL ϩⲣⲏⲉⲓ, BM ϩⲣⲏⲓ, F ϩⲁⲏⲉⲓ, S ϩⲣⲁⲓ "up"

A ϩⲣⲏⲓ, B ϧⲣⲏⲓ, F ϩⲁⲏⲓ, L ϩⲣⲏⲉⲓ, M ϩⲣⲏⲓ, S ϩⲣⲁⲓ "down"

FLS ϭⲉⲡⲏ "quickly" — verb "hasten"

Coptic also makes use of Greek adverbs, such as ⲕⲁⲗⲱⲥ (καλῶς) "well."

5.4 Prepositional Phrases Used as Adverbs

Coptic also has a number of words that are used primarily as adverbs, consisting of a preposition plus a noun or other element. Among the more common are:

(a) with the preposition AL ⲁ-, BFMS ⲉ- "to"

    AL ⲁⲃⲁⲗ, BS ⲉⲃⲟⲗ, FM ⲉⲃⲁⲗ "out"

    AL ⲁⲛⲏϩⲉ, BFMS ⲉⲛⲉϩ "ever"

    AL ⲁⲡⲁϩⲟⲩ, B ⲉⲫⲁϩⲟⲩ, FM ⲉⲡⲉϩⲟⲩ, S ⲉⲡⲁϩⲟⲩ "backward" — noun "end"

    AL ⲁⲡⲉⲥⲏⲧ, BFMS ⲉⲡⲉⲥⲏⲧ "downward" — ⲡⲉⲥⲏⲧ "the ground"

    AL ⲁⲧⲟ, B ⲉⲑⲱⲛ, FS ⲉⲧⲱⲛ, M ⲉⲧⲟⲛ "whither" ("to where")

    A ⲁⲧϩⲓ, BFMS ⲉⲧϩⲏ, L ⲁⲧⲉϩⲏ "beforehand" — ⲧϩⲓ/ⲧϩⲏ/ⲧⲉϩⲏ "the front"

    AL ⲁϩⲟⲩⲟ, BS ⲉϩⲟⲩⲟ, FM ⲉϩⲟⲩⲁ "more" — ϩⲟⲩⲟ/ϩⲟⲩⲁ "greater part"

    B ⲉⲙⲁϣⲱ, F ⲉⲙⲁϯ, M ⲉ́ⲙⲁϣⲁ, S ⲉⲙⲁⲧⲉ "very"

A ⲀⲘⲞ, BS ⲈⲘⲀⲨ, L ⲀⲘⲈⲨ "there" ("thither")

A ⲀⲌⲞⲨⲚ, B ⲈⲫⲞⲨⲚ, FS ⲈⲌⲞⲨⲚ, L ⲀⲌⲞⲨⲚ "in, inward"

AL ⲀⲌⲢⲎⲈⲒ, BM ⲈⲌⲢⲎⲒ, F ⲈⲌⲀⲎⲈⲒ, L ⲀⲌⲢⲎ "up"

A ⲀⲌⲢⲎⲒ, B ⲈⲫⲢⲎⲒ/ⲈⲌⲢⲎⲒ, F ⲈⲌⲀⲎⲒ, L ⲈⲌⲢⲎ, M ⲈⲌⲢⲎⲒ, S ⲈⲌⲢⲀⲒ "down"

(b) with the preposition ⲚⲦ/ⲘⲦ "in"

B Ⲙ̀ⲂⲈⲢⲒ, S Ⲛ̄Ⲃ̄Ⲣ̄ⲢⲈ "newly, recently" — ⲂⲈⲢⲒ/Ⲃ̄ⲢⲢⲈ "new"

B Ⲙ̀ⲘⲀⲱⲱ "very"

AMS Ⲙ̄ⲘⲎⲚⲈ, BF Ⲙ̀ⲘⲎⲚⲒ "daily"

A Ⲙ̄ⲘⲞ, BS Ⲙ̄ⲘⲀⲨ, FL Ⲙ̄ⲘⲈⲞⲨ, M Ⲙ̄ⲘⲈ "there" ("therein")

A ⲚⲀⲘⲒⲈ, S ⲚⲀⲘⲈ "truly" — ⲘⲒⲈ/ⲘⲈ "truth"

AFM Ⲛ̄ⲔⲈⲤⲀⲠ, BS Ⲛ̄ⲔⲈⲤⲞⲠ, L Ⲛ̄ⲔⲀⲒⲤⲀⲠ "again" ("in another time")

(c) with the preposition Ⲛ̄ⲤⲀⲦ/ⲤⲀⲦ "on the side"

AFM ⲤⲀⲂⲀⲖ, BS ⲤⲀⲂⲞⲖ "away"

B ⲤⲀⲠⲤⲀ, BS ⲤⲀⲞⲨⲤⲀ, FS Ⲛ̄ⲤⲀⲞⲨⲤⲀ "apart"

B ⲤⲀⲤⲀⲚⲒⲂⲈⲚ, F Ⲛ̄ⲤⲀⲤⲈⲚⲒⲘ, S Ⲛ̄ⲤⲀⲤⲀⲚⲒⲘ/ⲤⲀⲤⲀⲚⲒⲘ "everywhere"

FS ⲤⲀⲌⲢⲀⲒ "up"

(d) with the preposition ⲱⲀⲦ "toward"

AFM ⲱⲀⲂⲀⲖ, BS ⲱⲀⲂⲞⲖ "outward"

A ⲱⲀⲌⲞⲨⲚ, B ⲱⲀⲫⲞⲨⲚ, FLS ⲱⲀⲌⲞⲨⲚ "inward"

AL ⲱⲀⲌⲢⲎⲈⲒ, BF ⲱⲀⲈⲌⲢⲎⲒ, S ⲱⲀⲌⲢⲀⲒ "upward"

(e) with the preposition ⲌⲒⲦ "on"

AFM ⲌⲒⲂⲀⲖ, BS ⲌⲒⲂⲞⲖ "outside"

AFM ⲌⲒⲚⲈⲒ̈, BS ⲌⲒⲚⲀⲒ, L ⲌⲒⲚⲈⲈⲒ "thus" ("on that")

ALFM ⲌⲒⲞⲨⲤⲀⲠ, BS ⲌⲒⲞⲨⲤⲞⲠ "at once, together"

AFLMS ⲌⲒⲠⲀⲌⲞⲨ, B ⲌⲒⲫⲀⲌⲞⲨ "behind"

ABFLMS ⲌⲒⲠⲈⲤⲎⲦ "below"

A ⲌⲒⲌⲞⲨⲚ, B ⲌⲒⲫⲞⲨⲚ, FLS ⲌⲒⲌⲞⲨⲚ "inside"

AL ⲌⲒⲌⲢⲎⲈⲒ, BF ⲌⲒⲌⲢⲎⲒ, S ⲌⲒⲌⲢⲀⲒ "upward"

(f,) with the preposition Ⲍ̄Ⲛ̄Ⲧ/ⲫⲈⲚⲦ/Ⲍ̄Ⲛ̄Ⲧ "in"

B ⲫⲈⲚⲫⲞⲞⲨ, F Ⲍ̄ⲘⲠⲀⲞⲨ, LS Ⲍ̄ⲘⲠⲞⲞⲨ "by day" ("in the day")

A ⲌⲚⲞⲨⲘⲒⲈ, B ⲫⲈⲚⲞⲨⲘⲎⲒ, F Ⲍ̄ⲚⲞⲨⲘⲈⲒ̈, L Ⲍ̄ⲚⲞⲨⲘⲎⲈ, M Ⲍ̄ⲚⲞⲨⲘⲈⲈ, S Ⲍ̄ⲚⲞⲨⲘⲈ "truly"

FLS Ⲍ̄ⲚⲞⲨϬⲈⲠⲎ "at once"

EXERCISE 5

Translate the following phrases and sentences.

1. M ϩⲁⲑⲏ ⲉⲙⲡⲁⲧⲟⲩϣⲏ ⲉϩⲟⲩⲛ ⲙ̄ⲛ̄ⲡⲉⲩⲏⲣ ϩⲁϥϭⲛ̄ⲧⲥ̄ ⲉⲥⲏⲧ ⲉⲃⲁⲗ ϩ̄ⲛⲟⲩⲡⲛ̄ⲁ̄ ⲉⲧⲟⲩⲉⲃ
2. M ϩⲁⲩϩⲓⲧⲟⲩ ⲉⲡⲉⲥⲏⲧ
3. B ⲁⲩϣⲉ ⲛⲱⲟⲩ ϧⲉⲛⲟⲩⲟⲓ ϧⲁⲧⲉⲛⲡⲓϫⲁϫⲣⲓⲙ ⲉϧⲣⲏⲓ ⲉⲫⲓⲟⲙ
4. S ⲙ̄ⲡⲣ̄ⲥⲱⲟⲩϩ̄ ⲛⲏⲧⲛ ⲉϩⲟⲩⲛ ⲛ̄ϩ̄ⲛⲁϩⲟ ϩⲓϫⲙ̄ⲡⲕⲁϩ
5. M ⲡⲟⲩⲁⲉⲓⲛ ⲉⲧⲛ̄ϩⲏⲧⲕ̄
6. L ⲙⲛ̄ϭⲁⲧⲟⲩⲥ ⲛ̄ⲧⲟⲟⲧⲕ̄
7. L ⲉⲧⲛⲁⲣ̄ⲡⲓⲥⲧⲉⲩⲉ ⲁⲣⲁⲉⲓ ⲁⲃⲁⲗ ϩⲓⲧⲛ̄ⲡⲟⲩⲥⲉϫⲉ
8. S ϥⲣ̄ⲙⲛ̄ⲧⲣⲉ ⲉⲧⲃⲏⲏⲧϥ̄
9. S ⲁϥⲃⲱⲕ ⲉⲃⲟⲗ ϩ̄ⲛⲥⲓⲇⲱⲛ ⲉⲑⲁⲗⲁⲥⲥⲁ ⲛ̄ⲧⲅⲁⲗⲓⲗⲁⲓⲁ
10. B ϧⲉⲛⲛⲓⲉϩⲟⲟⲩ ⲉⲧⲉⲙⲙⲁⲩ

Vocabulary

ⲁⲩϣⲉ B “they went” (with **ⲛ-** plus reflexive pronominal suffix “away”)
ⲁϥⲃⲱⲕ S “he went”
ⲁϩⲟ S “treasure”
ⲅⲁⲗⲓⲗⲁⲓⲁ S “Galilee”
ⲉⲙⲡⲁⲧⲟⲩϣⲏ M “they had gone”
ⲉⲥⲏⲧ M “pregnant”
ⲉⲧ- M “that, which”
ⲉⲧⲛⲁⲣ̄ⲡⲓⲥⲧⲉⲩⲉ L “who shall believe” (with **ⲁ-** “in”)
ⲉϩⲟⲟⲩ B “day”
ⲏⲣ M “union”
ⲓⲟⲙ B “sea”
ⲕⲁϩ S “earth”
ⲙⲛ̄- L “there is not”
ⲟⲩⲁⲉⲓⲛ M “light”
ⲟⲩⲟⲓ B “rush”
ⲙ̄ⲛ̄ⲡⲉⲩⲏⲣ M “together” (literally, “with their associate”)
ⲙ̄ⲡⲣ̄ⲥⲱⲟⲩϩ S “don’t gather”
ⲡⲛ̄ⲁ̄ M “spirit” (abbreviation of **ⲡⲛⲉⲩⲙⲁ**, Greek πνεῦμα)
ⲥⲉϫⲉ L “word”
ⲥⲓⲇⲱⲛ S “Sidon”
ⲑⲁⲗⲁⲥⲥⲁ S “the sea”
ϥⲣ̄ⲙⲛ̄ⲧⲣⲉ S “he testifies”
ϩⲁϥϭⲛ̄ⲧⲥ M “he found her”
ϩⲁⲩϩⲓⲧⲟⲩ M “they threw themselves”
ϫⲁϫⲣⲓⲙ B “cliff”
ϭⲁⲧⲟⲩⲥ L “jar” (Greek κάδος)

6. Nominal and Adjectival Sentences

Nominal Sentences

Coptic could make sentences in which a noun or noun equivalent served as predicate, without a verb. These are commonly known as "nominal sentences." There are three patterns of such sentences in Coptic: A B, A ⲡⲉ, and A ⲡⲉ B.

A B Sentences

In the A B sentence pattern, A is always an independent pronoun, which can serve as either subject or predicate.

As subject, first- and second-person pronouns usually appear in the construct state in dialects other than Bohairic: S ⲁⲛⲅⲟⲩⲣⲱⲙⲉ vs. B ⲁⲛⲟⲕ ⲟⲩⲣⲱⲙⲓ "I am a person" (Matt. 8:9), L ⲛ̄ⲧⲕⲟⲩⲥⲁⲃ "You are a wise man" (John 3:2) vs. B ⲛ̀ⲑⲟⲕ ⲟⲩⲣⲱⲙⲓ "You are a person" (Matt. 25:24), M ⲛ̄ⲧⲕⲟⲩⲥⲕⲁⲛⲇⲁⲗⲟⲛ ⲛⲉⲓ̈ vs. B ⲛ̀ⲑⲟⲕ ⲟⲩⲥⲕⲁⲛⲇⲁⲗⲟⲛ ⲛⲏⲓ "You are a snare (Greek σκάνδαλον) for me" (Matt. 16:23).

The absolute forms in dialects other than Bohairic, and third-person pronouns in all dialects, are normally the predicate: M ⲁⲛⲁⲕ ⲉⲧⲛ̄ⲛⲏⲟⲩ "I am the one who is coming" (Matt. 8:7), M ⲛ̄ⲧⲁⲕ ⲉⲧⲛ̄ⲛⲏⲟⲩ and S ⲛ̄ⲧⲟⲕ ⲡⲉⲧⲛⲏⲩ "You are the one who is coming?" (Matt. 11:3), B ⲛ̀ⲑⲟϥ ⲡⲉⲧⲉⲣ̀ⲙⲉⲑⲣⲉ ⲉⲧⲃⲏⲧ and S ⲛ̄ⲧⲟϥ ⲡⲉⲛⲧⲁϥⲣ̄ⲙⲛ̄ⲧⲣⲉ ϩⲁⲣⲟⲓ "he is the one who testifies/testified about me" (John 5:37).

3

A ⲡⲉ Sentences

For third-person pronominal subjects, Coptic uses the A ⲡⲉ sentence pattern. The pronoun, often referred to as a "copula," is an enclitic pronoun that agrees with the predicate in gender (ms ⲡⲉ, fs ⲧⲉ) or number (pl ⲛⲉ). The predicate is a noun, noun equivalent, or independent pronoun in the absolute state: LS ⲡϣⲏⲣⲉ ⲙ̄ⲡⲣⲱⲙⲉⲡⲉ "he is the Son of Man" (John 5:27), B ⲧⲃⲁⲕⲓ ⲙ̀ⲡⲓⲛⲓϣϯ ⲛ̀ⲟⲩⲣⲟⲧⲉ "it is the city of the mighty king" (Matt. 5:35), M ϩⲉⲛⲟⲩⲟⲛⲱ̄ⲛⲉ "they are wolves" (Matt. 7:15), B ⲛⲁⲓⲛⲉ "they are these" (Matt. 10:2), S ⲛⲓⲙⲡⲉ "Who is it?" (John 9:36), L ⲁⲛⲁⲕⲡⲉ "it is I" (John 8:24).

The A ⲡⲉ pattern is also used after a topicalized subject: S ⲧⲉⲥϩⲓⲙⲉⲇⲉ ⲡⲉⲟⲟⲩ ⲙ̄ⲡⲉⲥϩⲁⲓⲧⲉ "but the woman, she is the glory of her husband" (1Cor. 11:7), B ⲡⲓⲱⲥϧ ⲙⲉⲛ ⲟⲩⲛⲓϣϯⲡⲉ ⲛⲓⲉⲣⲅⲁⲧⲏⲥ ⲇⲉ ϩⲁⲛⲕⲟⲩⲭⲓⲛⲉ "The harvest, it is a great one, but the workers (Greek ἐργάτης), they are sparse" (Matt. 9:37),[1] S ⲛ̄ⲧⲟϥ ⲟⲩⲭⲣⲏⲥⲧⲟⲥⲡⲉ "he, he is a kind one (Greek χρηστός)" (Luke 6:35).

---

1   ⲙⲉⲛ and ⲇⲉ are taken from Greek μέν ... δέ "on the one hand ... on the other."

6.4 A ⲡⲉ B Sentences

To identify two nouns with one another, Coptic connected them by means of ⲡⲉ. In this case, ⲡⲉ is a true copula, invariant (unlike in the A ⲡⲉ sentence) and linking the two sides of the expression, of which the first is the subject: e.g., L ⲡⲉⲕⲥⲉⲭⲉⲡⲉ ⲧⲙⲏⲉ "Your word is the truth" (John 17:17), S ⲧⲁⲡⲉ ⲛ̄ⲣⲟⲟⲩⲧ ⲛⲓⲙⲡⲉ ⲡⲉⲭⲥ̄ "The head of every man is Christ" (1Cor. 11:3).

Apparent exceptions to this pattern occur when the second element is the subject and the copula is not invariant, agreeing in gender or number with the subject rather than with the first element: S ⲟⲩⲕⲗⲟⲙ ⲛ̄ⲧⲣⲩⲫⲏⲧⲉ ⲧⲙⲛ̄ⲧⲅ̄ⲗⲗⲟ ⲉⲧⲛⲁⲛⲟⲩⲥ "Good old age is a crown of luxuriosness (Greek τρυφή)" (Prov. 16:31). Since the copula reflects the subject and not the predicate (ⲕⲗⲟⲙ "crown" is masculine), such uses are probably to be understood as appositive: i.e., "It (feminine ⲧⲉ), the good old age (feminine ⲧⲙⲛ̄ⲧⲅ̄ⲗⲗⲟ), is a crown of luxuriousness." Similarly, M ⲛⲓⲙⲧⲉ ⲧⲁⲙⲁⲩ ⲏ ⲛⲓⲙⲛⲉ ⲛⲁⲥⲛⲏⲟⲩ "Who is my mother, or who are my brothers?" (Matt. 12:48): i.e., "She is who, my mother; or they are who, my brothers?"

Examples also occur with an independent pronoun in first position: S ⲛ̄ⲧⲟϥⲡⲉ ⲍⲏⲗⲓⲁⲥ ⲡⲉⲧⲛⲏⲩ "He is Elias, who is to come" (Matt. 11:14), L ⲁⲛⲁⲕⲡⲉ ⲧⲁⲛⲁⲥⲧⲁⲥⲓⲥ "I am the resurrection (Greek ἀνάστασις)" (John 11:25). These seem to be meant to identify the pronoun as predicate: for example, S ⲡⲉⲧⲉⲩ̄ⲛⲧⲁϥ ⲛ̄ⲧϣⲉⲗⲉⲉⲧ ⲛ̄ⲧⲟϥⲡⲉ ⲡⲁⲧϣⲉⲗⲉⲉⲧ "He who has the bride, it is he (who is) the bridegroom" (John 3:28). The difference between these and A B sentences (§ 6.2) is analogous to that between a stressed pronoun and a cleft sentence in English: B ⲛ̀ⲑⲟϥ ⲡⲉⲧⲁϥⲭⲟⲥ ⲛⲏⲓ "he is the one who said it to me (John 1:33) vs. B ⲛ̀ⲑⲟϥⲡⲉ ⲡⲁⲥⲟⲛ "it is he (who is) my brother" (Matt. 12:50).

6.5 Adjectival Predicates

Coptic uses a noun of quality (§ 2.7) with the indefinite article as an adjectival predicate: for example, S ⲡⲉⲓ̈ⲙⲩⲥⲧⲏⲣⲓⲟⲛ ⲟⲩⲛⲟϭⲡⲉ "This mystery (Greek μυστήριον) is great" (Eph. 5:32; literally, "this-mystery it-a-great-one"), M ⲁⲛⲕⲟⲩⲁⲅⲁⲑⲟⲥ "I am good" (Matt. 20:15), S ⲟⲩⲇⲓⲕⲁⲓⲟⲥⲡⲉ ⲡⲭⲟⲉⲓⲥ "the lord is just" (Ps. 10:7), ⲛⲉⲟⲩⲁⲧϭ̄ⲣⲏⲛⲧⲉ ⲉⲗⲓⲥⲁⲃⲉⲧ "Elizabeth was barren" (Luke 1:7).[2]

The language has three specifically predicative adjectives, ⲛⲉϥⲣ- "good, advantageous" and BS ⲟⲩⲉⲧ-, F ⲟⲩⲁⲧ-, L ⲟⲩⲱⲧ "different," and ALF (ⲉ)ⲍⲛⲉ⸗, BS ⲉ̇ⲛⲉ-/ ⲉ̇ⲛⲁ⸗, F ⲍⲛⲏ⸗, M ⲍⲛⲉ-/ⲍⲛⲉ⸗, S ⲍⲛⲉ-/ⲍⲛⲁ⸗ "willing, happy." The first is used preceding a nominal subject: S ⲛⲉϥⲣ̄ⲡⲉⲣⲡⲁⲥ "the old wine is good" (Luke 5:39: sole example). The second is used the same way, but usually in pairs, meaning "is one thing … is another": L ⲟⲩⲱⲧ ⲡⲉⲧⲭⲟ ⲟⲩⲱⲧ ⲡⲉⲧⲱⲥⲍ "He who sows is one thing, and he who reaps is another" (John 4:37). The third is used with nominal or suffix pronominal subjects: S ⲉ̇ⲛⲉⲡⲭⲟⲉⲓⲥ ⲍ̄ⲛⲛⲉⲧⲣ̄ⲣ̄ⲟⲧⲉ ⲍⲏⲧϥ "The Lord is happy with those who fear him" (Ps. 146:11), B ⲙ̀ⲫⲣⲏⲧ̇ ⲉⲧⲉⲍⲛⲏⲓ ⲁⲛⲟⲕ ⲁⲛ ⲁⲗⲗⲁ ⲙ̀ⲫⲣⲏⲧ̇ ⲉⲧⲉⲍⲛⲁⲕ ⲛ̀ⲑⲟⲕ "not in the manner that I want myself, but in the manner that

---

2   The initial ⲛⲉ is a past converter (§ 8.5).

you want yourself" (Mark 14:36). It is often used with following ⲁ-/ⲉ- plus infinitive: S ⲉϩⲛⲁⲛ ⲉⲧ ⲛⲏⲧⲛ "we are willing to give to you" (1 Thess. 2:8). The pronominal form is also used as a noun: S ⲡⲉϩⲛⲁⲛ ⲉⲛⲁⲩ ⲉⲣⲱⲧⲛ "our wish to see you" (Crum 690b).

Eight other predicative adjectives are formed from older or contemporary adjectives with the prefix ⲛⲁ-/ⲛⲉ-. Most have construct forms, and all have pronominal states:

ALSF ⲛⲁⲛⲟⲩ-/ⲛⲁⲛⲟⲩ꞊, B ⲛⲁⲛⲉ-/ⲛⲁⲛⲉ꞊, M ⲛⲁⲛⲟⲩ꞊ "good"
ABFLS ⲛⲁϣⲉ-/ⲛⲁϣⲱ꞊, M ⲛⲁϣⲉ-/ⲛⲁϭⲟ꞊ "many, plentiful"
S ⲛⲁϩⲗⲱϭ꞊/ⲛⲁϩⲗⲟϭ꞊ "pleasant, sweet"
AL ⲛⲉⲉ꞊, BS ⲛⲁⲁ-/ⲛⲁⲁ꞊, F ⲛⲁⲉ-, M ⲛⲁⲉ꞊, S ⲛⲁⲁⲁ꞊ "great"
AL ⲛⲉⲓⲉⲧ꞊, BS ⲛⲁⲓⲁⲧ꞊, F ⲛⲁⲓⲏⲧ꞊, M ⲛⲁⲉⲓⲉⲧ꞊ "blessed"
S ⲛⲉⲥⲃⲱⲱ꞊ "wise"
ALF ⲛⲉⲥⲱ꞊, BS ⲛⲉⲥⲉ-/ⲛⲉⲥⲱ꞊, AFMS ⲛⲉⲥⲟ꞊ "beautiful"
S ⲛⲉϭⲱ꞊/ⲛⲉϭⲱⲱ꞊ "ugly"

These are used with nominal or suffix pronominal subjects: B ⲛⲁⲛⲉⲡⲓϩⲙⲟⲩ "Salt is good" (Mark 9:50), S ⲛⲁⲓⲁⲧϥ ⲙⲡϩⲙϩⲁⲗ ⲉⲧⲙⲙⲁⲩ "Blessed is that servant" (Matt. 24:6).

.6 Negation

Nominal sentences and adjectival predicates are negated by means of initial ⲛ̄- and final AFM ⲉⲛ, BS ⲁⲛ; as with French *ne ... pas*, the initial element can be omitted, but not the final one: S ⲛ̄ⲛⲟⲩⲥ ⲁⲛⲛⲉ "they are not hers" (Matt. 2:18), B ⲁⲛⲟⲕ ⲁⲛ ⲡⲉ ⲡⲭ̄ⲥ̄ "I am not the Christ" (John 1:20), S ⲛ̄ⲛⲁⲛⲟⲩⲥ ⲁⲛ, B ⲛⲁⲛⲉⲥ ⲁⲛ "it is not good" (Matt. 15:26).

Exercise 6

Translate the following phrases and sentences.

1. L ⲁⲛⲁⲕⲡⲉ ⲉⲧⲥⲉϫⲉ ⲛ̄ⲙⲙⲉ
2. M ⲁⲛⲕⲟⲩⲣ̄ⲙⲣⲉϣ
3. S ⲡⲉϥⲣⲁⲛⲡⲉ ⲧⲓⲙⲟⲑⲉⲟⲥ
4. S ⲟⲩϣⲗⲟϭⲡⲉ ⲛ̄ⲟⲩⲣⲱⲙⲉ ⲛ̄ⲓ̈ⲟⲩⲇⲁⲓ̈
5. S ⲡⲉϥⲉⲓⲱⲧⲇⲉ ⲛⲉⲟⲩⲅⲉⲓ̈ⲉⲛⲓⲛⲡⲉ
6. S ⲧⲡⲩⲗⲏ ⲉⲧⲛⲉⲥⲱⲥ ⲛ̄ⲧⲉⲡⲣⲡⲉ
7. B ⲛⲁⲓⲛⲉ ⲛⲓϣⲏⲣⲓ ⲛ̄ⲧⲉⲧⲙⲉⲧⲟⲩⲣⲟ
8. M ⲧⲉⲓ̈ⲧⲉ ⲧϣⲁⲣⲡⲉ ⲁⲩⲱ ⲧⲛⲁϭ ⲛ̄ⲉⲛⲧⲟⲗⲏ
9. S ⲛⲉⲓ̈ⲣⲱⲙⲉ ϩⲉⲛⲓ̈ⲟⲩⲇⲁⲓ̈ⲛⲉ
10. S ⲡⲁⲓ ⲟⲩⲙⲉⲡⲉ ⲛ̄ⲧⲁϫⲟⲟϥ

Vocabulary

ⲉⲛⲧⲟⲗⲏ M "commandment" (Greek ἐντολή)

ⲉⲧ S "which"

ⲉⲧⲥⲉϫⲉ L "who speaks"

ïⲟⲩⲇⲁï S "Jew"

ⲙⲉ S "true"

ⲙⲉⲧⲟⲩⲣⲟ B "kingdom"

ⲛⲁϭ M see § 2.7

ⲛⲉ S "was"

ⲛ̄ⲙⲙⲉ L see §§ 5.3 and 3.4

ⲛ̄ⲧⲁϫⲟⲟⲩ S "what you (fs) said"

ⲟⲩⲉïⲉⲛⲓⲛ S "Greek"

ⲡⲩⲗⲏ S "gate" (Greek πύλη)

ⲣⲁⲛ S "name"

ⲣ̄ⲙⲣⲉϣ M "gentle person"

ⲣ̄ⲡⲉ S "temple"

ⲥⲱϥ B "abomination"

ϣⲁⲣⲡⲉ M see § 4.3

ϣⲗⲟϥ S "disgrace"

7. Verbs

Verb Forms

Every Coptic verb exists in one to four forms: in order of frequency, these are the infinitive, stative, conjunct participle (§ 2.6), and imperative. Most verbs are attested in the infinitive and stative. Few verbs have all four forms.

The Infinitive

Coptic infinitives belong to eleven major morphological classes, and verbs of a single class generally behave the same. Infinitives of transitive verbs can have three states, like those of nouns: absolute, construct, and pronominal. Intransitive verbs usually occur only in the absolute state.

(a) **1v** Infinitives

These have final -ⲱ, -ⲉ, or -ɪ: A ϫⲟⲩ, BFLMS ϫⲱ "say," construct ABFLMS ϫⲉ-; pronominal AL ϫɪ⸗, B ϫⲟ⸗/ϫⲟⲧ⸗, FM ϫⲁ⸗, S ϫɪⲧ⸗; ABLMS ϣⲉ, F ϣH "go"; ABFLMS ϥɪ "carry"; construct ABFLMS ϥɪ-; pronominal ABFLMS ϥɪⲧ⸗; also ALMS ⲉɪ, BF ɪ "come," with no initial consonant.

(b) **1v2** Infinitives

The class is exemplified by ABFLS ϣⲱⲡ, M ϣⲟⲡ "receive"; construct ABLS ϣⲡ̄-, F ϣⲁⲡ-, M ϣⲉⲡ-; pronominal AFLM ϣⲁⲡ⸗, BS ϣⲟⲡ⸗; also ABFLMS ⲙⲟⲩⲛ "remain" (see § 1.8). A few verbs of this class have no initial consonant: e.g., ABFLS ⲱⲡ, M ⲟⲡ "reckon"; construct A ϩⲉⲡ-, BFMS ⲉⲡ-; pronominal AFM ⲁⲡ⸗, BS ⲟⲡ⸗. The absolute vowel is ⲱ/ⲟ, with some exceptions: A ⲛⲟ, BS ⲛⲁⲩ, FL ⲛⲉⲩ "see," M ⲛⲉ; AL ⲟⲩⲉⲛ (BFS ⲟⲩⲱⲛ, M ⲟⲩⲟⲛ) "open"; ABFMS ⲕɪⲙ "move."

(c) **1v2v** Infinitives

There are five kinds of these infinitives, with different first vowels in the absolute state. Examples are

A ϣⲉϫⲉ, B ϣⲁϫɪ, F ⲥⲉϫɪ/ϣⲉϫɪ, L ⲥⲉϫⲉ/ϣⲉϫⲉ, M ⲥⲉϫⲉ, S ϣⲁϫⲉ "speak"

A ⲙⲉïⲉ, BF ⲙHɪ, L ⲙⲁïⲉ, M ⲙHɪⲉ, S ⲙⲉ "love"; construct AL ⲙ̄ⲡⲡⲉ-, B ⲙⲉⲛⲡⲉ-, F ⲙⲉⲗⲗɪ-, M ⲙⲉⲡⲡⲉ, S ⲙⲉⲡⲉ-; pronominal ALMS ⲙⲉⲡɪⲧ⸗, B ⲙⲉⲛⲡɪⲧ⸗

ALMS ⲡɪⲕⲉ, B ⲡɪⲕɪ, F ⲗɪⲕɪ "turn"; construct B ⲣⲁⲕ-, F ⲗⲉⲕⲧ-, M ⲣⲉⲕⲧ-, S ⲣⲁⲕⲧ-; pronominal AMS ⲣⲉⲕⲧ⸗, B ⲣⲁⲕⲧ⸗, F ⲗⲉⲕⲧ⸗

A ϣⲉⲟⲩⲉ, B ϣⲱⲟⲩɪ, F ϣⲁⲩⲉɪ, L ϣⲁⲩⲉɪⲉ, M ϣⲁⲟⲩⲉ, S ϣⲟⲟⲩⲉ "dry"

ALS ⲕⲱⲧⲉ, BF ⲕⲱϯ, M ⲕⲟⲧⲉ "turn"; construct BMS ⲕⲉⲧ-, F ⲕⲁⲧ-; pronominal ALFM ⲕⲁⲧ⸗, BS ⲕⲟⲧ⸗.

(d) **12v2** Infinitives

These have ⲁ/ⲟ as the standard absolute vowel: A ϩⲙⲁⲙ, B ϧⲙⲟⲙ, FLM ϩⲙⲁⲙ, S ϩⲙⲟⲙ "become warm."

(e) **122ⲓⲉ** Infinitives

These are a feature of some dialects, reduced to **122ⲉ** in others: A ⲕ̄ⲛⲛⲓⲉ, B ⲕⲉⲛⲓ, F ⲕϩⲛⲛⲓ, S ⲕ̄ⲛⲛⲉ "be fat"; A ⲡ̄ⲣⲣⲓⲉ, L ⲡ̄ⲣⲣⲉⲓⲉ, S ⲡ̄ⲣⲣⲉ "emerge."

(f) **1v23** Infinitives

These have ⲱ as the standard absolute vowel: ABLS ⲥⲱⲧ̄ⲡ̄, F ⲥⲱⲓⲧ̄ⲧ, M ⲥⲟⲧ̄ⲡ̄ "choose"; construct A ⲥⲱⲧ̄ⲡ̄-, BS ⲥⲉⲧ̄ⲡ̄-, FL ⲥⲁⲓⲧ̄-; pronominal ALM ⲥⲁⲧ̄ⲡ̄⸗, BS ⲥⲟⲧ̄ⲡ̄⸗, F ⲥⲁⲓⲧ̄⸗. The medial radical can also be a lost original consonant: A ϣⲟⲩⲟⲩⲧ, BM ϣⲱⲧ, FLS ϣⲱⲱⲧ "cut"; construct BFMLS ϣⲉⲧ-, B ϣⲁⲧ-, FS ϣⲉⲉⲧ-; pronominal ABS ϣⲁⲧ⸗, F ϣⲉⲉⲧ, LS ϣⲁⲁⲧ⸗.

(g) **12v3** Infinitives

These are largely intransitive, with three patterns: with final radical ⲉⲓ/ⲓ̄, with absolute vowel ⲁ/ⲟ, and with absolute vowel ⲏ:

> A ⲥϩⲉⲉⲓ, B ⲥϧⲁⲓ, F ⲥϩⲉ, LS ⲥϩⲁⲓ, M ⲥϩⲉⲓ̈ "write"; construct A ⲥϩⲉⲓ-, B ⲥϧⲉ-, F ⲥϩⲉ-, L ⲥⲁϩ-, S ⲥϩⲉ-; pronominal A ⲥⲁϩ⸗/ⲥϩⲉⲓⲧ⸗, B ⲥϧⲏⲧ⸗, F ⲥϩⲏⲧ⸗, LS ⲥⲁϩ⸗, S ⲥϩⲁⲓⲥ⸗/ⲥϩⲁⲓⲧ⸗/ⲥϩⲁⲓ⸗/ⲥⲁϩⲧ⸗
>
> AFLM ⲙ̄ⲧⲁⲛ, BS ⲙ̄ⲧⲟⲛ "rest." The first radical can be ⲁ, and the third one can be absent: S ⲁⲣⲟϣ, B ϩⲣⲟϣ "become cold"; ABLS ϩⲕⲟ, FM ϩⲕⲁ "hunger"
>
> ABFLMS ϣⲗⲏⲗ "pray"; AL ⲁⲣⲏϩ, B ⲁⲣⲉϩ, F ⲁⲗⲉϩ, MS ϩⲁⲣⲉϩ "keep, guard."

(h) **1v23v** Infinitives

This class has four patterns, with different first vowels in the absolute state, ⲁ, ⲉ, ⲁ/ⲟ, and ⲱ/ⲟⲩ:

> B ⲥⲁⲑⲙⲓ, S ⲥⲁⲧⲃⲉ "chew"
>
> AFLS ⲥⲉⲉⲡⲉ, B ⲥⲉⲡⲓ "remain, be left"; ALMS ϣ̄ⲙϣⲉ, BF ϣⲉⲙϣⲓ "serve"; construct B ϣⲉⲙϣⲉ-, S ϣ̄ⲙϣⲉ-; pronominal B ϣⲉⲙϣⲏⲧ⸗, S ϣ̄ⲙϣⲏⲧ⸗
>
> ALM ⲥⲁⲃⲧⲉ, B ⲥⲟⲃϯ, F ⲥⲁⲃϯ, S ⲥⲟⲃⲧⲉ "prepare"; construct AMS ⲥ̄ⲃⲧⲉ-, B ⲥⲉⲃⲧⲉ-; pronominal AFLS ⲥ̄ⲃⲧⲱⲧ⸗, B ⲥⲉⲃⲧⲱⲧ⸗, M ⲥ̄ⲃⲧⲟⲧ⸗; also with lost second consonant: AS ⲥⲟⲟϩⲉ "erect," construct S ⲥⲁϩⲉ-, pronominal AL ⲥⲉϩⲱ⸗, S ⲥⲁϩⲱ⸗
>
> A ⲡⲟⲩⲛⲉ, LS ⲡⲱⲱⲛⲉ, F ⲡⲱⲱⲛⲓ, M ⲡⲟⲛⲉ "change"; construct A ⲡⲉⲉⲛⲉ-, F ⲡⲁⲛⲉ-, M ⲡⲉⲛⲉ-; pronominal AFS ⲡⲁⲁⲛⲉ⸗, LM ⲡⲁⲛⲉ⸗, with a lost original consonant as the second consonant.

(i) **1v21v2** and **12v32v3** Infinitives

Infinitives of this type are known as "reduplicated." Most have the first vowel ⲁ/ⲟ in the absolute state, with the second vowel usually either ⲉ or elided. Examples are A ϩⲁⲧϩ̄ⲧ, B ⲫⲟⲧⲡⲉⲧ, F ⲍⲁⲧⲍⲉⲧ, L ⲍⲁⲧⲍ̄ⲧ, S ⲍⲟⲧⲍ̄ⲧ "examine"; construct B ⲫⲉⲧⲫⲉⲧ-, F ⲍⲁⲧⲍⲉⲧ-, S ⲍⲉⲧⲍ̄ⲧ-; pronominal A ⲍⲉⲧⲍⲱⲧ⸗, B ⲫⲉⲧⲫⲱⲧ⸗, FS ⲍⲉⲧⲍⲱⲧ⸗; and A ⲍⲧⲁⲣⲧⲣⲉ, B ⲱϣⲟⲟⲣⲧⲉⲣ, F ϣⲧⲁⲣⲧⲉⲣ, L ϣⲧⲁⲣⲧⲣ̄, M ϣⲧⲁⲣⲧⲏⲣ, S ϣⲧⲟⲣⲧⲣ̄ "disturb"; construct B ϣⲟⲉⲣⲧⲉⲣ-, S ϣⲧⲣ̄ⲧⲣ̄-; pronominal A ⲍⲧⲣⲧⲱⲣ⸗, B ϣⲧⲉⲣⲑⲱⲣ⸗. The second radical of some **1v21v2** verbs is a lost original consonant, with two vowel patterns: AS ⲃⲁⲁⲃⲉ "despise," construct ⲃⲁⲃⲉ-, pronominal ⲃⲁⲃⲱ⸗; A ⲃⲉⲃⲉ, B ⲃⲉⲃⲓ, S ⲃⲉⲉⲃⲉ "bubble." Intransitive verbs often have ⲉ or ⲁ as a second vowel: A ⲕⲉⲥⲕⲥ, B ⲭⲁⲥⲕⲉⲥ, F ⲕⲉⲥⲕⲉⲥ, S ⲕⲁⲥⲕ̄ⲥ "whisper"; B ⲭⲣⲉⲙⲣⲉⲙ, F ⲕⲗⲉⲙⲗⲉⲙ, LMS ⲕⲣ̄ⲙⲣ̄ⲙ "grumble."

(j) **1v234** Infinitives

A few infinitives have four different radicals, with an absolute vowel that is either ⲟ or ⲁ: A ⲥⲁⲩⲧⲛⲉ, B ⲥⲱⲟⲩⲧⲉⲛ, F ⲥⲁⲩⲧⲉⲛ, LS ⲥⲟⲟⲩⲧⲛ̄, M ⲥⲁⲩⲧⲛ̄ "stretch"; construct ABFS ⲥⲟⲩⲧⲱⲛ⸗; pronominal ABS ⲥⲟⲩⲧⲱⲛ⸗, M ⲥⲟⲩⲧⲟⲛ⸗; A ⲥⲁⲁⲛⲍ, B ϣⲁⲛϣ, F ϣⲏⲛϣ, L ⲥⲁⲛⲉϣ, M ⲥⲉⲛϣ, S ⲥⲁⲁⲛϣ "enliven"; construct B ϣⲁⲛⲟⲩϣ-, F ⲥⲁⲛⲟⲩϣ⸗; pronominal A ⲥⲁⲛⲟⲩⲍ⸗, BF ϣⲁⲛⲟⲩϣ⸗, LMS ⲥⲁⲛⲟⲩϣ⸗. Here also 12v(3)4 B ⲍⲁⲟⲗⲓ, S ⲍⲁⲟⲟⲗⲉ "nurse (a child)," with lost original consonant.

(k) ⲧ...ⲁ/ⲟ Infinitives

A large number of transitive Coptic infinitives have the initial radical ⲧ[1] and a final vowel ⲁ or ⲟ, depending on dialect. These are causative constructions, consisting of a construct of the verb ⲧ "give" and a second verb form serving as its object. They have a number of radicals, depending on those of the object verb. Examples are:

ALS ⲭⲟ, B ⲧϭⲟ/ϭⲟ, F ⲭⲁ, M ⲭⲭⲁ "send"; construct AFS ⲭⲉ-, B ϭⲉ-, M ⲭⲭⲉ-; pronominal ALF ⲭⲁ⸗, B ϭⲟ⸗, M ⲭⲭⲁ⸗, S ⲭⲟ⸗ — object verb ϣⲉ "go"

ABLS ⲧⲁⲉⲓⲟ, F ⲧⲁⲓⲁ, M ⲧⲁⲉⲓⲁ "honor"; construct BFS ⲧⲁⲉⲓⲉ-, L ⲧⲁⲉⲓⲁ-, M ⲧⲁⲓⲉ-; pronominal AL ⲧⲁⲉⲓⲁ⸗, BS ⲧⲁⲉⲓⲟ⸗ — object verb ⲁⲓⲁⲓ "become great"

ABLS ⲧⲥⲓⲟ, M ⲧⲥⲓⲁ "sate"; construct ABLS ⲧⲥⲉ-, F ⲧⲥⲁ-; pronominal AFL ⲧⲥⲁ⸗, BS ⲧⲥⲟ⸗ — object verb ⲥⲉⲓ "be satisfied"

AL ⲧⲉⲍⲟ, BS ⲧⲁⲍⲟ, FM ⲧⲁⲍⲁ "set up"; construct A ⲧⲉⲍⲉ-, BFMS ⲧⲁⲍⲉ-, L ⲧⲉⲍⲁ-; pronominal —object verb ⲱⲍⲉ "stand up"

AS ⲧⲙ̄ⲍⲟ, B ⲧⲉⲙⲍⲟ "set on fire"; construct ABS ⲧⲙ̄ⲍⲉ-; pronominal B ⲧⲙ̄ⲙⲟ⸗, S ⲧⲙ̄ⲍⲟ⸗ — object verb ⲙⲟⲩⲍ "burn"

BS ⲧⲁⲣⲕⲟ, FM ⲧⲁⲣⲕⲁ, L ⲧⲉⲣⲕⲁ "make swear"; construct BS ⲧⲁⲣⲕⲉ-, F ⲧⲓⲗⲕⲁ-; pronominal BS ⲧⲁⲣⲕⲟ⸗ — object verb ⲱⲣⲕ "swear"

A ⲧⲥⲉⲃⲟ, BS ⲧⲥⲁⲃⲟ, M ⲧⲥⲁⲃⲁ "instruct"; construct A ⲧⲥⲉⲃⲟ-, BS ⲧⲥⲃⲁⲉ-, F ⲧⲥⲉⲃ-, L ⲧⲥⲉⲃⲁ-, M ⲧⲥⲁⲃⲉ-; pronominal AL ⲧⲥⲉⲃⲁ⸗, BS ⲧⲥⲁⲃⲟ⸗, F ⲧⲥⲁⲃⲁ⸗, M ⲧⲥⲁⲃⲁ⸗ — object verb ⲥⲁⲃⲉ "wise"

---

1 Or ⲭ < ⲧϣ. The initial ⲧ is also sometimes elided: e.g., S ⲕⲃⲟ, B ⲧⲕⲃⲟ "cool."

A ⲦⲘⲀⲤⲈⲒⲞ, B ⲐⲘⲈⲤⲒⲞ, S ⲘⲈⲤⲒⲞ "bring to birth"; construct B ⲐⲘⲈⲤⲒ-; pronominal S ⲘⲈⲤⲒⲞ⸗ — object verb ⲘⲒⲤⲈ "give birth to"

AS ⲐⲂⲂⲒⲞ, B ⲐⲈⲂⲒⲞ, FM ⲐⲂⲂⲒⲀ/ⲐⲈⲂⲒⲀ, L ⲐⲂⲈⲒⲞ "humiliate"; construct AS ⲐⲂⲂⲒⲈ-, L ⲐⲂⲒⲞ-; pronominal AM ⲐⲂⲂⲒⲀ⸗, B ⲐⲈⲂⲒⲞ⸗, F ⲐⲈⲂⲒⲀ⸗, L ⲐⲂⲒⲀ⸗, S ⲐⲂⲂⲒⲞ⸗ — object verb ⲌⲂⲂⲈ "become low"

B ⲦⲌⲈⲘⲤⲞ, S ⲐⲘⲤⲞ "seat"; construct AS ⲐⲘⲤⲈ-, B ⲦⲌⲈⲘⲤⲈ-, L ⲦⲌⲘⲤⲈ-; pronominal A ⲐⲘⲤⲀ⸗, B ⲦⲌⲈⲘⲤⲞ⸗, F ⲦⲌⲈⲘⲤⲀ⸗, S ⲐⲘⲤⲞ⸗ — object verb ⲌⲘⲞⲞⲤ "sit"

A few Coptic infinitives of this class do not conform to the regular pattern with final Ⲁ/Ⲟ, but instead have a final ⲀⲨ/ⲞⲞⲨ/ⲞⲨ in the absolute state:

AL ⲦⲀⲨ, S ⲦⲞⲞⲨ "buy"; construct A ⲦⲀⲨ-, L ⲦⲀⲨⲈ-, S ⲦⲈⲨ-; pronominal S ⲦⲞⲞⲨ⸗ — object verb ⲧ "give"

ALF ⲬⲀⲨ, B ⲬⲈⲨ, M ⲬⲬⲀⲨ/ⲬⲀⲨ, S ⲬⲞⲞⲨ "send"; construct FL ⲬⲀⲨ-, S ⲬⲈⲨ-; pronominal AL ⲬⲀⲨ⸗, F ⲬⲀⲞⲨⲦ⸗, M ⲬⲀⲞⲨ⸗, S ⲬⲞⲞⲨ⸗ — object verb ⲬⲒ "take"

AFLS ⲬⲚⲞⲨ, B ϬⲚⲞⲨ "question"; construct F ⲬⲚⲞⲨ-, LS ⲬⲚⲈ-; pronominal AFLS ⲬⲚⲞⲨ⸗, B ϬⲚⲞⲨ⸗ — object verb ϢⲒⲚⲈ "ask"

ALM ⲦⲚⲚⲀⲨ, F ⲦⲈⲚⲚⲀⲨ, S ⲦⲚⲚⲞⲞⲨ "send"; construct F ⲦⲚⲀⲨ/ⲦⲚⲀⲨⲦ-, S ⲦⲚⲚⲈⲨ-; pronominal ALM ⲦⲚⲚⲀⲞⲨ⸗, S ⲦⲚⲚⲞⲨⲦ⸗ — object verb ⲈⲒⲚⲈ "get"

One further irregular infinitive of this type is A ⲦⲞⲨⲚⲞⲨⲤ, BS ⲦⲞⲨⲚⲞⲤ, M ⲦⲦⲞⲨⲚⲈⲤ "wake," construct ABMS ⲦⲞⲨⲚⲈⲤ-, FL ⲦⲞⲨⲚⲀⲤ-, pronominal AFL ⲦⲞⲨⲚⲀⲤ⸗, BS ⲦⲞⲨⲚⲞⲤ⸗, M ⲦⲦⲞⲨⲚⲀⲤ⸗, originally from ⲧ plus ⲞⲨⲰⲚ "open."

(l) Greek Verbs

Coptic also uses Greek verbs as loan words. Those that appear in Coptic texts are usually treated in three different ways:[2] ⲣ̄/ⲈⲢ- (construct of ⲈⲒⲢⲈ "do") plus the Greek infinitive, ⲣ̄/ⲈⲢ- plus the Greek infinitive without ending, and the Greek infinitive without ending alone: e.g., Greek κελεύειν "command" → ⲣ̄ⲔⲈⲖⲈⲄⲈⲒⲚ, ⲣ̄ⲔⲈⲖⲈⲄⲒ, or ⲔⲈⲖⲈⲄⲒ. Bohairic prefers the first of these; Fayumic, the first or second; Akhmimic and Lycopolitan, the second or third; and Oxyrhynchite and Saidic, the third: for example, B ⲀϤⲈⲢⲡⲢⲞⲪⲎⲦⲈⲄⲒⲚ, L ⲈϤⲢ̄ⲡⲢⲞⲪⲎⲦⲈⲄⲈ, S ⲀϤⲣ̄ⲡⲢⲞⲪⲎⲦⲈⲄⲈ "he prophesied" (John 11:51, Greek ἐπροφήτευσεν). The construct ⲣ̄/ⲈⲢ- is also used with Coptic nouns: for example, AS ⲣ̄ⲞⲨⲰ, B ⲈⲢⲞⲨⲰ, F ⲈⲖⲞⲨⲰ, "reply," literally, "make report (ⲞⲨⲰ)."

7.3 The Causative Infinitive

In addition to ⲧ...Ⲁ/Ⲟ infinitives, which are lexical items, Coptic has a grammatical means of expressing causation, through the element A ⲦⲈ-, B ⲐⲢⲈ- and ⲐⲢⲞ Ⲛ̀-, F ⲦⲀⲈ-, LS ⲦⲢⲈ-, M

---

2   Grossman and Richter 2017. A fourth method, use of the Greek infinitive itself, is rare.

ETPE-, construct of B ⲐⲢⲞ, LS ⲦⲢⲞ "make do," with the infinitive: S ⲦⲢⲈⲠⲈⲔⲈⲞⲞⲨ ⲞⲨⲰⲚϨ ⲈⲂⲞⲖ "making your glory show forth" (Crum 430a). Pronominal forms are

1s	A ⲦⲀ, B ⲐⲢⲒ, L ⲦⲢⲒ, FMS ⲦⲢⲀ		1pl	A ⲦⲚ̄, B ⲐⲢⲈⲚ, FLMS ⲦⲢⲈⲚ
2ms	A ⲦⲔ̄, B ⲐⲢⲈⲔ, FLMS ⲦⲢⲈⲔ		2pl	A ⲦⲢⲈⲦⲈⲦⲚ̄/ⲦⲈⲦⲈⲦⲚ̄/ⲦⲈⲦⲚ̄,
2fs	A ⲦⲈ, B ⲐⲢⲈ, FLMS ⲦⲢⲈ			B ⲐⲢⲈⲦⲈⲚ, FLMS ⲦⲢⲈⲦⲈⲦⲚ̄/ⲦⲢⲈⲦⲚ̄
3ms	A Ⲧϥ̄, B ⲐⲢⲈϥ, FLMS ⲦⲢⲈϥ		3pl	A ⲦⲞⲨ, B ⲐⲢⲞⲨ, F ⲦⲢⲞⲨ/ⲦⲢⲈⲨ,
3fs	A ⲦⲤ̄, B ⲐⲢⲈⲤ, FLMS ⲦⲢⲈⲤ			L ⲦⲢⲞⲨ, MS ⲦⲢⲈⲨ

for example, L ⲀⲦⲢⲞⲨⲘⲀⲞⲨⲦϥ "to have him killed" (John 7:1). literally, "to-make-them-kill-him" Despite its causative origin, however, the form also acts like the infinitive of the underlying verb, without causative meaning, particularly when it is nominalized by the definite article: e.g., S ϨⲘ̄ⲠⲦⲢⲈϥⲈⲒⲀⲈ Ⲙ̄ⲘⲀⲦⲈ ⲀⲚ ⲀⲖⲖⲀ ϨⲘ̄ⲠⲔⲈⲘ̄ⲦⲞⲚ Ⲛ̄ϨⲎⲦ "And not only in his coming but in contentment as well" (2Cor. 7:7—literally, "in-the-making-him-come-and only not but in-the-other-ease of-heart."

7.4 The Stative

The Coptic stative expresses the state resulting from the action of a verb: for example, ALS ⲂⲰⲔ "go" → ⲂⲎⲔ "gone," F ⲀϢⲈⲈⲒ "become many" → ⲀϢ "many, multiple" M ϨⲘⲀⲘ "become warm" → ϨⲨⲘ "warm," B ϧⲞⲦϧⲈⲦ "examine" → ϧⲈⲦϧⲰⲦ "examined." It is descended from an older verb form that had obligatory suffixes for first, second, and third-person subjects. Of these, only the 3ms and 3fs forms have survived, the former as the regular Coptic stative, the latter as an alternate form for some verbs: for example, S ϨⲔⲞ "hunger" → ϨⲞⲔⲢ (3ms) and ϨⲔⲞⲈⲒⲦ "hungry" (3fs).

Because of the stative's origin, its morphological patterns are not as regular or predictable as those of the infinitive. Nevertheless, a few general principles can be stated. The stative of **1v2** and **12v2** verbs is regularly **1Ⲏ2**: ABFS ϢⲰⲠ "receive" → ϢⲎⲠ "received," FL ϨⲘⲀⲘ "become warm" → ϨⲎⲘ "warm, warmed." The stative of most other verbs has a stressed Ⲁ, Ⲟ, or ⲱ in its penultimate or final syllable: e.g., **1ⲱ23** → **1Ⲁ/ⲟ23** (BLS ϨⲰⲦⲠ "reconcile" → BS ϨⲞⲦⲠ̄, L ϨⲀⲦⲠ̄ "reconciled"), **1Ⲓ2v** → **1Ⲁ2v** (AS ⲢⲒⲔⲈ, B ⲢⲒⲔⲒ "bend" → AS ⲢⲀⲔⲈ, B ⲢⲀⲔⲒ "bent"), **1ⲟ21(v)2** → **1ⲉ21ⲱ2** (B ϢⲞⲦϢⲈⲦ, S ϢⲞⲦϢⲦ̄ "carve" → BS ϢⲈⲦϢⲰⲦ "carved"). Some Ⲧ...Ⲁ/ⲟ infinitives have the stative ending ⲎⲨ or ⲎⲞⲨⲦ: e.g., S ⲐⲘ̄ⲔⲞ, B ⲦϨⲈⲘⲔⲞ "humiliate" → S ⲐⲘ̄ⲔⲎⲨ, B ⲦϨⲈⲘⲔⲎⲞⲨⲦ "humiliated."

The stative of some verbs is morphologically irregular compared to that of other members of their class: for example, AFLMS ⲈⲒ, BF Ⲓ "come, go" → ABFLMS ⲚⲎⲨ/ⲚⲎⲞⲨ "come, gone"; ALMS ⲈⲒⲢⲈ, B ⲒⲢⲒ, F ⲒⲀⲒ "act, do, make" → A ⲈⲒⲈ, BF ⲞⲒ, LS Ⲟ, M Ⲁ "done." Coptic also has a stative with the ending ⲰⲞⲨ, used primarily for less common infinitive classes: for example, A Ⲡ̄ⲢⲢⲒⲈ "emerge" → Ⲡ̄ⲢⲈⲒⲰⲞⲨ "emergent."

7.5 The Conjunct Participle

The "conjunct participle" (§ 2.6) is a noun of agent that exists only in the construct form. It is attested for verbs of the six most basic infinitival classes, regularly with the main vowel ⲁ:

> **1v → 1ⲁ1** — AFLMS ϫⲓ, B ϭⲓ "take" → AFLMS ϫⲁⲓ-, B ϭⲁⲓ- "taker": AS ϫⲁⲓⲃⲉⲕⲉ "wage-taker"; but A ϫⲟⲩ, BFLMS ϫⲱ "say" → LS ϫⲁⲧ- "sayer": L ϫⲁⲧⲃⲱⲱⲛ "evil-speaker" (originally **1v2**: see next)

> **1v2 → 1ⲁ2** — ABFLS ⲟⲩⲱⲙ, M ⲟⲩⲟⲙ "eat" → BFS ⲟⲩⲁⲙ- "eater": S ⲟⲩⲁⲙⲣⲱⲙⲉ "man-eater"

> **1v2v → 1ⲁ2 or 1ⲁ2ⲓ/ⲉ** — AS ⲡⲓⲥⲉ, B ⲫⲓⲥⲓ, F ⲡⲓⲥⲓ "cook" → B ⲫⲁⲥ-, S ⲡⲁⲥ- "cooker": B ⲡⲁⲥⲥⲟϫⲉⲛ, S ⲡⲁⲥⲥⲟ6ⲛ "ointment-cooker"; ALMS ϫⲓⲥⲉ, B ϭⲓⲥⲉ, F ϫⲓⲥⲓ "rise, raise" → AFLS ϫⲁⲥⲓ-, B ϭⲁⲥⲓ- "raiser, mounter": B ϭⲁⲥⲓ⳿ⲑⲟ "horseman (horse-mounter)"

> **1v23 and 12v3 → 1ⲁ23** — ABS ⲛⲟⲩϣⲡ "scare away" → BF ⲛⲁϣⲡ- "scarer"; AFLM ⳓⲣⲁϣ, BS ⳓⲣⲟϣ "become slow" → ALFS ⳓⲁⲣϣ- "slow": BF ⲛⲁϣⲡⲏⲣⲓ "scarecrow" (from ⲛⲁϣⲡ- plus ⲡⲏⲣⲓ "quail"), S ⳓⲁⲣϣ2ⲏⲧ "long-suffering"

> **1v23v → 1ⲁ23 or 1ⲁ23ⲉ** — ALM ⲙⲁⲥⲧⲉ, B ⲙⲟⲥϯ, F ⲙⲁⲥⲧ, S ⲙⲟⲥⲧⲉ "hate" → B ⲙⲁⲥⲧⲉ-, S ⲙⲁⲥⲧ- "hater": B ⲙⲁⲥⲧⲉⲥⲟⲛ "brother-hater"

7.6 The Imperative

Coptic regularly uses the infinitive as an imperative: e.g., S ⲁⳓ̅ⲣ2ⲟⲧⲉ ⲉⲃⲱⲕ ⲉⲡⲙⲁ ⲉⲧⲙ̅ⲙⲁⲩ "he was afraid to go to that place" (Matt. 2:22 — infinitive ⲃⲱⲕ) and ⲃⲱⲕ ⲉ2ⲟⲩⲛ ⲉⲡⲉⲕⲧⲁⲙⲓⲟⲛ "go into your chamber" (Matt. 6:3 — imperative ⲃⲱⲕ). Ten specifically imperative forms survive from older phases of the language:

> A ⲁⲩⲉⲉⲓ, B ⲁⲩⲓⲥ, F ⲁⲟⲩⲉⲓ, L ⲁⲩⲉⲓ/ⲁⲩⲉⲓⲥ, S ⲁⲩ/ⲁⲩⲉ/ⲁⲩⲉⲓ/ⲁⲩⲉⲓⲥ "give, come" — all forms also used as constructs

> ALMS ⲉⲓ, BF ⲓ "come" → 2ms ABFLMS ⲁⲙⲟⲩ, 2fs BFLS ⲁⲙⲏ, 2pl AM ⲁⲙⲏⲉⲓⲛⲉ, BF ⲁⲙ-ⲱⲓⲛⲓ, F ⲁⲙⲱⲓⲧⲛ, L ⲁⲙⲏⲏⲧⲛ, S ⲁⲙⲱⲓⲛⲉ/ⲁⲙⲏⲉⲓⲧⲛ

> AMS ⲉⲓⲛⲉ, BF ⲓⲛⲓ, L ⲓⲛⲉ "get" → A ⲁⲛⲓ⳿, B ⲁⲛⲓⲟⲩⲓ/ⲁⲛⲓ-/ⲁⲛⲓⲧ⳿, F ⲁⲛⲓ-/ⲁⲛⲓⲧ⳿/ⲁⲛⲉⲛⲧ⳿, L ⲉⲛⲓ⳿, M ⲁⲛⲓⲛⲉ/ⲁⲛⲓ⳿/ⲁⲛⲓⲧ⳿, S ⲁⲛⲉⲓⲛⲉ/ⲁⲛⲓ-/ⲁⲛⲓ⳿

> ALMS ⲉⲓⲣⲉ, B ⲓⲣⲓ, F ⲓⲁⲓ "do, act, make" → A ⲁⲣⲓ-/ⲉⲣⲓ-, B ⲁⲣⲓⲟⲩⲓ/ⲁⲣⲓ-/ⲁⲣⲓⲧ⳿, F ⲁⲗⲓ-/ⲁⲗⲓⲧ⳿, L ⲉⲣⲓ-/ⲁⲣⲓ⳿, MS ⲁⲣⲓⲣⲉ/ⲁⲣⲓ-/ⲁⲣⲓ⳿

> F ⲗⲁ, LS ⲗⲟ "stop" → 2ms ⲁⲗⲟⲕ, 2fs ⲁⲗⲟ, 2pl ⲁⲗⲱⲧⲛ̅

> A ⲛⲟ, BS ⲛⲁⲩ, FLM ⲛⲉⲩ "look, see" → A ⲉⲛⲟ, BS ⲁⲛⲁⲩ, FL ⲁⲛⲉⲩ

> AL ⲟⲩⲉⲛ, BSF ⲟⲩⲱⲛ, M ⲟⲩⲟⲛ "open" → A ⲉⲩⲉⲛ/ⲁⲟⲩⲛ̅-, BF ⲁⲟⲩⲱⲛ, M ⲁⲟⲩⲟⲛ, S ⲁⲟⲩⲱⲛ/ⲟⲩⲛ̅-

> ABFLMS ϯ "give" → ⲙⲁ- "give"; ⲙⲁ- plus infinitive "make" something happen: e.g., S ⲙⲁⲧⲁϫⲣⲟ "strengthen" ("make strong")

> AFLS ⲱⲗ, B ⲱⲗⲓ "hold" → B ⲁⲗⲓ/ⲁⲗⲓⲟⲩⲓ, ⲁⲗⲓⲧ⳿ "hold, take hold of"

A ϫⲟⲩ, BFLMS ϫⲱ "say" → AL ⲁϫⲓ⸗/ⲉϫⲓ⸗, B ⲁϫⲉ-/ⲁϫⲟ⸗/ⲁϫⲟⲧ⸗, F ⲁϫⲉ-/ⲁϫⲓ⸗, M ⲁϫⲱ/ⲁϫⲓ⸗, S ⲁϫⲉ-/ⲁϫⲓ-/ⲁϫⲓ⸗

The particle A ⲗⲟⲩ, FLMS ⲁⲩⲱ "and" (§ 4.5) is also originally an imperative "add," from ⲟⲩⲱϩ/ⲟⲩⲟϩ "put"; Bohairic uses the infinitive ⲟⲩⲟϩ.

7 Vocatives

Coptic uses either proper nouns or common nouns with the definite article or possessive as vocatives, occasionally with an interjection such as ⲱ "oh": L ⲗⲁⲍⲁⲣⲟⲥ ⲁⲙⲟⲩ ⲁⲃⲁⲗ "Lazarus, come out" (John 11:43), B ⲡⲁⲓⲱⲧ ϫⲱ ⲛⲱⲟⲩ ⲉⲃⲟⲗ "My father, forgive them" (Luke 23:34), S ⲱ ⲧⲉⲥϩⲓⲙⲉ ⲟⲩⲛⲟϭⲧⲉ ⲧⲟⲩⲡⲓⲥⲧⲓⲥ "Oh woman, great is your faith (Greek πίστις)" (Matt. 15:28).

8 Negations

The infinitive is negated by ALMS ⲧⲙ-, BF ϣⲧⲉⲙ-/ϣⲧⲙ-: B ⲉϣⲧⲉⲙⲕⲟⲧⲟⲩ, S ⲉⲧⲙⲕⲟⲧⲟⲩ "to not return" (Matt. 2:12: literally, "to-not-turn-themselves"). The imperative is negated by ALMS ⲙⲡⲣ-, B ⲙⲡⲉⲣ-, F ⲙⲡⲉⲗ- plus the infinitive: M ⲙⲡⲣⲟⲣⲕ "do not swear" (Matt. 5:34). The absolute form of the latter is also used as a general imperative negation: ALS ⲙⲡⲱⲣ, B ⲙⲫⲱⲣ, M ⲙⲡⲟⲣ "don't, by no means, no."

Exercise 7

Translate the following phrases and sentences.

1. S ⲙⲡⲣⲣϩⲟⲧⲉ ⲉϫⲓ ⲙⲙⲁⲣⲓⲁ ⲧⲉⲕⲥϩⲓⲙⲉ
2. B ⲙⲁⲧⲁⲙⲟⲓ
3. B ⲙⲡⲉⲣⲣⲙⲉⲩⲓ ϫⲉⲉⲧⲁⲓⲓ ⲉⲃⲉⲗⲡⲓⲛⲟⲙⲟⲥ ⲉⲃⲟⲗ
4. B ⲛⲉⲧⲁⲓⲓ ⲉⲃⲟⲗⲟⲩ ⲁⲛ ⲁⲗⲗⲁ ⲉϫⲟⲕⲟⲩ
5. M ⲥⲁⲗⲡⲥ ϩⲓⲧⲥ ϩⲁⲃⲁⲗ
6. L ϥⲓ ⲛⲉⲧⲛⲃⲉⲗ ⲁϩⲣⲏⲓ
7. S ⲙⲡⲣⲉⲓⲣⲉ ⲙⲡⲏⲉⲓ ⲙⲡⲁⲉⲓⲱⲧ ⲙⲙⲁⲛⲉϣⲱⲧ
8. S ⲉⲧⲁϩⲟϥ ⲉⲣⲁⲧϥ ⲙⲡⲭⲟⲉⲓⲥ
9. S ⲡϫⲟⲉⲓⲥ ⲙⲁⲧⲁⲛϩⲟⲛ
10. B ⲁⲙⲱⲓⲛⲓ ⲙⲟϣⲓ ⲛⲥⲱⲓ

Vocabulary

ⲃⲉⲗ L "eye"
ⲃⲱⲗ ⲉⲃⲟⲗ B "throw out"
ⲉⲓⲣⲉ S "make"

ⲉⲧⲁⲓⲓ ... ⲛⲉⲧⲁⲓⲓ B "I have come ... I have not come"

ⲏⲉⲓ S "house"

ⲙⲁⲛⲉ̄ⲱⲟⲧ S "market" ("place of merchant")

ⲙⲟ ϣⲓ B "walk"

ⲛⲟⲙⲟⲥ B "law" (Greek νόμος)

ⲣ̀ⲙⲉ ⲩⲓ B "think"

ⲣ̄ϩⲟⲧⲉ S "fear, be afraid"

ⲥⲟ ⲗ̄ⲡ M "cut off"

ⲥϩⲓⲙⲉ S "wife"

ⲧⲁⲙⲟ B "inform"

ⲧⲁⲛϩⲟ S "make live"

ⲧⲁϩⲟ ⲉⲣⲁⲧ⸗ S "present" ("make stand to foot")

ϥⲓ L "lift up"

ϩⲁⲃⲁⲗ M "out"

ϩⲓⲟ ⲩⲉ M "throw"

ϫⲓ S "take" (with ⲙ̄-)

ϫⲟⲉⲓⲥ S "lord"

ϫⲱⲕ B "complete"

8. The Bipartite Construction

1 Definition

Coptic verbal constructions are traditionally designated according to the nature of the verb phrase. The bipartite construction, also known as durative, consists of a nominal or pronominal subject preceding an infinitive or a stative, as well as a prepositional or adverbial predicate. Pronominal subjects are expressed by the subject pronouns (§ 3.6). The construction is essentially situational, placing the subject in a situation (prepositional phrase or adverb), action (infinitive), or state (stative), without inherent regard to time.

2 Adverbial Predicates

Coptic uses a prepositional phrase or an adverb as predicate, without a verb. Such predicates follow their subject: S ⲡⲛⲟⲩⲧⲉ ⲅ̄ⲛⲧⲉⲥⲙⲏⲧⲉ "God is in her midst" (Ps. 45:5) S ϥ̄ϩ̄ⲙⲡ̄ⲭⲁⲓⲉ "he is in the desert" (Matt. 24:26), S ⲡⲉⲧⲣⲟⲥ ⲙ̄ⲙⲁⲩ "Peter was there" (Acts 9:38).[1] An undefined nominal subject is always preceded by ALMS ⲟⲩⲛ̄-, B ⲟⲩⲟⲛ, FM ⲟⲩⲁⲛ "there is/are/was/were": S ⲟⲩⲛ̄ϩⲉⲛⲧ̄ⲧⲱⲛ ⲛ̄ϩⲏⲧⲧⲏⲩⲧⲛ̄ "there are some disputes among you" or "disputes are among you" (1Cor. 1:11).

3 Infinitival Predicates

Infinitives, in the absolute form, are the most common bipartite predicates. If the infinitive has an object, it is always marked by ⲛ̄-/ⲙ̄ⲙⲟ⸗:[2] S ⲥⲉⲟⲩⲱⲙ ⲙ̄ⲡⲉⲩⲟⲉⲓⲕ "they eat their bread" (Mark 7:2), B ϯϫⲱ ⲙ̀ⲙⲟⲥ ⲛⲱⲧⲉⲛ "I say it to you" (Matt. 5:18). The construction is used for both gnomic and progressive statements; S ⲟⲩⲛⲟⲩϭⲟⲛ ϫⲓϩⲁⲡ ⲙ̄ⲛ̄ⲡⲉϥⲥⲟⲛ "a brother goes to court with his brother" (1Cor. 6:6), M ⲥⲉⲉⲓⲣⲉ ⲙ̄ⲡⲉⲧⲉⲛ̄ϣ̄ϣⲉ ⲉⲛ ϩ̄ⲛ̄ⲡⲥⲁⲃⲃⲁⲧⲟⲛ "they are doing that which is not right on the Sabbath" (Matt. 12:2). This construction is traditionally called the First Present.

4 Stative Predicates

Statives follow the same rules as other bipartite predicates; unlike infinitives, they do not take objects: B ⲫⲁⲓ ϥⲭⲏ "this one, he is set" (Luke 2:34), S ⲟⲩⲛⲟⲩⲛⲟϭ ⲛ̄ⲭⲁⲥⲙⲁ ⲧⲁϫⲣⲏⲟⲩ "a great chasm (Greek χάσμα) is set firm" (Luke 16:26). The stative of ϣⲱⲡⲉ "become, happen"—A ϩⲟⲟⲡ, B ϣⲟⲡ, F ϣⲁⲁⲡ, LS ϣⲟⲟⲡ, M ϣⲁⲡ—is particularly common; in most cases it has the sense of "existent": L ⲡⲛⲟⲩⲧⲉ ϣⲟⲟⲡ ⲛ̄ⲙ̄ⲙⲉϥ "God is with him" (John 3:2).

---

1   Bohairic tends to verbalize these with the stative ⲭⲏ "set": ⲧⲉⲛⲭⲏ ⲙ̀ⲡⲁⲓⲙⲁ ⲃⲉⲛⲟⲩⲙⲁⲛ̀ϣⲁϥⲉ "we are set in this place in a desert" (Luke 9:12), for which Saidic has ⲥⲉϩⲛ̄ⲟⲩⲙⲁⲛ̄ϫⲁⲓⲉ "they (were) in a desert."

2   Because it was originally a genitival expression: e.g., S ϫⲓ ⲛ̄ⲟⲩⲧⲁⲉⲓⲟ "take honor," literally, "taking of an honor" (Rom. 13:3).

8.5 The Past Converter

Coptic specifies that a statement applies to the past by means of a prefix, known as the past converter. This has two forms. When the subject is a noun, the converter is ABM ⲚⲀⲢⲈ-, F ⲚⲀⲖⲈ-, S ⲚⲈⲢⲈ-: for example, M ⲚⲀⲢⲈⲦⲈϤⲤⲚⲦⲈ ⲬⲬⲀⲢⲎⲞⲨⲦ ϨⲒⲜⲚⲦⲠⲈⲦⲢⲀ "Its foundation was set firm on the rock (Greek πέτρα)" (Matt. 7:25). When the subject is pronominal, the converter is AFM ⲚⲀ⸗, BS ⲚⲈ⸗, with suffix pronouns: M ⲚⲀⲨⲦⲞⲂϨ Ⲙ̄ⲘⲀϤ "they were beseeching him" (Matt. 8:34).

1s	ABFM ⲚⲀⲒ		3fs	ABFM ⲚⲀⲤ	
	LS ⲚⲈⲒ, ⲚⲈⲈⲒ			LS ⲚⲈⲤ	
2ms	ABFM ⲚⲀⲔ		1pl	ABFM ⲚⲀⲚ	
	LS ⲚⲈⲔ			LS ⲚⲈⲚ	
2fs	ABM ⲚⲀⲢⲈ		2pl	AFM ⲚⲀⲦⲈⲦⲚ̄	
	F ⲚⲀⲖⲈ			B ⲚⲀⲢⲈⲦⲈⲚ	
	LS ⲚⲈⲢⲈ			LS ⲚⲈⲦⲈⲦⲚ̄	
3ms	ABFM ⲚⲀϤ		3pl	ABFM ⲚⲀⲨ	
	LS ⲚⲈϤ			LS ⲚⲈⲨ	

Statements with this converter often have ⲡⲉ added at the end: S ⲚⲈϤϪⲰⲢⲘ ⲞⲨⲂⲎⲨⲠⲈ "he was beckoning toward them" (Luke 1:22). The ⲚⲀ⸗/ⲚⲈ⸗ form of the converter is used before ⲞⲨⲚ̄-/ⲞⲨⲞⲚ/ⲞⲨⲀⲚ: B ⲚⲈⲞⲨⲞⲚ ⲞⲨⲘⲎϢⲈ Ⲛ̀ⲤϨⲒⲘⲒ ⲘⲘⲀⲨ "And there was a multitude of women there" (Matt. 27:55). The same converter is also used with nominal sentences: B ⲚⲈϨⲀⲚⲞⲨⲞϨⲒ ⲄⲀⲢⲚⲈ "for they were fishermen" (Matt. 4:18).

8.6 First Future

The bipartite construction with infinitival predicate is specified for future reference by insertion of the prefix ABLS ⲚⲀ-, FM ⲚⲈ- immediately before the infinitive: S ϨⲎⲖⲈⲒⲀⲤ ⲚⲀⲈⲒ "Elias will come" (Mark 15:36); M ϤⲚⲈϨⲞⲚ Ⲛ̄ⲚⲈϤⲀⲄⲄⲈⲖⲞⲤ ⲈⲦⲂⲎⲦⲔ̄ "he will charge his angels concerning you" (Matt. 4:6).[3] The infinitive can have a direct object: S ϮⲚⲀⲬⲞⲞⲤ "I will say it" (Matt. 13:30).

This construction is traditionally called the First Future. Its prefix is derived from a prepositional phrase meaning "going to," so the construction is actually present in meaning rather than future, like English "Elias is going to come." For that reason, it can also be made past by use of the past converter: L ⲚⲈϤⲚⲀⲘⲞⲨ ⲄⲀⲢ "for he was going to die" (John 4:47). The First Future with past converter is particularly common in the apodosis of conditional sentences after a counter-to-fact protasis: e.g., B ⲈⲚⲀⲔⲬⲎ Ⲙ̀ⲠⲀⲒⲘⲀ ⲚⲀⲢⲈⲠⲀⲤⲞⲚ ⲚⲀⲘⲞⲨ ⲀⲚⲠⲈ "if you

---

3   The prefix derives from an original adverbial predicate: ϮⲚⲀⲬⲞⲞⲤ "I will say it" < *tw.j m n'j r ḏd.s* "I am in going to its saying."

had been in this place, my brother would not have died" (John 11:21; for the negation, see next).

7 Negation

The negation of the bipartite construction has an initial N- and a final AFM ⲉⲛ, BS ⲁⲛ; as in nominal sentences (§ 6.6), the initial element can be omitted, but not the final one: S ⲛϥϩ̄ⲙⲡⲉⲓ̈ⲙⲁ ⲁⲛ "he is not in this place" (Mark 16:6), S ⲛⲉϥⲛⲁⲕⲁⲁⲩ ⲁⲛ ⲉϭⲱⲧϩ̄ ⲉⲡⲉϥⲏⲓ̈ "he would not have permitted them to break into his house" (Luke 12:39).

8 Existential Statements

ALMS ⲟⲩⲛ̄-, B ⲟⲩⲟⲛ, FM ⲟⲩⲁⲛ (§ 8.2) is derived from an older verb meaning "exist." Apart from its function in introducing undefined subjects, it is also used as a verb in its own right: B ⲛⲉⲟⲩⲟⲛ ⲟⲩⲣⲱⲙⲓ ⲛ̀ⲛⲉⲃⲓⲟϩⲓ, M ⲛⲉⲟⲩⲛ̄ⲟⲩⲣⲟⲙⲉ ⲛ̄ⲟⲓⲕⲟⲇⲉⲥⲡⲟⲧⲏⲥ "There was a man who was a landowner" (Matt. 21:33). The negative counterpart of this verb is AFLS ⲙ̄ⲙⲛ̄-/ⲙ̄ⲛ-, B ⲙ̀ⲙⲟⲛ, M ⲙ̄ⲙⲁⲛ/ⲙ̄ⲙⲛ̄-: B ⲙ̀ⲙⲟⲛ ϩⲁⲓ ⲥⲱⲟⲩⲛ ⲙ̄ⲡϣⲏⲣⲓ, S ⲙ̄ⲛⲗⲁⲁⲩ ⲥⲟⲟⲩⲛ ⲙ̄ⲡϣⲏⲣⲉ "there is not anyone (who) knows the son" (Matt. 11:27).

Both verbs are also used with ABMS ⲛ̄ⲧⲉ-, BS ⲛ̄ⲧⲁ⸗, F ⲛ̄ⲧⲏ⸗, LM ⲛ̄ⲧⲉ⸗, from a prepositional phrase meaning "with," to express possession. Reduced forms of this combination are A ⲟⲩⲛ̄ⲧⲉ⸗/ⲟⲩⲛ̄ⲧ⸗, B ⲟⲩⲟⲛⲧⲉ-/ⲟⲩⲟⲛⲧⲁ⸗, F ⲟⲩⲁⲛⲧⲁ-/ⲟⲩⲁⲛⲧⲏ⸗, LMS ⲟⲩⲛ̄ⲧⲉ-/ⲟⲩⲛ̄ⲧⲉ⸗/ⲟⲩⲛ̄ⲧ⸗, and AFLS ⲙ̄ⲛ̄ⲧⲉ⸗/ⲙ̄ⲛⲧ⸗, B ⲙ̀ⲙⲟⲛⲧ⸗, M ⲙ̄ⲙⲛ̄ⲧⲉ⸗/ⲙ̄ⲙⲛ̄ⲧ⸗: B ⲟⲩⲟⲛ ⲛ̄ⲧⲁⲛ ⲙ̄ⲡⲉⲛⲓⲱⲧ ⲁⲃⲣⲁⲁⲙ, M ⲟⲩⲛ̄ⲧⲉⲛ ⲙ̄ⲡⲉⲛⲓⲟⲧ ⲁⲃⲣⲁϩⲁⲙ "We have our father, Abraham" (Matt. 3:9), S ⲙ̄ⲙⲛ̄ⲧⲉⲡ̄ⲛ̄ⲁ ⲕⲁⲥ ϩⲓⲥⲁⲣⲝ "A spirit has not bone and body (Greek σάρξ)" (Luke 24:39).[4] These are often followed by A ⲙ̄ⲙⲟ, BS ⲙ̄ⲙⲁⲩ, FL ⲙ̄ⲙⲉⲟⲩ, M ⲙ̄ⲙⲉ "there": S ⲟⲩⲛ̄ⲧϥ ⲙⲁⲁϫⲉ ⲙ̄ⲙⲁⲩ "he has ears" (Matt. 11:15).

EXERCISE 8

Translate the following phrases and sentences.

1. M ⲙ̄ⲙⲛ̄ⲧⲉⲧⲛ̄ ⲃⲉⲕⲏ ⲙ̄ⲙⲉ ⲛ̄ⲧⲛ̄ⲡⲉⲧⲛ̄ⲓⲟⲧ
2. B ⲛⲉⲟⲩⲟⲛ ⲛ̀ⲧⲉⲟⲩⲁⲓ ⲛ̀ⲟⲩⲃⲱ ⲛ̀ⲕⲉⲛⲧⲉ
3. S ⲥⲛⲁϫⲡⲟⲇⲉ ⲛ̄ⲟⲩϣⲏⲣⲉ
4. S ⲛⲉⲩⲛⲁⲃⲱⲕ ⲉϩⲣⲁⲓ ⲉⲡⲉⲣⲡⲉ
5. L ϩⲉⲱⲥ ϯϩ̄ⲛ̄ⲡⲕⲟⲥⲙⲟⲥ ⲁⲛⲁⲕ ⲡⲟⲩⲁⲉⲓⲛ ⲙ̄ⲡⲕⲟⲥⲙⲟⲥ
6. M ⲡⲉⲧϩⲓϫⲛ̄ⲡⲭⲉⲛⲉⲡⲟⲣ
7. M ⲡⲉⲧϩ̄ⲛ̄ⲥⲟϣⲉ
8. A ⲛⲁⲣⲉⲓ̈ⲱⲛⲁⲥ ⲛ̄ϩⲏⲧϥ ⲙ̄ⲡⲕⲏⲧⲟⲥ

---

4 ⲡ̄ⲛ̄ⲁ is an abbreviation of ⲡⲛⲉⲩⲙⲁ (Greek πνεῦμα).

9. S ⲛⲉϥⲘⲙⲁⲩⲡⲉ

10. B ⲓⲥ ⲍⲟⲩⲟ ⲉⲡⲓⲉⲣⲫⲉⲓ Ⲛⲡⲁⲓⲙⲁ

VOCABULARY

ⲃⲉⲕⲏ M "reward"

ⲃⲱ Ⲛ̀ⲕⲉⲛⲧⲉ B "fig tree"

ⲃⲱⲕ S "go"

ⲉⲣⲫⲉⲓ B "temple"

ⲓⲟⲧ M "father"

ⲓ̈ⲱⲛⲁⲥ S "Jonas"

ⲕⲏⲧⲟⲥ S "whale" (Greek κῆτος)

ⲕⲟⲥⲙⲟⲥ L "world" (Greek κόσμος)

ⲙⲁ B "place"

Ⲙ̄ⲙⲉ M "there"

ⲟⲩⲁⲉⲓⲛ L "light"

ⲟⲩⲁⲓ B "one, a certain person"

ⲡⲉⲧ- M "the one who"

Ⲣ̄ⲡⲉ S "temple"

ⲥⲱϣⲉ M "field"

ϩⲉⲱⲥ L "as long as" (Greek ἕως)

ϩⲏⲧ꞊ A "belly" (with obligatory pronominal suffix)

ϩⲟⲩⲟ B "one great"

ⲝⲉⲛⲉⲡⲟⲣ M "roof"

ⲭⲡⲟ S "create, give birth to"

9. The Tripartite Construction

.1 Definition

The tripartite verbal construction consists of a prefix, nominal or suffix-pronominal subject, and the infinitive. Most Coptic verb forms belong to this category, and most have affirmative and negative counterparts. With few exceptions, the predicate is only the infinitive; the stative is never used in the tripartite construction. The infinitive takes a direct object rather than one introduced by **ⲛ̄-/ⲙ̄ⲙⲟ⸗**. It therefore has three forms: absolute, without object; construct, with a nominal object; and pronominal, with a suffix pronoun as object: e.g., S **ⲥⲱⲗ̄ⲡ** "sever," **ⲥⲉⲗⲡⲟⲩϩⲱⲃ** "cut off a thing," and **ⲥⲟⲗⲡ̄ϥ** "sever it."

.2 Past Tenses

The most basic tripartite construct in all dialects except Oxyrhynchite is a past tense, called First Perfect, formed with the prefix **ⲁ-/ⲁ⸗**, in origin a form of **ⲉⲓⲣⲉ/ⲓⲣⲓ** "do": S **ⲁⲡⲛⲟⲩⲧⲉ ϣⲁϫⲉ ⲛ̄ⲙ̄ⲙⲱϋⲥⲏⲥ** "God spoke with Moses" (John 9:29)—literally, "did-God speak with-Moses." With pronominal subject, the forms are:

1s	ABFS **ⲁⲓ**, L **ⲁⲉⲓ**	1pl	**ⲁⲛ**
2ms	**ⲁⲕ**	2pl	ALS **ⲁⲧⲉⲧⲛ̄**,
2fs	AL **ⲁⲣ**, BS **ⲁⲣⲉ**		BF **ⲁⲧⲉⲧⲉⲛ**
	F **ⲁⲗ**	3pl	**ⲁⲩ**
3ms	**ⲁϥ**		
3fs	**ⲁⲥ**		

The Third Perfect, which exists in Oxyrhynchite, is formed with the prefix **ϩⲁ-/ϩⲁ⸗**, a form of **ⲟⲩⲱϩ** "set" It is used instead of the First Perfect: M **ϩⲁϥϭⲛ̄ⲧⲥ ⲉⲥⲏⲧ** "he found her pregnant" vs. B **ⲁⲩϫⲉⲙ̄ⲥ ⲉⲥⲙ̀ⲃⲟⲕⲓ** "they found her pregnant" (Matt. 1:18). The Coptic dialects other than Akhmimic have a periphrastic perfect, used in contrast to the First or, in Oxyrhynchite, Third Perfect, formed with the verb **ⲟⲩⲱ** "stop": M **ϩⲁϥⲟⲩⲱ ⲉϥⲉⲣⲛⲁⲉⲓⲕ** "he has committed adultery" (Matt. 5:28). Bohairic formed a similar periphrastic perfect using the verb **ⲕⲏⲛ** "cease": **ⲁϥⲕⲏⲛ ⲉϥⲟⲓ ⲛ̀ⲛⲱⲓⲕ** "he has committed adultery" (Matt. 5:28).

Two negative counterparts of the First and Third Perfect exist in Coptic, one with the prefix **ⲙ̄ⲡⲉ-** and other with **ⲙ̄ⲡⲁⲧⲉ-**. The former is a simple past or perfect negation; the latter is perfect, often with the connotation "not yet": B **ⲙ̀ⲡⲉⲡⲓⲭⲁⲕⲓ ⲧⲁϩⲟϥ** "the darkness did not understand it" (John 1:5), M **ⲙ̄ⲡⲁⲧⲉⲑⲁⲏ ϣⲟⲡⲉ** "the end has not yet happened" (Matt. 24:6). Pronominal forms are:

1s	**ⲙ̄ⲡⲓ; ⲙ̄ⲡⲁϯ**	1pl	**ⲙ̄ⲡⲉⲛ; ⲙ̄ⲡⲁⲧⲛ̄/ⲙ̄ⲡⲁⲧⲉⲛ**

2ms	ⲙ̄ⲡⲉⲕ; ⲙ̄ⲡⲁⲧⲕ̄	2pl	ALS ⲙ̄ⲡⲉⲧⲛ̄, BF ⲙ̄ⲡⲉⲧⲉⲛ;
2fs	ⲙ̄ⲡⲉ; ⲙ̄ⲡⲁⲧⲉ		ⲙ̄ⲡⲁⲧⲉⲧⲛ̄/ⲙ̄ⲡⲁⲧⲉⲧⲉⲛ
3ms	ⲙ̄ⲡⲉϥ; ⲙ̄ⲡⲁⲧϥ̄	3pl	ⲙ̄ⲡⲟⲩ; ⲙ̄ⲡⲁⲧⲟⲩ
3fs	ⲙ̄ⲡⲉⲥ; ⲙ̄ⲡⲁⲧⲥ̄		

Examples are B ⲙ̄ⲡⲉⲧⲉⲛϭⲟⲥϫⲉⲥ "you have not danced" (Matt. 11:17), L ⲙ̄ⲡⲁϯⲃⲱⲕ ⲁϩⲣⲏⲓ "I have not yet gone up" (John 20:17).

The verb A ϫⲟⲩ, BFLMS ϫⲱ "say" has both a regular past tense—e.g., B ⲁϥϫⲱ ⲙⲙⲟⲥ ⲉⲑⲃⲏⲧⲟⲩ, M ϩⲁϥϫⲱ ⲙ̄ⲙⲁⲩ ⲉⲧⲃⲏⲧⲟⲩ "he said it/them about them" (Matt. 21:45)—but also a construct and pronominal form used to introduce direct or indirect quotations. The construct is AL ⲡⲁϫⲉ-, BFMS ⲡⲉϫⲉ- with nominal subject: L ⲡⲁϫⲉⲡⲉⲧⲣⲟⲥ ⲛⲉϥ "Peter said to him" (John 13:8). Pronominal forms are:

1s	AL ⲡⲁϫⲉⲓ, B ⲡⲉϫⲏⲓ,	1pl	AL ⲡⲁϫⲉⲛ, B ⲡⲉϫⲁⲛ, M ⲡⲉϫⲉⲛ
	M ⲡⲉϫⲉï, S ⲡⲉϫⲁⲓ	2pl	AL ⲡⲁϫⲏⲧⲛⲉ, B ⲡⲉϫⲱⲧⲉⲛ,
2ms	M ⲡⲉϫⲉⲕ, S ⲡⲉϫⲁⲕ		M ⲡⲉϫⲉⲧⲛ̄, S ⲡⲉϫⲏⲧⲛ̄
3ms	AL ⲡⲁϫⲉϥ, BS ⲡⲉϫⲁϥ,	3pl	AL ⲡⲁϫⲉⲩ, B ⲡⲉϫⲱⲟⲩ,
	FM ⲡⲉϫⲉϥ		FM ⲡⲉϫⲉⲩ, S ⲡⲉϫⲁⲩ
3fs	AL ⲡⲁϫⲉⲥ, BS ⲡⲉϫⲁⲥ,		
	FM ⲡⲉϫⲉⲥ		

Examples: S ⲡⲉϫⲏⲧⲛ̄ ϫⲉⲟⲩⲛ̄ⲟⲩⲇⲁⲓⲙⲟⲛⲓⲟⲛ ϩⲓⲱⲱϥ "you say that there is a demon (Greek δαιμόνιος) on him" (Luke 7:33), M ⲡⲉϫⲉⲩ ⲛⲉϥ ϫⲉϩⲛ̄ⲧⲃⲏⲑⲗⲉⲉⲙ "They said to him, 'In Bethlehem'" (Matt. 2:5).

9.3 Gnomic Tenses

Although the First Present is used for gnomic statements (§ 8.3), Coptic also has a specific verb form for this use, known as the First Aorist. It is marked by the prefix A ϩⲁⲣⲉ-, BLMS ϣⲁⲣⲉ-, F ϣⲁⲗⲉ- before nominal subjects: S ϣⲁⲣⲉⲡⲉⲙⲛⲟⲩⲧ ⲟⲩⲱⲛ ⲛⲁϥ ⲁⲩⲱ ϣⲁⲣⲉⲛⲉⲥⲟⲟⲩ ⲥⲱⲧⲙ̄ ⲉⲧⲉϥⲥⲙⲏ "the doorkeeper opens to him and the sheep listen to his voice" (John 10:3). With pronominal subject, the prefix is

1s	A ϩⲁⲣⲓ, BFS ϣⲁⲓ, LM ϣⲁⲣⲓ	1pl	A ϩⲁⲣⲉⲛ, BFS ϣⲁⲛ, LM ϣⲁⲣⲉⲛ
2ms	A ϩⲁⲣⲉⲕ, BFS ϣⲁⲕ, LM ϣⲁⲣⲉⲕ	2pl	A ϩⲁⲣⲉⲧⲛ̄, B ϣⲁⲣⲉⲧⲉⲛ,
2fs	A ϩⲁⲣⲉ, BLMS ϣⲁⲣⲉ		F ϣⲁⲧⲉⲧⲉⲛ, LM ϣⲁⲣⲉⲧⲛ̄,
3ms	A ϩⲁⲣⲉϥ, BFS ϣⲁϥ, LM ϣⲁⲣⲉϥ		S ϣⲁⲧⲉⲧⲛ̄
3fs	A ϩⲁⲣⲉⲥ, BFS ϣⲁⲥ, LM ϣⲁⲣⲉⲥ	3pl	A ϩⲁⲣⲟⲩ, BFS ϣⲁⲩ, LM ϣⲁⲣⲟⲩ

for example, L ⲡⲉⲧϣⲟⲟⲡ ⲁⲃⲁⲗ ϩⲛ̄ⲡⲛⲟⲩⲧⲉ ϣⲁⲣⲉϥⲥⲱⲧⲙ̄ ⲁⲛⲥⲉϫⲉ ⲙ̄ⲡⲛⲟⲩⲧⲉ "The one who is from God, he listens to the speech of God" (John 8:47).

The negative counterpart of the First Aorist has the prefix AL ⲙⲁⲣⲉ-, B ⲙ̀ⲡⲁⲣⲉ-, F ⲙⲉⲗⲉ-, MS ⲙⲉⲣⲉ-: B ⲙ̀ⲡⲁⲣⲉⲛⲓ̈ⲟⲩⲇⲁⲓ ⲙⲟⲩϫⲧ̄ ⲛⲉⲙⲛⲓⲥⲁⲙⲁⲣⲓⲧⲏⲥ "The Jews do not mix with the Samaritans" (John 4:9). Pronominal forms are

1s	AL ⲙⲁⲓ, B ⲙ̀ⲡⲁⲓ, FMS ⲙⲉⲓ	1pl	AL ⲙⲁⲛ, B ⲙ̀ⲡⲁⲛ, FMS ⲙⲉⲛ
2ms	AL ⲙⲁⲕ, B ⲙ̀ⲡⲁⲕ, FMS ⲙⲉⲕ	2pl	AL ⲙⲁⲧⲉⲧⲛ̄, B ⲙ̀ⲡⲁⲣⲉⲧⲉⲛ,
2fs	AL ⲙⲁⲣⲉ, B ⲙ̀ⲡⲁⲣⲉ, FMS ⲙⲉⲣⲉ		FMS ⲙⲉⲧⲉⲧⲛ̄
3ms	AL ⲙⲁϥ, B ⲙ̀ⲡⲁϥ, FMS ⲙⲉϥ	3pl	AL ⲙⲁⲩ, B ⲙ̀ⲡⲁⲩ, FMS ⲙⲉⲩ
3fs	AL ⲙⲁⲥ, B ⲙ̀ⲡⲁⲥ, FMS ⲙⲉⲥ		

for example, S ⲙⲉⲩϫⲉⲗⲉⲉⲗⲟⲟⲗⲉ ⲉⲃⲟⲗ ⲍ̄ⲛⲃⲁⲧⲟⲥ "they do not harvest grape from bramble (Greek βάτος)" (Luke 6:44).

.4 Prospective Tenses

Two tripartite constructions have reference to prospective actions, both modally non-indicative. One, called the Third Future, expresses inevitability or desirability. It is actually a quadripartite construct, consisting of the prefix ⲁ-/ⲉ-, a nominal or pronominal subject, and (in ALM) ⲁ-/ⲉ- plus the infinitive. With nominal subject, the prefix is A ⲁ- ... ⲁ-, B ⲉⲣⲉ̀-, F ⲉⲗⲉ-, L ⲉⲣⲉ- ... ⲁ-, M ⲉⲣⲉ- ... ⲉ- (ⲉ- also omitted), S ⲉⲣⲉ-: s ⲍ̄ⲙⲡⲣⲁⲛ ⲛ̄ⲓⲥ ⲉⲣⲉⲡⲁⲧ ⲛⲓⲙ ⲕⲱⲗ̄ⲭ̄ "at the name of Jesus every knee should bend" (Phil. 2:10). With pronominal subject, the forms are

1s	A ⲁⲓⲁ, BFMS ⲉⲓ̈ⲉ, L ⲉⲓ̈ⲁ	1pl	A ⲁⲛⲁ, BFMS ⲉⲛⲉ, L ⲉⲥⲁ
2ms	A ⲁⲕⲁ, BFMS ⲉⲕⲉ, L ⲉⲕⲁ	2pl	A ⲁⲧⲉⲧⲛⲁ, B ⲉⲣⲉⲧⲉⲛⲉ,
2fs	A ⲁⲣⲁ, BMS ⲉⲣⲉ, F ⲉⲗⲉ, L ⲉⲣⲁ		FMS ⲉⲧⲉⲧⲛⲉ, L ⲉⲣⲉⲧⲛⲁ
3ms	A ⲁϥⲁ, BFMS ⲉϥⲉ, L ⲉϥⲁ	3pl	A ⲁⲩⲁ, BFMS ⲉⲩⲉ, L ⲉⲩⲁ
3fs	A ⲁⲥⲁ, BFMS ⲉⲥⲉ, L ⲉⲥⲁ		

for example, M ⲉⲃⲁⲗⲇⲉ ⲍ̄ⲛⲛⲉⲩⲕⲁⲣⲡⲟⲥ ⲉⲧⲉⲧⲛⲉⲥⲟⲩⲟⲛⲟⲩ "And by their fruits (Greek καρπός) you shall know them" (Matt. 7:16).

The negative counterpart of the Third Future is tripartite, with the prefix A ⲛⲉ-, BSFM ⲛ̄ⲛⲉ- before a nominal subject: B ⲛ̀ⲛⲉⲟⲩⲁⲓ ⲥⲱⲧⲉⲙ ⲉⲧⲉⲥⲙⲏ "one shall not listen to his voice" (Matt. 12:19). The pronominal prefixes are

1s	A ⲛⲁ, BFMS ⲛ̄ⲛⲁ	1pl	A ⲛⲉⲛ, BFMS ⲛ̄ⲛⲉⲛ
2ms	A ⲛⲉⲕ, BFMS ⲛ̄ⲛⲉⲕ	2pl	A ⲛⲉⲧⲛ, BF ⲛ̄ⲛⲉⲧⲉⲛ,
2fs	A ⲛⲉ, BFMS ⲛ̄ⲛⲉⲕ		MS ⲛ̄ⲛⲉⲧⲛ̄
3ms	A ⲛⲉϥ, BFMS ⲛ̄ⲛⲉϥ	3pl	A ⲛⲟⲩ, BFM ⲛ̄ⲛⲟⲩ, S ⲛ̄ⲛⲉⲩ
3fs	A ⲛⲉⲥ, BFMS ⲛ̄ⲛⲉⲥ		

An example is M ⲛ̄ⲛⲉⲩⲕⲁⲧⲧⲟⲩ ⲉⲣⲉⲧϥ̄ ⲛ̄ⲍⲏⲣⲱⲇⲏⲥ "they should not return to Herod" (Matt. 2:12).

The second prospective tense is the Optative, with optative/jussive meaning. Its prefix is ABLMS ⲙⲁⲣⲉ-, F ⲙⲁⲗⲉ-: L ⲙⲁⲣⲉⲛⲣⲱⲙⲉ ⲛⲁϫⲟⲩ ⲁⲍⲣⲏⲓ "Let the people set themselves down" (John 6:10). With pronominal subject, the prefix is

1s	ABLMS ⲙⲁⲣⲓ, F ⲙⲁⲗⲓ		1pl	ABLMS ⲙⲁⲣⲉⲛ, F ⲙⲁⲗⲉⲛ
2s	— (imperative)		2pl	— (imperative)
3ms	ABLMS ⲙⲁⲣⲉϥ, F ⲙⲁⲗⲉϥ		3pl	ABLMS ⲙⲁⲣⲟⲩ, F ⲙⲁⲗⲟⲩ
3fs	ABLMS ⲙⲁⲣⲉⲥ, F ⲙⲁⲗⲉⲥ			

e.g., B ⲙⲁⲣⲟⲩⲑⲱⲙⲥ ⲛ̄ⲛⲟⲩⲣⲉϥⲙⲱⲟⲩⲧ "let them bury their dead" (Matt. 8:22). There is also an absolute form, A ⲙⲁⲣⲁⲛ, BS ⲙⲁⲣⲟⲛ, meaning "let's" or "let's go." The Optative is negated with the negative imperative (§ 7.8) plus the Causative Infinitive (§ 7.3): S ⲙ̄ⲡⲣ̄ⲧⲣⲉⲛⲛ̄ⲕⲟⲧⲕ̄ "let us not sleep" (1 Thess. 5:6).

9.5 The Past Converter

The past converter (§ 8.5) is used with tripartite forms to indicate a stage of action prior to that designated by the verb form: S ⲛⲉⲁϥⲉⲓ̈ⲡⲉ ⲉⲑⲓ̈ⲗⲏⲙ ⲉⲟⲩⲱϣ̄ⲧ "he had come to Jerusalem to worship" (Acts 8:27), B ⲛⲉϣⲁⲣⲉⲓⲏ̄ⲥ ⲑⲱⲟⲩⲧ ⲉⲙⲁⲡⲉ ⲛ̄ⲛⲟⲩⲙⲏϣ ⲛ̄ⲥⲟⲡ "Jesus used to gather there on many occasions" (John 18:2), L ⲓⲏ̄ⲥ ⲛⲉⲙ̄ⲡⲁⲧϥ̄ϫⲓ ⲉⲁⲩ "Jesus had not yet taken glory" (John 7:39).

9.6 Passives

Coptic does not have dedicated passive forms; instead, it uses third-person plural pronominal subjects to paraphrase the passive. In some cases, the sense is less passive than active with an unspecified subject: B ⲥⲉⲛⲁⲑⲉⲃⲓⲟϥ "they will humble him" or "he will be humbled" (Luke 14:11). In others, however, the passive sense is clear: B ⲁⲩⲛⲁⲙⲉⲥⲡⲭ̄ⲥ̄ ⲑⲱⲛ "where the Christ was going to be born," literally, "they-were-going-to-birth-the-Christ where" (Matt. 2:4). Passive participles are similarly paraphrased: M ⲡⲉⲧⲟⲩⲙⲟⲩⲧⲉ ⲉⲣⲁϥ ϫⲉⲡⲉⲭⲣ̄ⲥ̄ "the one called the Christ," literally, "the-who-they-say about-him that-the-Christ" (Matt. 27:17).

Some transitive verbs can also be used intransitively. An example is ⲟⲩⲱⲛ "open": S ⲁⲩⲟⲩⲱⲛ ⲛ̄ⲛⲉⲩⲁⲍⲱⲱⲣ "they opened their treasures" (Matt. 2:11) and ⲛⲉⲙϩⲁⲁⲩ ⲁⲩⲟⲩⲱⲛ "the tombs opened" (Matt. 27:52).

9.7 Ability

Coptic expresses the ability to do something by means of the infinitival prefix A ⲍ-, BFLMS ϣ-, FS ⲉϣ-: for example, S ⲙⲉⲩⲉϣⲁⲙⲁⲍⲧⲉ ⲙ̄ⲙⲟϥ "they could not lay hold of him" (Job 31:11): ⲙⲉⲩ "they could not" (§ 9.3) – ⲉϣ – ⲁⲙⲁⲍⲧⲉ "lay hold" – ⲙ̄ⲙⲟϥ "of him"; B ⲙ̄ⲡⲉϩⲗⲓ ϣⲉⲣⲧⲟⲗⲙⲁⲛ ⲉϣⲉⲛϥ "no one could find the courage to ask him" (Mark 12:34): ⲙ̄ⲡⲉ (§ 9.2) – ϩⲗⲓ "anyone" – ϣ – ⲉⲣ "do" (construct of ⲓⲣⲓ) – ⲧⲟⲗⲙⲁⲛ "courage" (Greek τόλμα) – ⲉ "to" – ϣⲉⲛϥ "ask him" (pronominal form of ϣⲓⲛⲓ). A frequent combination is A ϭⲙ̄ϭⲁⲙ, FLM ϣ̄ⲙ̄ϭⲁⲙ, B ϣϫⲉⲙϫⲟⲙ, S ϣ̄ϭⲙ̄ϭⲟⲙ "be able," literally, "be able" (ϩ/ϣ) "to find" (ϭⲙ/ϫⲉⲙ,

construct of ϭⲓⲛⲉ/ⲭⲓⲙⲓ/ϭⲓⲛⲓ "find") "strength" (ϭⲁⲙ/ⲭⲟⲙ/ϭⲟⲙ): B ⲙⲡⲟⲩϣⲭⲉⲙⲭⲟⲙ
ⲛⲉⲣⲫⲁ̣ϩⲣⲓ ⲉⲣⲟϥ "they could not cure him" (Matt. 17:16): ⲙ̄ⲡⲟⲩ "they did not" (§ 9.2) –
ϣⲭⲉⲙⲭⲟⲙ – ⲛ̀ "of" – ⲉⲣ "making" (construct of ⲓⲡⲓ) – ⲫⲁ̣ϩⲣⲓ "treatment" – ⲉⲣⲟϥ "to him."

Exercise 9

Translate the following phrases and sentences.

1. A ϥⲛⲁⲡⲱⲧ ϩⲓⲭ̄ⲛⲑⲁⲗⲁⲥⲥⲁ ⲛ̄ⲧϩⲉ ⲛ̄ⲟⲩⲙⲟⲩⲓ
2. A ⲁϥϣ̄ⲛϩⲧⲏϥ ϩⲁⲣⲱⲧⲛⲉ
3. A ⲡⲁⲭⲉⲡⲭⲁⲉⲓⲥ ⲭⲉⲧⲛⲁⲥϩⲉⲓ ⲙ̄ⲡⲁⲣⲉⲛ ⲁⲭ̄ⲛⲧⲟⲩⲧⲉϩⲛⲉ
4. A ⲛ̄ⲣⲉϥⲣ̄ⲛⲁⲃⲉⲗⲉ ⲛ̄ⲧⲁⲩ ⲥⲉⲛⲁⲭⲓϣⲓⲡⲉ
5. A ⲥⲉⲭⲓⲧⲟⲩ ⲁⲧⲙⲏⲧⲣⲟⲡⲟⲗⲓⲥ
6. F ⲁϥⲉⲗϩⲟⲙⲟⲗⲟⲅⲓⲛ ⲁⲩⲱ ⲙ̄ⲡⲉϥⲉⲗⲁⲣⲛⲓⲥⲑⲉ
7. F ⲁⲛⲁⲕ ϯⲭⲱⲕⲉⲙ ⲙ̄ⲙⲱⲧⲉⲛ ϩ̄ⲛⲟⲩⲙⲁⲟⲩ
8. L ⲙ̄ⲡ̄ⲣⲧⲣⲉⲡⲉⲧⲛ̄ϩⲏⲧ ϣⲧⲁⲣⲧ̄ⲣ
9. L ⲉⲣⲉⲧ̄ⲛⲛⲁϣⲱⲡⲉ ⲛ̄ϣⲏⲣⲉ ⲙ̄ⲡⲟⲩⲁⲉⲓⲛ
10. B ⲙⲁⲣⲉⲛ̄ϩⲟⲑⲃⲉϥ

Vocabulary

ⲁⲭ̄ⲛ A § 5.4

ⲉⲗⲁⲣⲛⲓⲥⲑⲉ F "deny" (construct of ⲓⲁⲓ "do" plus Greek ἀρνεῖσθαι)

ⲉⲗϩⲟⲙⲟⲗⲟⲅⲓⲛ F "confess" (construct of ⲓⲁⲓ "do" plus Greek ὁμολογεῖν)

ⲙⲁⲟⲩ F "water"

ⲙⲏⲧⲣⲟⲡⲟⲗⲓⲥ A "city" (Greek μητρόπολις)

ⲙⲟⲩⲓ A "lion"

ⲟⲩⲁⲉⲓⲛ L "light"

ⲡⲱⲧ A "run"

ⲣⲉⲛ A "name"

ⲣⲛⲁⲃⲉ A "sin" (see § 2.6)

ⲥϩⲉⲓ A "write"

ⲧⲉϩⲛⲉ A "forehead"

ⲑⲁⲗⲁⲥⲥⲁ A "the sea" (Greek θάλασσα) (for ⲑⲁⲗⲁⲥⲥⲁ)

ϣⲓⲡⲉ A "shame"

ϣ̄ⲛϩⲧⲏ⸗ A "be merciful" (with pronominal suffix; ϩⲁ- "to")

ϣⲧⲁⲣⲧ̄ⲣ L "be troubled"

ϣⲱⲡⲉ L "become"

ϩⲉ A "manner" (ⲛ̄ⲧϩⲉ "in the manner" = "like")

ϩⲏⲧ L "heart"

ϧⲱⲧⲉⲃ B "kill"

ⲭⲁⲉⲓⲥ A "lord"

ⲭⲓ A "receive, take"

ⲭⲱⲕⲉⲙ F "wash"

10. DEPENDENT FORMS

0.1 Definition

In addition to the bipartite and tripartite verbal constructions, Coptic also has a number of specific verb forms for dependent, rather than main clause, usage. All are marked by a prefix before a nominal or pronominal subject and predicate. The prefix can be thought of as a converter, designating an independent form for dependent function.

0.2 The Circumstantial Converter

The primary dependent converter is called "circumstantial," although it is used in continuative clauses as well. Before nominal subjects, the converter is A ⲉ-, BLMS ⲉⲣⲉ- F ⲉⲗⲉ-: B ⲁϥϣⲉ ⲛⲁϥ ⲉⲣⲉⲡⲉϥϩⲏⲧ ⲙⲟⲕϩ "he went away with his heart grieved," "he went away, his heart being grieved" (Matt. 19:22)—ⲁϥϣⲉ "he went" (§ 9.2) – ⲛⲁϥ "for him(self)" – ⲉⲣⲉ DEP – ⲡⲉϥϩⲏⲧ "his heart" – ⲙⲟⲕϩ "grieved" (stative of ⲙ̄ⲕⲁϩ "grieve").[1] The pronominal forms of the converter for bipartite constructions are:

1s	ⲉⲓ	3fs	ⲉⲥ
2ms	ⲉⲕ	1pl	ⲉⲛ
2fs	ABLMS ⲉⲣⲉ, F ⲉⲗⲉ	2pl	ALMS ⲉⲧⲉⲧⲛ̄, B ⲉⲣⲉⲧⲉⲛ, F ⲉⲧⲉⲧⲉⲛ
3ms	ⲉϥ	3pl	ⲉⲩ

for example, M ϩⲁϥϣⲉ ⲛⲉϥ ⲉϥⲗⲩⲡⲏ "he went away vexed" (Matt. 19:22)—ϩⲁϥϣⲉ "he went" (§ 9.2) – ⲛⲉϥ "for him(self)" – ⲉϥ DEP 3MS – ⲗⲩⲡⲏ vexed" (Greek λυπεῖν); M ⲉⲛⲉ ⲉⲩⲣⲟⲙⲉ ⲉϥϩⲛ̄ϩⲁⲓⲧⲉ "to see a man in clothing" (Matt. 11:8)—ⲉ "to" – ⲛⲉ "look" – ⲉ "at" – ⲩⲣⲟⲙⲉ "a man" – ⲉϥ DEP 3MS – ϩⲛ̄ "in" – ϩⲁⲓⲧⲉ "garment."

The circumstantial converter ⲉ- is used before the past converter and tripartite verb forms: S ⲁⲩⲃⲱⲕ ⲉϩⲣⲁⲓ ⲉⲡⲙⲁ ⲛ̄ⲧⲡⲉ ⲉⲛⲉⲩⲟⲩⲏϩ ⲛ̄ϩⲏⲧϥ "they went up to the upper room (literally, "to the place of the sky"), while they were settled in it" (Acts 1:13); L ⲛⲉⲩⲁϩⲉ ⲁⲣⲉⲧⲟⲩⲡⲉ ... ⲉⲁⲩⲭⲉⲣⲉⲟⲩϣⲁϩ "They were standing ... having kindled a fire" (John 18:18), B ⲙ̄ⲫⲣⲏϯ ⲙ̄ⲡⲓⲙⲁⲛⲉⲥⲱⲟⲩ ⲉϣⲁϥⲫⲱⲣⲝ ⲛ̄ⲛⲓⲉⲥⲱⲟⲩ ⲉⲃⲟⲗ ϧⲉⲛⲛⲓⲃⲁⲉⲙⲡⲓ "in the manner of the shepherd, when he separates the sheep from the goats" (Matt. 25:32), S ϩⲛ̄ⲧⲉⲓⲟⲩϣⲏ ⲉⲙⲡⲁⲧⲉⲟⲩⲁⲗⲉⲕⲧⲱⲣ ⲙⲟⲩⲧⲉ ⲛ̄ⲥⲉⲡⲥⲛⲁⲩ "in this night, before a rooster speaks two times" (Mark 14:30; literally, "a rooster having not yet spoken"). Circumstantial use is common after verbs of perception: e.g., ⲁϥϭⲉⲙⲟⲩ ⲉⲩⲛⲕⲟⲧ "he found them sleeping" (Matt. 26:40). It is also used with ϩⲱⲡⲉ/ϣⲱⲡⲉ/ϣⲱⲡⲓ/ϣⲟⲡⲉ "become," particularly as a substitute for non-

---

[1] ⲉ- rather than ⲉⲡⲉ- is used in nominal sentences: L ⲉⲁⲛⲁⲕ ⲟⲩⲥϩⲓⲙⲉ ⲛ̄ⲥⲁⲙⲁⲣⲓⲧⲏⲥ "since I am a Samaritan woman" (John 4:9).

existent forms: e.g., S ⲉⲓⲥ ϩⲏⲏⲧⲉ ⲧⲉⲧⲛ̄ⲃⲉⲕⲉ ϥⲛⲁϣⲱⲡⲉ ⲉϥⲛⲁϣⲱϥ ϩⲛ̄ⲧⲡⲉ "Behold (§ 4.5), your reward will be plentiful (§ 6.5) in heaven" (Luke 6:23) — ϥⲛⲁϣⲱⲡⲉ "it will become" ⲉϥⲛⲁϣⲱϥ "it being plentiful" (for *ϥⲛⲁⲛⲁϣⲱϥ). Continuative use is primarily with the First Perfect, and not common: S ⲁⲫⲓⲗⲓⲡⲡⲟⲥⲇⲉ ⲟⲩⲱⲛ ⲛ̄ⲣⲱϥ ⲉⲁϥⲁⲣⲭⲉⲓ ϩⲛ̄ⲧⲉⲓ̈ⲅⲣⲁⲫⲏ "And Phillip opened his mouth and began with this writing (Greek γραφή)" (Acts 8:35).

10.3 Temporal Forms

Most Coptic dialects have two temporal prefixes for the First Present with infinitival predicate. The first is A ⲛ̄ⲧⲁⲣⲉ/ⲧⲁⲣⲉ, F ⲛ̄ⲧⲉⲗⲉ, L ⲛ̄ⲧⲁⲣⲉ, MS ⲛ̄ⲧⲉⲣⲉ "when," used with nominal subjects: S ⲁⲥϣⲱⲡⲉⲇⲉ ⲛ̄ⲧⲉⲣⲉⲓ̅ⲥ̅ ⲟⲩⲱ ⲛ̄ⲛⲉⲓ̈ⲡⲁⲣⲁⲃⲟⲗⲏ ⲁϥⲡⲱⲱⲛⲉ ⲉⲃⲟⲗ ϩⲙ̄ⲡⲙⲁ ⲉⲧⲙ̄ⲙⲁⲩ "And it happened, when Jesus ended these parables (Greek παραβολή), he moved out of that place" (Matt. 13:53). With pronominal subjects, the forms are:

1s	A ⲛ̄ⲧⲁⲣⲓ/ⲧⲁⲣⲓ, MS ⲛ̄ⲧⲉⲣⲓ		1pl	A ⲛ̄ⲧⲁⲣⲉⲛ/ⲧⲁⲣⲉⲛ, MS ⲛ̄ⲧⲉⲣⲉⲛ	
2ms	A ⲛ̄ⲧⲁⲣⲉⲕ/ⲧⲁⲣⲉⲕ, MS ⲛ̄ⲧⲉⲣⲉⲕ		2pl	A ⲛ̄ⲧⲁⲣⲉⲧⲛ̄/ⲧⲁⲣⲉⲧⲉⲛ,	
2fs	A ⲛ̄ⲧⲁⲣⲉ/ⲧⲁⲣⲉ, MS ⲛ̄ⲧⲉⲣⲉ			F ⲛⲧⲉⲗⲉⲧⲉⲛ, MS ⲛⲧⲉⲣⲉⲧⲛ̄	
3ms	AL ⲛ̄ⲧⲁⲣⲉϥ/ⲧⲁⲣⲉϥ, MS ⲛ̄ⲧⲉⲣⲉϥ		3pl	AL ⲛ̄ⲧⲁⲣⲟⲩ/ⲧⲁⲣⲟⲩ, F ⲛ̄ⲧⲉⲗⲟⲩ,	
3fs	AL ⲛ̄ⲧⲁⲣⲉⲥ/ⲧⲁⲣⲉⲥ, MS ⲛ̄ⲧⲉⲣⲉⲥ			MS ⲛ̄ⲧⲉⲣⲟⲩ	

For example, S ⲛ̄ⲧⲉⲣⲉϥⲛⲁⲩⲇⲉ ⲉⲙ̄ⲙⲏⲏϣⲉ ⲁϥⲁⲗⲉ ⲉϩⲣⲁⲓ ⲉϫⲙ̄ⲡⲧⲟⲟⲩ "and when he saw the multitudes, he went up to the top of the hill" (Matt. 5:1). Bohairic uses the Second Perfect (§ 11,2) instead of this form.

The other temporal prefix is AB ϣⲁⲧⲉ-, FLMS ϣⲁⲛⲧⲉ- "until": B ⲛ̄ⲛⲉϥⲥⲓⲛⲓ ⲉⲃⲟⲗ ϧⲉⲛⲡⲓⲛⲟⲙⲟⲥ ϣⲁⲧⲉⲛⲁⲓ ⲧⲏⲣⲟⲩ ϣⲱⲡⲓ "it shall not pass out of the law (Greek νόμος) until these all happen" (Matt. 5:18). Pronominal forms are:

1s	AB ϣⲁϯ, FLMS ϣⲁⲛⲧⲁ/ϣⲁⲛϯ		1pl	A ϣⲁⲧⲛ̄, B ϣⲁⲧⲉⲛ,	
2ms	AB ϣⲁⲧⲉⲕ, FLS ϣⲁⲛⲧⲉⲕ			F ϣⲁⲛⲧⲉⲛ, LMS ϣⲁⲛⲧⲛ̄	
2fs	AB ϣⲁⲧⲉ, LS ϣⲁⲛⲧⲉ, F ϣⲁⲛⲧⲉⲗ		2pl	A ϣⲁⲧⲉⲧⲛ̄, B ϣⲁⲧⲉⲧⲉⲛ,	
3ms	AB ϣⲁⲧⲉϥ, FLS ϣⲁⲛⲧⲉϥ			F ϣⲁⲛⲧⲉⲧⲉⲛ, LS ϣⲁⲛⲧⲉⲧⲛ̄	
3fs	AB ϣⲁⲧⲉⲥ, FLS ϣⲁⲛⲧⲉⲥ		3pl	AB ϣⲁⲧⲟⲩ, FLMS ϣⲁⲛⲧⲟⲩ	

for example, M ⲛ̄ⲛⲉⲕⲉⲓ ⲉⲃⲁⲗ ϩⲙ̄ⲡⲙⲉ ⲉⲧⲙ̄ⲙⲉ ϣⲁⲛⲧⲉⲕⲧⲟⲩⲓⲁ ⲙ̄ⲡϩⲁⲏ ⲛ̄ⲕⲟⲛⲇⲣⲁⲛⲧⲏⲥ "you shall not come out of that place until you repay the last penny (Greek κοδράντης)" (Matt. 5:26).

10.4 The Conjunctive

The Conjunctive extends the temporal and modal range of a preceding verb form to a succeeding one. It consists of a prefix and the First Present with infinitival predicate. For a nominal subject, the prefix is A ⲧⲉ-, BFLMS ⲛ̄ⲧⲉ-: B ⲟⲩⲛ̄ϩⲉⲛϩⲟⲟⲩ ⲛⲏⲟⲩ ⲉϩⲣⲁⲓ̈ ⲉϫⲱ ⲛ̄ⲧⲉⲛⲟⲩϫⲁϫⲉ ⲕⲧⲉⲟⲩϣⲱⲗϩ ⲉⲣⲟ "Days are coming upon you (f), and your enemies will stake a boundary against you" (Luke 19:43). The forms with pronominal subject are:

1s	A ⲧⲁ, BM ⲛ̄ⲧⲁ, FLS ⲛ̄ⲧⲁ/ⲧⲁ	1pl	A ⲧⲛ̄, BF ⲛ̄ⲧⲉⲛ, LMS ⲛ̄ⲧⲛ̄
2ms	A ⲕ, B ⲛ̀ⲧⲉⲕ, FM ⲛ̄ⲕ/ⲛⲉⲕ, LS ⲛ̄ⲅ̄	2pl	A ⲧⲉⲧⲛ̄, BF ⲛ̄ⲧⲉⲧⲉⲛ,
2fs	A ⲧⲉ, BFLS ⲛ̄ⲧⲉ		LMS ⲛ̄ⲧⲉⲧⲛ̄
3ms	A ⲅ, B ⲛ̀ⲧⲉⲅ, FLMS ⲛ̄ⲅ	3pl	A ⲥⲉ, B ⲛ̀ⲧⲟⲩ,
3fs	A ⲥ, B ⲛ̀ⲧⲉⲥ, FLS ⲛ̄ⲥ		BFLMS ⲛ̄ⲥⲉ/ⲛ̄ⲥⲟⲩ

The quotation above continues, in Saidic, ⲛ̄ⲥⲉⲟⲧⲡⲉ ⲉϩⲟⲩⲛ ⲛ̄ⲥⲁⲥⲁ ⲛⲓⲙ "and enclose you in on every side" (Luke 19:43). In the case of Akhmimic, the Conjunctive with pronominal subject is identical with the First Present, except for the first person singular (ⲧⲁ- vs. ϯ-). The negative counterpart of the Conjunctive is the negated infinitive (§ 7.7): S ⲁⲙⲟⲩ ⲉⲃⲟⲗ ⲙ̄ⲙⲟⲅ ⲛ̄ⲅ̄ⲧ̄ⲙⲕⲟⲧⲕ̄ ⲉⲃⲱⲕ ⲉϩⲟⲩⲛ ⲉⲣⲟⲅ "Come out of him and don't return to go into him" (Mark 9:25).

The Conjunctive can be used after most verb forms. It is particularly common after an imperative: M ⲙⲉϣⲉ ⲛⲉⲕⲥⲁϩⲱⲅ ⲟⲩⲧⲟⲕ ⲟⲩⲧⲟⲅ "Go and accuse him between you and him" (Matt. 18:15). In some cases, the Conjunctive follows a circumstantial clause (§ 10.2) and must be translated as if it were the main clause: S ⲉⲁⲧⲉⲧⲛ̄ⲛⲁⲩ ⲉⲣⲟⲅ ⲛ̄ⲧⲉⲧⲉⲧⲛ̄ⲣⲁϣⲉ ⲟⲛ "having seen him, you rejoice again" (Phil. 2:28). It is also used in this sense after certain Greek proclitic particles (§ 4.5): M ϩⲁⲅⲑⲉⲣⲁⲡⲉⲩⲉ ⲙ̄ⲙⲁⲅ ϩⲱⲥⲧⲉ ⲛ̄ⲧⲉⲡⲉⲙⲡⲁ ⲥⲉⲭⲉ "He healed (Greek θεραπεύειν) him, so that the dumb spoke" (Matt. 12:22), B ⲙⲁⲧⲁⲙⲟⲓ ϩⲓⲛⲁ ⲛ̄ⲧⲁⲓ ϩⲱ ⲛ̀ⲧⲁⲟⲩⲱϣⲧ ⲙ̄ⲙⲟⲅ "Let me know so that I can come myself and worship him" (Matt. 2:8). The Conjunctive is standard when two actions are treated as a single event: B ⲙ̄ⲡⲁⲩϭⲉⲣⲉⲟⲩⲏⲃⲥ ⲛ̄ⲥⲉⲭⲁⲅ ϧⲁⲟⲩⲙⲉⲛⲧ "they don't light a lamp and put it under a bushel" (Matt. 5:15).

10.5 The Prospective Conjunctive

In addition to the Conjunctive, Coptic has a form that marks an action that follows or results from another. Also known as the Finalis, it is mostly found in Saidic, where it is marked by the prefix ⲧⲁⲣⲉ- before nominal subjects and by the following pronominal forms:

1s	ⲧⲁⲣⲓ	1pl	ⲧⲁⲣⲛ
2fs	ⲧⲁⲣⲉ	2pl	ⲧⲁⲣⲉⲧⲛ̄/ⲧⲁⲣⲉⲧⲉⲧⲛ̄
2ms	ⲧⲁⲣⲉⲕ	3pl	ⲧⲁⲣⲟⲩ
3ms	ⲧⲁⲣⲉⲅ		
3fs	ⲧⲁⲣⲉⲥ		

The same forms are attested in Akhmimic and Lycopolitan; Fayumic has 2pl ⲧⲁⲗⲉⲧⲉⲧⲉⲛ· Oxyrhynchite has 2ms ⲛ̄ⲧⲁⲣⲉⲕ, 1pl ⲛ̄ⲧⲁⲣⲛ̄, 3pl ⲛ̄ⲧⲁⲣⲟⲩ; the same initial ⲛ̄ is also found in Bohairic (twice) and in Fayumic 2pl ⲛ̄ⲧⲁⲗⲉⲧⲉⲧⲉⲛ.

The Prospective Conjunctive is used primarily after an imperative: S ⲁⲓⲧⲓ ⲧⲁⲣⲟⲩϯ ⲛⲏⲧⲛ ϣⲓⲛⲉ ⲧⲁⲣⲉⲧⲛ̄ϭⲓⲛⲉ ⲧⲱϩⲙ̄ ⲧⲁⲣⲟⲩⲟⲩⲱⲛ ⲛⲏⲧⲛ "Ask (Greek αἰτεῖν) and they will give to you, seek and you will find, knock and they will open to you" (Luke 11:9). It is also used as the second element of a question: S ⲚⲦⲞⲔ ⲠⲈⲦⲚⲎⲨ ⲬⲚⲦⲀⲢⲚϬⲰϢⲦ ϨⲎⲦϤ ⲚⲔⲈⲞⲨⲀ "Are *you* the one who is coming, or should we wait for another one?" (Matt. 11:3)—for these, Bohairic has ⲀⲢⲒⲈⲦⲒⲚ[2] ⲞⲨⲞϨ ⲤⲈⲚⲀϮ ⲚⲰⲦⲈⲚ ⲔⲰⲦ ⲞⲨⲞϨ ⲦⲈⲦⲈⲚⲚⲀⲬⲒⲘⲒ ⲔⲰϨⲌ ⲞⲨⲞϨ ⲤⲈⲚⲀⲞⲨⲰⲚ ⲚⲰⲦⲈⲚ, with ⲞⲨⲞϨ "and" and the First Future (§ 8.6); and Oxyrhynchite, ⲚⲦⲀⲔ ⲈⲦⲚⲚⲎⲞⲨ ⲬⲚⲀⲚⲚⲈϬⲟϢⲦ ϨⲎⲦϤ ⲚⲔⲈⲞⲨⲈ, with the Second Future (Chapter 11).

10.6 Relative Clauses

Coptic formed relative clauses both with a relative pronoun (§ 10.8) and with dedicated verb forms (§ 10.9). These were considered defining elements, like the definite article and possessive pronouns, and were therefore incompatible with undefined antecedents. For the latter, circumstantial clauses were used with relative as well as adverbial function (§ 10.7).[3]

10.7 Relative Clauses with an Undefined Antecedent

The circumstantial converter allows bipartite and tripartite constructions to serve as relative clauses after a demonstrative or an undefined antecedent. The converter is ⲈⲢⲈ- when the subject of the relative clause is a noun not identical with the antecedent and the predicate is bipartite: S ⲞⲨⲢⲰⲘⲈ ⲈⲢⲈⲞⲨϢⲞϢⲞⲨ ⲘⲘⲞⲞⲨ ϨⲒⲬⲰϤ "a man with a jar of water on his head" (Mark 14:13), M ⲞⲨⲢⲰⲘⲈ ⲈⲢⲈⲦⲈϤϬⲒⲜ ϢⲞⲨⲞⲞⲨ "a man who hand was dried up" (Matt. 12:10). Otherwise, it is Ⲉ-:

- with nominal predicate: S ⲚⲈⲨⲚⲞⲨϨⲎⲔⲈⲆⲈ ⲈⲠⲈϤⲢⲀⲚⲠⲈ ⲖⲀⲌⲀⲢⲞⲤ "And there was a poor man, whose name was Lazarus" (Luke 16:20)

- with ⲞⲨⲚⲦ⸗: S ⲞⲨⲢⲰⲘⲈ ⲢⲢⲘⲘⲀⲞ[4] ⲈⲨⲚⲦⲀϤ ⲘⲘⲀⲨ ⲚⲞⲨⲞⲒⲔⲞⲚⲞⲘⲞⲤ "a rich man who had a steward (Greek οἰκονόμος)" (Luke 16:1)

- with adjectival predicate: L ϨⲈⲚϨⲂⲎⲨⲈ ⲈⲚⲈⲈⲈⲨ ⲀⲚⲈⲈⲒ "works that are greater than these" (John 5:20)

- with adverbial predicate: M ⲞⲨⲢⲞⲘⲈ ⲈϤϨⲚϨⲈⲚϨⲀⲒⲦⲈ ⲈⲨϬⲎⲚ "a man in soft garments" (Matt. 11:8)

- with the First Present: B ⲞⲨⲢⲰⲘⲒ ⲈϤϤⲀⲒ ⲚⲞⲨϢⲞϢⲞⲨ ⲘⲘⲰⲞⲨ "a man carrying a jar of water" (Mark 14:13)

- with the First Future, negated: S ⲘⲘⲚⲖⲀⲀⲨ ... ⲈⲚϤⲚⲀⲬⲒⲦⲞⲨ ⲀⲚ "There is no one ... who will not receive them" (Luke 18:30–31)

- with the First Perfect: B ⲞⲨⲤⲀⲄⲎⲚⲎ ⲈⲀⲨϨⲒⲦⲤ ⲈⲪⲒⲞⲘ "a dragnet (Greek σαγήνη) that was cast into the sea" (Matt. 13:47)

---

2 See §§ 7.2(l): ⲀⲢⲒ "do" (§ 7.6) plus ⲈⲦⲒⲚ = Greek αἰτεῖν.

3 For an extended discussion, see Müller 2015, 142–67.

4 For ⲚⲢⲘⲘⲀⲞ with assimilation of Ⲛ to Ⲣ.

- with the Third Perfect: M ACⲦNTONT EYPOME EⲀⲀϤⲬⲬⲀ ⲚOYⲞPⲀ6 ENⲀNOYϤ
  ⲌⲚTEϤCOϢE "It is likened to a man who sowed good seed in his field" (Matt. 13:24)
- with the First Aorist: B OYⲌⲀⲀHT EϢⲀϤⲐϢOYϮ ⲚNEϤMⲀC EⲂOYN ⲃⲀNEϤTENⲌ "a
  bird that gathers in its young under its wings" (Matt. 23:37)
- with the Third Future, negated: S ⲌOINE ... ENNEYⲬIϮⲠE ⲘⲠMOY "some ... who shall
  not taste death" (Luke 9:27)

Although they are defined, absolute demonstrative pronouns can also take circumstantial
clauses as modifiers: S ⲠⲀI EYNO6NE6 ⲘMOϤ "the one they reproach" (Matt. 27:44), S NⲀI
EYEBOⲖ ⲚⲌHTOYTE MⲀPIⲀ TMⲀⲄⲆⲀⲖHNH ⲘⲚMⲀPIⲀ TⲀIⲀKⲰBOC "among whom were
Mary Magdalene and James's Mary" (Matt. 27:56).

0.8 The Relative Converter

The converter used to introduce relative clauses after defined antecedents has two sets of
forms, depending on whether it serves as subject of the relative clause or not. In the first case,
the converter is ET- or ETE-:

- with nominal predicate: B ⲠϢEMHP ⲚTENIⲪⲀPICEOC ETETOYMETϢOBITE "the
  leaven of the Pharisees, which is their hypocrisy" (Luke 12:1)
- with OYⲚT⸗: S ⲠCⲀϢϤ ⲚⲀⲄⲄEⲖOC ETEOYⲚTOY TCϢⲀϤE MⲪIⲀⲖH "the seven angels
  that had the seven vials (Greek φιάλη)" (Rev. 17:1)
- with adjectival predicate: L ⲠϢⲰC ETNⲀNOYϤ "the good shepherd" (John 10:11)
- with adverbial predicate: M NⲀⲞYⲖⲀOYE ET⸗ⲚBHⲐⲖEEM "the children who were in
  Bethlehem" (Matt. 2:16)
- with the First Present: B ⲐH ETⲬⲰ ⲘMOC "the one that says it" (Matt. 13:14), S ⲠϢHN
  ETPHT ⲌIⲬⲚⲘMⲀⲚⲌⲀTE "the tree that was sprouted on the water-courses" (Ps. 1:3)
- with the First Future: S ⲠⲀI ETNⲀMOONE ⲘⲠⲀⲖⲀOC "this one who will shepherd my
  people" (Matt. 2:6)

When the subject of the relative clause is different from the antecedent, the converter is AM
ETE- BLS ETEPE- F ETEⲖE- if the subject is nominal: L ⲠMⲀ ETEPEIⲰⲀNNHC ⲚⲌHTϤ
"the place that John was in" (John 10:40). Pronominal subjects have the following forms:

1s	ET	1pl	ALMS ETⲚ, BF ETEN
2ms	ALMS ETⲔ, BF ETEK	2pl	ALMS ETETⲚ, BF ETETEN
2fs	ETE	3pl	ETOY
3ms	ALMS ETϤ, BF ETEϤ		
3fs	ALMS ETC, BF ETEC		

Examples: B OY ⲘMETⲌOYO ETETENIPI ⲘMOC "what is the excess that you do?" (Matt.
5:47), M TETⲚENEϢCE ⲠⲀⲠⲀT ETNⲀCⲀϤ ⲀNⲀK "Will you be able to drink the cup that I
myself will drink?" (Matt. 20:22). Oxyrhynchite uses ET- with the Third Perfect (TⲀ → Ⲑ):

ⲡⲉⲑⲁⲡ⳪ ϫⲁϥ "what which the Lord said" (Matt. 1:22), ⲡⲥⲓⲟⲩ ⲉⲑⲁⲩⲛⲉ ⲉⲣⲁϥ "the star that they saw" (Matt. 2:9).

10.9   Relative Forms

A few Coptic verb forms have specific relative counterparts, which are used instead of the relative converter plus the verb form. These are constructed with a prefix added to the verb form:

> ⲉ- with the past converter and the First Aorist, in Bohairic and Saidic: B ⲡⲓⲙⲁ ⲉⲛⲁⲣⲉⲡⲓⲁⲗⲟⲩ ⲭⲏ ⲙ̀ⲙⲟϥ "the place that the baby was laid in" (Matt. 2:9), S ⲡⲙⲁ ⲉϣⲁⲩϫⲉ ⲡϣⲁϫⲉ ⲛ̄ϩⲏⲧϥ "the place that the word is sown in" (Mark 4:15)

> ⲛ̄- with the First Aorist, in Fayumic: F ϩⲁⲓⲛⲓ ⲛ̄ϣⲁⲩⲙⲟⲩⲧ ⲉⲣⲁⲩ ϫⲉⲛⲟⲩϯ "some they call god" (1Cor. 8:5)

> ⲛ̄ⲧ- with the First Perfect, in Lycopolitan and Saidic: L ⲡⲥⲉϫⲉ ⲛ̄ⲧⲁⲓ⳪ ϫⲟⲟϥ "the speech that Jesus said" (John 2:22), S ⲧⲁⲓ ⲛ̄ⲧⲁⲩϫⲡⲉⲓ⳪ ⲉⲃⲟⲗ ⲛ̄ϩⲏⲧⲥ "she of whom Jesus was born" (Matt. 1:16)

10.10   Independent Relatives

Relative clauses are also used in Coptic without an expressed antecedent, in which case they are preceded by the definite article: S ⲡⲉⲧⲉⲣⲉⲧⲉⲕⲟⲩⲛⲁⲙ ⲉⲓⲣⲉ ⲙ̄ⲙⲟϥ "that which your right hand is doing" (Matt. 6:3), S ⲧⲉϣⲁⲩⲙⲟⲩⲧⲉ ⲉⲣⲟⲥ ϫⲉⲃⲏⲑⲗⲉⲉⲙ "the one they call Bethlehem" (Luke 2:4), ⲛⲉⲛⲧⲁⲩϫⲱϩ ⲁⲩⲟⲩϫⲁⲓ "those who touched became whole" (Matt. 14:36).

EXERCISE 10

Translate the following phrases and sentences.

1. S ⲁⲩϩⲉ ⲉⲣⲟϥ ϩ̄ⲙⲡⲉⲣⲡⲉ ⲉϥϩⲙⲟⲟⲥ ⲛ̄ⲧⲙⲏⲧⲉ ⲛ̄ⲛⲥⲁϩ ⲉϥⲥⲱⲧⲙ̄ ⲉⲣⲟⲟⲩ ⲁⲩⲱ ⲉϥϫⲛⲟⲩ ⲙ̄ⲙⲟⲟⲩ

2. B ⲁϥⲛⲁⲩ ⲉⲛⲓⲫⲏⲟⲩⲓ ⲉⲁⲩⲫⲱϩ

3. L ⲛ̄ⲧⲁⲣⲉϥⲧⲱⲱⲛⲉ ⲁⲃⲁⲗ ϩ̄ⲛⲛⲉⲧⲙⲁⲟⲩⲧ ⲁⲩⲣ̄ⲡⲙⲉⲉⲩⲉ ϫⲓⲛⲉϥⲙⲁⲑⲏⲧⲏⲥ ϫⲉⲡⲉⲉⲓⲛⲉ ⲉⲛⲉϥϫⲱ ⲙ̄ⲙⲁϥ

4. M ϩⲁϥϭⲱ ⲙ̄ⲙⲉ ϣⲁⲛⲧⲉϩⲏⲣⲱⲇⲏⲥ ⲙⲟⲩ

5. S ⲧⲱⲱⲃⲉ ⲉⲣⲛ̄ⲛⲉⲛⲧⲁⲩϫⲟⲟⲩ ⲛ̄ϭⲓⲛ̄ϩⲣⲟⲩⲃⲃⲁⲓ ⲛ̄ⲧⲙⲥⲁϩⲟⲩ

6. S ⲕⲱ ⲉⲃⲟⲗ ⲧⲁⲣⲟⲩⲕⲱ ⲛⲏⲧⲛ̄ ⲉⲃⲟⲗ

7. B ⲡⲓϫⲱⲛⲧ ⲉⲑⲛⲏⲟⲩ

8. L ⲧⲕⲟⲗⲩⲙⲃⲏⲑⲣⲁ ⲛ̄ⲥⲓⲗⲟⲩⲁⲙ ⲡⲉⲉⲓ ⲉϣⲁⲣⲟⲩⲟⲩⲁϩⲙ̄ϥ ϫⲉ ⲡⲉⲛⲧⲁⲩⲧⲛ̄ⲛⲁⲟⲩϥ

9. B ⲡⲓⲥⲏⲟⲩ ⲉⲧⲁϥϧⲉⲧϧⲱⲧϥ̄ ⲛ̄ⲧⲟⲧⲟⲩ ⲛ̄ⲛⲓⲙⲁⲅⲟⲥ

10. L **ⲡⲉⲛⲧⲁⲩϫⲡⲁϥⲇⲉ ⲁⲃⲁⲗ ϩⲛ̄ⲧⲥⲁⲣⲝ ⲟⲩⲥⲁⲣⲝⲡⲉ**

Vocabulary

ⲕⲟⲗⲩⲃⲏⲑⲣⲁ L "bathing pool" (Greek κολυμβήθρα)

ⲕⲱ S "put, throw"; with **ⲉⲃⲟⲗ** "out" = "forgive"

ⲙⲁⲅⲟⲥ B "sage"

ⲙⲁⲟⲩⲧ L "dead" (stative)

ⲙⲁⲑⲏⲧⲏⲥ L "disciple" (Greek μαθητής)

ⲙⲏⲧⲉ S "midst"

ⲙⲟⲩ M "die"

ⲛⲁⲩ B "look"; "look at" = "see"

ⲛⲏⲩ B "coming" (stative of **ⲓ** "come")

ⲟⲩⲱϩⲙ̄ L "interpret" (when passive)

ⲫⲏⲟⲩⲓ B "skies"

ⲫⲱϧ B "burst open"

ⲣ̄ⲡⲉ S "temple"

ⲣ̄ⲡⲙⲉⲉⲩⲉ L "remember" ("do the thought")

ⲥⲁⲣⲝ L "flesh" (Greek σάρξ)

ⲥⲁϩ S "scribe"; see also **ⲥϩⲁï**

ⲥⲛⲟⲩ B "time"

ⲥⲓⲗⲟⲩⲁⲙ L "Siloam"

ⲥⲱⲧⲙ̄ S "listen"

ⲥϩⲁï "write"

ⲧⲛ̄ⲛⲁⲟⲩ L "send"

ⲧⲱⲱⲃⲉ S "put a seal," with **ⲉⲣ-** "to the mouth" = "seal up"

ⲧⲱⲱⲛ L "rise"

ϩⲉ S "fall"; with **ⲉ-** "come upon"

ϩⲏⲣⲱⲇⲏⲥ M "Herod"

ϩⲙⲟⲟⲥ S "seated" (stative)

ϩⲣⲟⲩⲃⲃⲁï S "thunder"

ϧⲟⲧϧⲉⲧ B "learn by examination"

ϫⲛⲟⲩ S "question"

ϫⲡⲟ L "create"

ϫⲱ L "say"

ϫⲱⲛ̄ⲧ B "wrath"

ϭⲱ M "stay"

11. SECOND TENSES

11.1 Definition

Four Coptic verbal constructions—Present, Future, Aorist, and Perfect—have additional forms known as Second Tenses, with the same temporal reference as the First Tenses but with a different semantic function. These are traditionally labeled Second Present, Second Future, Second Aorist, and Second Perfect.

11.2 Forms

The Second Present and Second Future are formed by the addition of a prefix to the First-Tense forms. For nominal subjects, this is ABM ⲁⲣⲉ-, F ⲁⲗⲉ-, LS ⲉⲣⲉ- (Present) and A ⲁ/ⲁⲣⲉ- … ⲛⲁ-, B ⲁⲣⲉ- … ⲛⲁ-, F ⲁⲗⲉ- … ⲛⲉ, LS ⲉⲣⲉ- … ⲛⲁ, M ⲁⲣⲉ- … ⲛⲉ- (Future). Pronominal forms of the Second Present are:

1s	ABFM ⲁⲓ, LS ⲉ̈ⲓ		1pl	ABFM ⲁⲛ, LS ⲉⲛ
2ms	ABFM ⲁⲕ, LS ⲉⲕ		2pl	A ⲁⲧⲉⲧⲛ̄, B ⲁⲣⲉⲧⲉⲛ,
2fs	ABFM ⲁⲣⲉ, LS ⲉⲣⲉ			F ⲁⲧⲉⲧⲉⲛ LS ⲉⲧⲉⲧⲛ̄/ⲉⲣⲉⲧⲛ̄,
3ms	ABFM ⲁϥ, FLS ⲉϥ			M ⲁⲧⲉⲧⲛ̄/ⲁⲧⲛ̄
3fs	ABFM ⲁⲥ, LS ⲉⲥ		3pl	ABFM ⲁⲩ, FLS ⲉⲩ

Those of the Second Future are:

1s	AB ⲁⲓⲛⲁ, FM ⲁⲓⲛⲉ, LS ⲉ̈ⲓⲛⲁ		1pl	AB ⲁⲛⲛⲁ, FM ⲁⲛⲛⲉ, LS ⲉⲛⲛⲁ
2ms	AB ⲁⲕⲛⲁ, FM ⲁⲕⲛⲉ, LS ⲉⲕⲛⲁ		2pl	A ⲁⲧⲉⲧⲛⲁ, B ⲁⲣⲉⲧⲉⲛⲛⲁ,
2fs	ABFM ⲁⲣⲉⲛⲁ, LS ⲉⲣⲉⲛⲁ			FM ⲁⲧⲉⲧⲉⲛⲛⲉ, LS ⲉⲧⲉⲧⲉⲛⲛⲁ
3ms	AB ⲁϥⲛⲁ, FM ⲁϥⲛⲉ, LS ⲉϥⲛⲁ		3pl	AB ⲁⲩⲛⲁ, FM ⲁⲩⲛⲉ, LS ⲉⲩⲛⲁ
3fs	AB ⲁⲥⲛⲁ, FM ⲁⲥⲛⲉ, LS ⲉⲥⲛⲁ			

The Second Aorist also has a prefix before the First Aorist forms: A ⲁ-, F ⲛ-, MS ⲉ-. With a nominal subject, therefore, A ⲁϣⲁⲣⲉ-, F ⲛ̄ϣⲁⲣⲉ-, MS ⲉϣⲁⲣⲉ-. Pronominal forms are:

1s	A ⲁϣⲁⲣⲓ, F ⲛ̄ϣⲁⲓ, MS ⲉϣⲁⲓ		1pl	A ⲁϣⲁⲣⲉⲛ, F ⲛ̄ϣⲁⲛ, MS ⲉϣⲁⲛ
2ms	A ⲁϣⲁⲣⲉⲕ, F ⲛ̄ϣⲁⲕ, MS ⲉϣⲁⲕ		2pl	A ⲁϣⲁⲣⲉⲧⲛ̄, B ⲉϣⲁⲣⲉⲧⲉⲛ,
2fs	A ⲁϣⲁⲣⲉ, F ⲛ̄ϣⲁⲣⲉ MS ⲉϣⲁⲣⲉ			F ⲛ̄ϣⲁⲧⲉⲧⲛ̄, MA ⲉϣⲁⲧⲉⲧⲛ̄
3ms	A ⲁϣⲁⲣⲉϥ, F ⲛ̄ϣⲁϥ, MS ⲉϣⲁϥ		3pl	A ⲁϣⲁⲣⲟⲩ, F ⲛ̄ϣⲁⲩ, MS ⲉϣⲁⲩ
3fs	A ⲁϣⲁⲣⲉⲥ, F ⲛ̄ϣⲁⲥ, MS ⲉϣⲁⲥ			

The Second Perfect has the prenominal prefix ABF ⲉⲧⲁ-, FLS ⲛ̄ⲧⲁ-, M ⲉ2ⲁ-. With pronominal subject, the forms are:

1s	BF ⲉⲧⲁⲓ, FLS ⲛ̄ⲧⲁⲓ, M ⲉ2ⲁⲓ		3fs	BF ⲉⲧⲁⲥ, FLS ⲛ̄ⲧⲁⲥ, M ⲉ2ⲁⲥ

2ms	BF ⲉⲧⲁⲕ, FLS ⲛ̄ⲧⲁⲕ, M ⲉ̄ⲁⲕ	1pl	BF ⲉⲧⲁⲛ, FLS ⲛ̄ⲧⲁⲛ, M ⲉ̄ⲁⲛ
2fs	B ⲉⲧⲁⲣⲉ, LS ⲛ̄ⲧⲁⲣⲉ	2pl	B ⲉⲧⲁⲣⲉⲧⲉⲛ, LS ⲛ̄ⲧⲁⲧⲉⲧ̄ⲛ
3ms	A ⲛⲁⲿ, BF ⲉⲧⲁⲿ, F ⲁⲁⲿ, FLS ⲛ̄ⲧⲁⲿ, M ⲉ̄ⲁⲿ	3pl	BF ⲉⲧⲁⲩ, FLS ⲛ̄ⲧⲁⲩ, M ⲉ̄ⲁⲩ

In Fayumic, the prefix is also ⲉⲧⲉⲁ- before nouns and pronominal ⲉⲧⲉⲁⲓ-, etc.

11.3   Primary Use

The Second Tenses have two functions. The first, and most common, was not fully understood until 1944, when H.J. Polotsky's *Études de syntaxe copte* was published. Based on Polotsky's work, the Second Tenses are now understood to serve as non-rhematic predicates: that is, as predicate in a clause in which the primary interest is not in the predicate, where it normally is, but in another element of the clause.[1]

The primary function of the Second Tenses is analogous—*not* equivalent—to that of the cleft sentence in English, with which Second Tenses are often translated: e.g., First Perfect S ⲁⲿϣⲱⲡⲉ ⲉⲃⲟⲗ ϩ̄ⲛⲟⲩⲥϩⲓⲙⲉ "He came about from a woman" (Gal. 4:4) vs. Second Perfect S ⲡⲁⲓ ⲛ̄ⲧⲁⲿϣⲱⲡⲉ ⲉⲃⲟⲗ ϩⲓⲧⲟⲟⲧⲿ ⲙ̄ⲡϫⲟⲉⲓⲥ "This, it is by the hand of the Lord that it came about" (Matt. 21:42). English marks the predicate as a noun clause, inherently identified with themes, by *that*, which is then removed to the end of the statement and replaced by *it*:

it came about		by the hand of the Lord →
that it came about	is	by the hand of the Lord →
it	is	by the hand of the Lord	that it came about.

Coptic performs a similar function with the Second Tenses, derived from relative forms (another nominalizing strategy):

| ⲁⲿϣⲱⲡⲉ | ⲉⲃⲟⲗ ϩⲓⲧⲟⲟⲧⲿ ⲙ̄ⲡϫⲟⲉⲓⲥ → |
| ⲛ̄ⲧⲁⲿϣⲱⲡⲉ | ⲉⲃⲟⲗ ϩⲓⲧⲟⲟⲧⲿ ⲙ̄ⲡϫⲟⲉⲓⲥ. |

Like the cleft sentence, this strategy privileges an element other than the predicate by "thematizing" the predicate.

---

1   The predicate is a syntactic element, the rheme, a semantic one; similarly, for subject and theme, respectively. In most cases, the predicate and rheme coincide, as do the subject and theme. The theme is what the statement is about, and the rheme is what is said about the theme. For example, in the statement *lions ate the gazelles*, the theme and subject is *lions* and the rheme and predicate is *ate the gazelles*: the sentence states what the lions did. But the two pairs do not necessarily coincide. In the similar statement *lions ate the gazelles* (and not the zebras), the subject and predicate are the same as in the revious statement, but the theme in this case is *lions ate* and the rheme is *the gazelles*: the fact that *lions ate* is a given, and the statement reveals what the lions ate.

This function can be illustrated by the following sentence, in which the same verb phrase appears in both the First and Second Perfect: S ⲉⲫⲟⲥⲟⲛ ⲁⲧⲉⲧⲛⲁⲁⲥ ⲛ̄ⲟⲩⲁ ⲛ̄ⲛⲉⲓⲥⲛⲏⲩ ⲉⲧⲥⲟⲃⲕ̄ ⲛ̄ⲧⲁⲧⲉⲧⲛ̄ⲁⲁⲥ ⲛⲁⲓ "As long as you did it (ⲁⲧⲉⲧⲛⲁⲁⲥ) to one of these least brothers, you did it (ⲛ̄ⲧⲁⲧⲉⲧⲛ̄ⲁⲁⲥ) to me" (Matt. 25:40). In the second clause, the Second Perfect appears instead of the First Perfect because the purpose of the clause is not to state, "you did it," which has been stated by the First Perfect in the preceding clause, but that "you did it *to me*." The stress laid on the prepositional phrase ⲛⲁⲓ "to me" is shown by the paraphrase of this passage in Bohairic: ⲉⲫⲟⲥⲟⲛ ⲁⲧⲉⲧⲉⲛⲁⲓⲧⲟⲩ ⲛⲟⲩⲁⲓ ⲛ̄ⲛⲁⲓⲕⲟⲩϫⲓ ⲛ̄ⲥⲛⲏⲟⲩ ⲛ̄ⲧⲏⲓ ⲁⲛⲟⲕ ⲡⲉⲧⲁⲣⲉⲧⲉⲛⲁⲓⲧⲟⲩ ⲛⲏⲓ "As long as you did them to one of these least brothers of mine, I am the one you did them to"; Oxyrhynchite is similar: ⲁⲛⲁⲕ ⲡⲉⲑⲁⲧⲛ̄ⲉⲩ ⲛⲉⲓ̈ "I am the one you did them to."

Second Tenses are prevalent in sentences with an interrogative adverb or prepositional phrase following the predicate, where the interrogative, and not the predicate, is always the rheme: e.g., B ⲉⲧⲁ̄ⲫⲁⲓ ϫⲉⲙ̄ⲧⲁⲓⲥⲃⲱ ⲑⲱⲛ "Where did this one find this teaching?" (Matt. 13:54), S ⲉⲣⲉⲧⲛⲱⲁϫⲉ ⲛⲙ̄ⲛⲉⲧⲛ̄ⲉⲣⲏⲩ ϩⲛ̄ⲧⲉϩⲓⲏ ⲉⲧⲃⲉⲟⲩ "Why (ⲉⲧⲃⲉⲟⲩ "on account of what") do you speak with your companions on the road?" (Mark 9:33), L ⲉⲕⲓⲣⲉ ⲙ̄ⲙⲁⲕ ⲛ̄ⲛⲓⲙ "Into whom are you making yourself?" (John 8:53). When the interrogative precedes the predicate, the First Tenses can be used: M ⲉⲧⲃⲉⲟⲩ ⲧⲉⲧⲛ̄ϥⲓⲣⲁⲟⲩⲱ ϩⲁⲑⲃⲥⲱ "Why do you care about clothes?" (Matt. 6:28).

This indicates that the purpose of the Second Tenses in such sentences is to "de-rhematize" the predicate and thus to point to a subsequent element as the rheme. The rhematized element need not be an adverb or prepositional phrase. Second Tenses are also used in some questions with a focalized subject or object: S ⲉϣⲁⲣⲉⲟⲩ ⲅⲁⲣ ϣⲱⲡⲉ "What happens?" (Rom. 3:3), B ⲛⲑⲱⲧⲉⲛⲇⲉ ⲉⲣⲉⲧⲉⲛϫⲱ ⲙ̄ⲙⲟⲥ ϫⲉⲁⲛⲟⲕ ⲛⲓⲙ "But who do *you* say I am?" (Matt. 16:15), M ⲉϩⲁϥⲧⲁⲙⲓⲁ ⲛ̄ⲟⲩϩⲁⲟⲩⲧ ⲙ̄ⲛⲟⲩⲥϩⲓⲙⲉ "Male and female he created" (Matt. 19:4).

Coptic also uses the prefix of the Second Present without a predicate, to focalize an adverbial element: B ϯⲙⲉⲧⲟⲩⲣⲟ ⲅⲁⲣ ⲛ̄ⲧⲉⲫ̄ϯ ⲛⲁⲥϧⲉⲛⲥⲁϫⲓ ⲁⲛ ⲁⲗⲗⲁ ⲁⲥϧⲉⲛⲟⲩϫⲟⲙ "For the kingdom of God, it is not in word but it is in power" (1Cor. 4:20).

1.4 Secondary Use

The second function of the Second Tenses is less common: as a statement intended to draw special attention to the predicate itself: S ⲁⲛⲁⲩ ⲉⲧⲃ̄ⲛⲕ̄ⲛⲧⲉ ⲛ̄ⲧⲁⲕⲥϩⲟⲩⲱⲣⲥ̄ ⲛ̄ⲧⲁⲥϣⲟⲟⲩⲉ "Look at the fig tree that you cursed: it has dried up!" (Mark 11:21), L ⲙⲏⲧⲓ ⲛ̄ⲧⲁⲟⲩⲉⲉ ⲉⲓⲛⲉ ⲛⲉϥ ⲁⲧⲣⲉϥⲟⲩⲱⲙ "Hasn't (Greek μήτι) anyone even brought him something to eat?" (John 4:33), B ⲙ̄ⲡⲉⲥⲙⲟⲩ ⲛ̄ϫⲉⲧⲁⲗⲟⲩ ⲁⲗⲗⲁ ⲁⲥⲛ̄ⲕⲟⲧ "She has not died, namely the girl, but she is *sleeping*" (Mark 5:39), S ⲉⲧⲉⲧⲛ̄ⲗⲟⲃⲉ "You are *mad*!" (1Cor. 14:23).

11.5 Negation

In negative statements, Second Tenses mostly occur with post-verbal ⲁⲛ/ⲉⲛ (§ 4.6) or ⲛ ... ⲁⲛ/ⲉⲛ, which is a negation of the sentence rheme (the predicate is affirmative): S ⲛ̄ⲧⲁⲓⲉⲓ ⲅⲁⲣ ⲁⲛ ⲭⲉⲉⲓⲉⲕⲣⲓⲛⲉ ⲙ̄ⲡⲕⲟⲥⲙⲟⲥ ⲁⲗⲗⲁ ⲭⲉⲕⲁⲥ ⲉⲉⲓⲉⲛⲁϩⲙⲉϥ "For I have come not that I might judge (Greek κρίνειν) the world, but that I might save it" (John 12:47), M ⲛⲁⲣⲉⲡⲣⲟⲙⲉ ⲛⲉⲟⲛ̄ϩ ⲉⲡⲁⲉⲓⲕ ⲙ̄ⲙⲉⲧⲉ ⲉⲛ ⲁⲗⲗⲁ ⲉⲥⲉϫⲉ ⲛⲓⲙ ⲉⲧⲛ̄ⲛⲏⲟⲩ ⲉⲃⲁⲗ ϩ̄ⲛⲣⲱϥ ⲙ̄ⲡϯ "It is not by the bread alone that the person will live, but by every speech that is coming from the mouth of God" (Matt. 4:4). The predicate itself is negated by an infixed ⲧⲙ̄/ϣⲧⲉⲙ: ⲁⲣⲉϣⲧⲉⲙⲧⲉⲧⲉⲛⲙⲉⲑⲙⲏⲓ ⲉⲣϩⲟⲩⲟ ⲉⲑⲁⲛⲓⲥⲁⲭ ⲛⲉⲙⲛⲓⲫⲁⲣⲓⲥⲉⲟⲥ ⲛ̄ⲛⲉⲧⲉⲛⲓ̀ ⲉϧⲟⲩⲛ ⲉ̀ϯⲙⲉⲧⲟⲩⲣⲟ ⲛ̄ⲧⲉⲛⲓⲫⲏⲟⲩⲓ "should your righteousness not be more than the scribes and the Pharisees, you shall not come into the kingdom of heaven" (Matt. 5:20).

EXERCISE 11

Translate the following phrases and sentences.

1. S ⲁⲓ̄ⲥ ⲟⲩⲟⲛϩ̄ϥ ⲉⲛⲉϥⲙⲁⲑⲏⲧⲏⲥ ϩⲓϫⲛ̄ⲑⲁⲗⲁⲥⲥⲁ ⲛ̄ⲧⲓⲃⲉⲣⲓⲁⲥ ⲛ̄ⲧⲁϥⲟⲩⲟⲛϩ̄ϥⲇⲉ ⲉⲃⲟⲗ ⲛ̄ⲧⲉⲓϩⲉ

2. L ⲛ̄ⲧⲁⲛⲉⲉⲓ ⲅⲁⲣ ϣⲱⲡⲉ ⲭⲉⲕⲁⲥ ⲉⲣⲉⲧⲅⲣⲁⲫⲏ ⲛⲁϫⲱⲕ ⲁⲃⲁⲗ

3. L ⲉⲓⲥⲁⲡⲥ̄ⲡ ⲉⲛ ⲭⲉⲉⲕⲁϥⲓⲧⲟⲩ ⲁⲃⲁⲗ ϩ̄ⲛⲡⲕⲟⲥⲙⲟⲥ ⲁⲗⲗⲁ ⲭⲉⲕⲁⲥⲉ ⲉⲕⲁⲁⲣⲏϩ ⲁⲣⲁⲩ ⲁⲃⲁⲗ ϩ̄ⲛⲡⲡⲟⲛⲏⲣⲟⲥ

4. B ⲁⲣⲉⲧⲉⲛⲛⲁⲩ ⲉⲣⲟϥ ⲙ̀ⲙⲁⲩ

5. M ⲙⲉⲩⲭⲭⲉⲣⲁ ⲛⲟⲩϩⲏⲃⲥ ⲛ̄ⲥⲉⲕⲉϥ ⲛ̄ϩⲟⲩⲛ ϩⲁⲟⲩⲙⲟⲇⲓⲟⲛ ⲁⲗⲗⲁ ⲉϣⲁⲩⲕⲉϥ ϩⲓϫⲛ̄ⲧⲁⲩⲭⲛⲓⲁ ⲛ̄ϥⲉⲣⲟⲩⲁⲉⲓⲛ ⲉⲛⲉⲧϩ̄ⲛⲡⲏⲓ ⲧⲏⲣⲟⲩ

6. A ⲛⲁⲡϩⲱⲡ̄ϣ ⲙ̄ⲡⲭⲁⲉⲓⲥ ⲟ̄ⲱⲡ ⲁⲛⲓⲙ

7. F ⲉⲩⲧⲱⲛ ⲛⲉⲧⲉⲛⲅⲣⲁⲙⲙⲁⲧⲉⲩⲥ ⲉⲩⲧⲱⲛ ⲛⲉⲧⲉⲛⲭⲓϣⲁⲭⲛⲓ ⲉϥⲧⲱⲛ ⲡⲉⲧⲱⲡ ⲛ̄ⲛⲉⲥⲓⲟⲩ

8. F ⲛ̄ⲧⲁⲧⲉϩⲃⲱ ϣⲏⲛ̄ϣ ⲙ̄ⲙⲉⲩ ⲛ̄ⲛⲉⲥϣⲏⲣⲓ

9. F ⲁⲭⲛⲡⲟⲥ̄ ⲛ̄ⲧⲁⲛⲓ ⲉϩⲣⲏⲓ ⲉⲧⲉⲓⲭⲱⲣⲁ

10. B ⲉⲧⲁⲕⲓ ⲉⲙⲛⲁⲓ ⲉⲧⲁⲕⲟⲛ ⲙ̄ⲡⲁⲧⲉⲡⲉⲛⲥⲏⲟⲩ ϣⲱⲡⲓ (question)

VOCABULARY

ⲁⲣⲏϩ L "guard" (with ⲁ-)

ⲁⲭⲛ̄ F see § 5.3

ⲅⲣⲁⲙⲙⲁⲧⲉⲩⲥ F "accountant" (Greek γραμματεύς)

ⲅⲣⲁⲫⲏ L "writing, scripture" (Greek γραφή)

ⲉⲙⲛⲁⲓ B see § 5.1

ⲉⲣⲟⲩⲁⲉⲓⲛ M "give light" (construct of ⲉⲓⲣⲉ "make" plus ⲟⲩⲁⲉⲓⲛ "light")

ϩⲓ M "house"

ⲐⲀⲗⲀⲤⲤⲀ S "the sea" (Greek θάλασσα) (for ⲦⲐⲀⲗⲀⲤⲤⲀ)

ⲓ BF "come"

ⲓⲤ S abbreviation for ⲓⲎⲤⲞⲨⲤ "Jesus" (Greek Ιησοῦς)

ⲔⲞⲤⲘⲞⲤ L "world" (Greek κόσμος)

ⲔⲰ M "put"

ⲬⲰⲢⲀ F "place" (Greek χώρα)

ⲗⲨⲬⲚⲒⲀ M "lampstand" (Greek λυχνία)

ⲘⲀⲐⲎⲦⲎⲤ S "disciple" (Greek μαθητής)

ⲘⲞⲇⲒⲞⲚ M "bushel" (Greek μόδιος, about 2 gallons)

ⲚⲀⲨ B "look" (with ⲉ- "see")

ⲞⲨⲰⲚϨ S "reveal"

ⲠⲞⲚⲎⲢⲞⲤ L "evil" (Greek πονηρός)

ⲤⲀⲠⲤⲛ̄ L "pray"

ⲤⲎⲞⲨ B "time"

ⲤⲒⲞⲨ F "star"

ⲦⲀⲔⲞ B "destroy"

ⲦⲒⲂⲈⲢⲒⲀⲤ S "Tiberias" (Greek Τιβεριάς)

ⲦⲰⲚ F "where?"

ⲰⲠ F "reckon"

ⲰⲎⲚϨ̄ⲱ F "give life"

ⲱⲎⲢⲒ F "child"

ⲱⲰⲠⲒ B, ⲱⲰⲠⲉ L "happen"

ϥⲓ L "lift"

ϨⲂⲰ F "snake" (f)

Ϩⲉ S "way, manner"

ϨⲎⲂⲤ M "lamp"

Ϩⲱⲡ̄ⲱ A "arm"

ⲬⲀⲉⲓⲤ A "Lord"

ⲬⲒⲱⲀⲬⲚⲒ F "advisor" (ⲬⲒ "take" plus ⲱⲀⲬⲚⲒ "counsel")

ⲬⲬⲉⲢⲀ M "light" (a fire)

ⲬⲰⲔ L "be fulfilled"

ⲟ̄ⲥ F for ⲬⲀⲉⲓⲤ (abbreviation borrowed from Bohairic)

ϬⲰⲗⲡ̄ A "be revealed"

12. COMPLEX SENTENCES

2.1 Definition

Complex sentences are those with two or more clauses that have an interdependent relationship—that is, each dependent clause is integral to the meaning of the sentence and not merely ancillary to it. These typically have at least one dependent clause that restricts the statement of the main clause. Such clauses include

- restrictive circumstance: the main clause is true under a specific circumstance
- purpose: the dependent clause states the reason for the action of the main clause
- result: the dependent clause states the consequence of the main clause
- cause: the dependent clause states the cause of the action of the main clause
- temporal: the dependent clause specifies a time when the main clause is true
- content: the dependent clause is the object of the verb in the main clause
- concession: the main clause emends what is stated or implied by the dependent clause
- real condition: the dependent clause (protasis) states a hypothetical situation under which the action of the main clause (apodosis) results
- unreal condition: a real condition in the past in which neither the protasis nor the apodosis were realized.

In Coptic the interrelationship between the clauses is usually marked either by a proclitic particle or a specific verb form.

2.2 Restrictive Circumstance

Coptic can use a Second-Tense construction to rhematize a restrictive circumstance: S ⲚⲦⲀⲨⲬⲠⲞϤ ⲈϤⲞ ⲚⲂⲖⲖⲈ "He was born made blind" (John 9:20), L ⲚⲦⲀϤϫⲈⲠⲈⲈⲓⲆⲈ ⲈϤⲢ̄ⲠⲓⲢⲀⲌⲈ ⲘⲘⲀϤ "He said this testing (Greek πειράζειν) him" (John 6:6), ⲚⲦⲀϤϢⲱⲠⲈ ϪⲈⲔⲀⲤ ⲈϤⲈϪⲱⲔ ⲈⲂⲞⲖ Ⲛ̄ϬⲒⲠⲈⲚⲦⲀⲠϪⲞⲈⲒⲤ ϪⲞⲞϤ "It happened so that it might be fulfilled, namely, what the Lord said"(Matt. 1:22). A rhematic predicate can also be used, in which case the restrictive connotation of the dependent clause is purely contextual: S ⲀϤϨⲈ ⲈⲢⲞⲞⲨ ⲈⲨⲚ̄ⲔⲞⲦⲔ̄ "He found them sleeping" (Matt. 26:40).

2.3 Clauses of Purpose

Purpose clauses are marked by ϪⲈ or ϪⲈⲔⲀⲤ (§ 4.5) in most dialects, usually with the Third Future or Conjunctive in the dependent clause: L ϢⲀⲢⲈϤⲈⲒ ⲀⲠⲞⲨⲀⲈⲒⲚ ϪⲈⲔⲀⲤⲈ ⲈⲢⲈⲚⲈϤϨⲂⲎⲨⲈ ⲞⲨⲰⲚϨ̄ ⲀⲂⲀⲖ "He comes to the light so that his deeds may be revealed" (John 3:21), S Ⲛ̄ⲦⲀⲨⲤⲈϨⲚⲀⲒⲆⲈ ϪⲈⲔⲀⲤ ⲈⲦⲈⲦⲚⲈⲠⲒⲤⲦⲈⲨⲈ "But these have been written so that you might believe" (John 20:31), M ϨⲀϤϢⲞⲠⲈ ϪⲈⲈϤⲈϪⲞⲔ ⲈⲂⲀⲖ Ⲛ̄ϬⲎ ⲠⲈⲐⲀⲠⲬ̄Ⲥ̄ϪⲀϤ "it happened so that it might be fulfilled, namely that which the Christ said" (Matt. 1:22), F ΝΕΑϢΕ ΕϨΛΗΙ ΕΠΠΟΛΙϹ ΚΕϹ ⲚϹΕϢⲰⲠ ⲚϨΕΝϨⲢⲎⲞⲨⲒ "they were going up to the city so that they could get supplies" (John 4:8). Bohairic uses the Greek conjunction ϨΙΝΑ (ἵνα) with the Conjunctive: ΑϢΕ ΝⲰⲞⲨ ΕⲐΒΑΚΙ ϨΙΝΑ ⲚⲦⲞⲨϢⲰⲠ ⲚϨΑΝϨⲢⲎⲞⲨⲒ ⲚⲰⲞⲨ "they went away to the town so that they could get supplies for themselves" (John 4:8).

Negative counterparts of purpose clauses are formed with a negated verb form or with the Greek conjunctions ΜΗΠΟⲦⲈ (μήποτε) and ΜΗΠⲰⲤ (μήπως) "lest" followed by the Conjunctive: S ⲘⲠⲢ̄ⲔⲢⲒⲚⲈ ΧⲈⲔⲀⲤ ⲚⲚⲈⲨⲔⲢⲒⲚⲈ ⲘⲘⲰⲦⲚ̄, B ⲘⲠⲈⲢϮϨⲀⲠ ϨⲒⲚⲀ ⲚⲦⲞⲨϢⲦⲈⲘϮϨⲀⲠ ⲈⲢⲰⲦⲈⲚ "Don't judge (S Greek κρίνειν), so that you won't be judged" (Matt. 7:1), M ⲘⲠⲈⲢϨⲒⲞⲨⲈ ⲚⲚⲈⲦⲚ̄ⲘⲀⲢⲄⲀⲢⲒⲦⲎⲤ ⲚⲚⲀϨⲢⲚ̄ⲚⲈϢⲈⲨ ΜΗΠⲰⲤ ⲚⲤⲈⲔⲀⲦⲀⲠⲀⲦⲒ ⲘⲘⲀⲨ ϨⲚ̄ⲚⲈⲨⲞⲨⲈⲢⲎⲦⲈ "Don't thrown your pearls (Greek μαργαρίτης) before the pigs, so that they don't trample (Greek καταπατεῖν) them with their feet" (Matt. 7:6), M ⲈⲨⲈϤⲒⲦⲔ̄ ϨⲒⲚⲈⲨϬⲒⲬ ΜΗΠΟⲦⲈ ⲚⲦⲈⲦⲈⲔⲞⲨⲈⲢⲎⲦⲈ ⲬⲒⲬⲢⲀⲠ ⲈⲞⲨⲞⲚⲈ "they shall carry you on their hands so that your foot doesn't trip[1] on a stone" (Matt. 4:6).

12.4 Clauses of Result

Result is regularly expressed with the Prospective Conjunctive (§ 10.5). It is also expressed by the proclitic particle ϨⲰⲤⲦⲈ (Greek ὥστε) introducing Ⲉ- plus the infinitive or Causative Infinitive, or the Conjunctive: S ⲀⲚϨⲞⲈⲒⲘ ϤⲰϬⲈ ⲈⲠⲬⲞⲈⲒ ϨⲰⲤⲦⲈ ⲈⲞⲘⲤϤ̄ "the waves surged at the boat so as to submerge it" (Mark 4:37), S ⲞⲨⲚⲞϬ ⲚⲔⲘ̄ⲦⲞ ⲀϤϢⲰⲠⲈ ϨⲚ̄ⲐⲀⲖⲀⲤⲤⲀ ϨⲰⲤⲦⲈ ⲈⲦⲢⲈⲠⲬⲞⲒ̈ ϨⲰⲂⲤ̄ ⲈⲂⲞⲖ ϨⲒⲦⲚ̄Ⲛ̄ϨⲒⲘⲎ "a great earthquake, it happened in the sea so that the boat was covered with the waves" (Matt. 8:24), M ⲞⲨⲚⲞϬ ⲚϬⲀⲤⲘ ϨⲀϤϢⲰⲠⲈ ϨⲚ̄ⲐⲀⲖⲀⲤⲤⲀ ϨⲰⲤⲦⲈ ⲚⲦⲈⲠⲬⲀⲒ̈ ⲞⲘⲤ̄ ⲚⲦⲚ̄Ⲛ̄ϨⲒⲘⲎ "a great tempest, it happened in the sea so that the boat was submerged by the waves" (Matt. 8:24).

12.5 Causal Clauses

Causality is expressed by the proclitic particle ⲬⲈ- (§ 4.5) or ⲈⲂⲞⲖ ⲬⲈ-: M ϨⲀϤⲢ̄ϨⲀⲦⲈ ⲈⲦⲂⲈⲠⲘⲎϢⲈ ⲬⲈⲚⲀⲨⲬⲒ ⲘⲘⲀϤⲠⲈ ϨⲰⲤ ⲠⲢⲞⲪⲎⲦⲎⲤ, S ⲀϤⲢ̄ϨⲞⲦⲈ ϨⲎⲦϤ̄ ⲘⲠⲘⲎⲎϢⲈ ⲈⲂⲞⲖ ⲬⲈⲈⲚⲈⲨⲬⲒ ⲘⲘⲞϤⲠⲈ ϨⲰⲤ ⲠⲢⲞⲪⲎⲦⲎⲤ "he feared the masses because they took him as a prophet (Greek προφήτης)" (Matt. 14:5), B ⲬⲈⲘ̄ⲘⲞⲚⲦⲞⲨ ⲚⲞⲨⲚⲒ ⲘⲘⲀⲨ ⲀⲨϢⲰⲞⲨⲒ, S ⲈⲂⲞⲖ ⲬⲈⲘ̄Ⲛ̄ⲚⲞⲨⲚⲈ ⲘⲘⲞⲞⲨ ⲀⲨϢⲞⲞⲨⲈ "because they do not have root, they dried up" (Matt. 13:6), L Ⲛ̄ⲦⲀⲨⲬⲈⲚⲈⲈⲒϬⲈ ⲬⲒⲚⲈϤⲈⲒⲀⲦⲈ ⲬⲈⲚⲈⲨⲢ̄ϨⲀⲦⲈ ϨⲎⲦⲞⲨ Ⲛ̄ⲚⲒⲞⲨⲦⲀⲒ̈ⲠⲈ "Moreover, it was because they feared the Jews that they, his parents, said these" (John 9:22).

12.6 Temporal Clauses

The negative Third Perfect (§ 9.2) with the circumstantial converter, and the temporal converters (§ 10.3), are both used to form temporal clauses: M ⲈⲘⲠⲀⲦⲈⲞⲨⲀⲖⲈⲔⲦⲰⲢ ⲘⲞⲨⲦⲈ ⲔⲚⲈⲀⲠⲀⲢⲚⲒ ⲘⲘⲀⲒ̈ Ⲛ̄ϢⲀⲘⲚ̄Ⲧ ⲚⲤⲀⲠ "Before the rooster (Greek ἀλέκτωρ) speaks, you will

---

1   ⲬⲒ "take" ⲬⲢⲀⲠ "obstacle."

deny (Greek ἀπαρνήσασθαι) me three times" (Matt. 26:75), S ⲚⲦⲈⲢⲈϤⲔⲞⲦϤⲆⲈ ⲚϬⲒⲤ ⲀϤ-
ⲚⲀⲨ ⲈⲢⲞⲞⲨ ⲈⲨⲞⲨⲎ𝟤 ⲚⲤⲰϤ "And when he turned, namely Jesus, he saw them stationed
behind him" (John 1:38), B ⲪⲰⲦ ⲈⲬⲎⲘⲒ ⲞⲨⲞ𝟤 ⲰⲰⲠⲒ ⲘⲘⲀⲨ ⲰⲀⲦϪⲞⲤ ⲚⲀⲔ "Flee to Egypt
and be there until I tell you" (Matt. 2:12).

Bohairic uses the Second Perfect in place of ⲚⲦⲈⲢⲈ-: S ⲚⲀⲒⲆⲈ ⲚⲦⲈⲢⲈϤⲘⲈⲈⲨⲈ ⲈⲢⲞⲞⲨ
ⲈⲒⲤ ⲠⲀⲄⲄⲈⲖⲞⲤ ⲘⲠⲬⲞⲈⲒⲤ ⲀϤⲞⲨⲞⲚ𝟤Ϥ ⲚⲀϤ ⲈⲂⲞⲖ 𝟤ⲚⲞⲨⲢⲀⲤⲞⲨ, B ⲚⲀⲒⲆⲈ ⲈⲦⲀϤⲘⲞⲔⲘⲈⲔ
ⲈⲢⲰⲞⲨ 𝟤ⲎⲠⲠⲈ ⲈⲒⲤ ⲞⲨⲀⲄⲄⲈⲖⲞⲤ ⲚⲦⲈⲠⳓⲤ ⲀϤⲞⲨⲞⲚ𝟤Ϥ ⲈⲒⲰⲤⲎⲪ ϧⲈⲚⲞⲨⲢⲀⲤⲞⲨⲒ "And
these, when he thought/pondered on them, behold, a messenger (Greek ἄγγελος) of the Lord
revealed himself to him/Joseph in a dream" (Matt. 1:20). This construction can also be introduced by 𝟤ⲞⲦⲈ "when" (Greek ὅτε): B 𝟤ⲞⲦⲈ ⲞⲨⲚ ⲈⲦⲀϤⲦⲰⲚϤ ⲈⲂⲞⲖ ϧⲈⲚⲚⲎ ⲈⲐⲘⲰⲞⲨⲦ
ⲀⲨⲈⲢⲪⲘⲈⲨⲒ ⲚϪⲈⲚⲈϤⲘⲀⲐⲎⲦⲎⲤ ϪⲈⲪⲀⲒ ⲈⲚⲀϤϪⲰ ⲘⲘⲞϤ "Then (Greek οὖν), when he
raised himself from those who were dead, they remembered, namely his disciples, that which
he used to say to them" (John 2:22).

Temporal clauses are also introduced by prepositions (§ 5.3) governing various forms of
the verb:

– 𝟤Ⲛ governing a nominalized Causative Infinitive (§ 7.3)—concomitance: S ⲀⲨⲰ
  𝟤ⲘⲠⲦⲢⲈϤϪⲞ Ⲁ𝟤ⲞⲒⲚⲈ 𝟤Ⲉ 𝟤ⲀⲦⲚⲦⲈ𝟤ⲒⲎ "and during the sowing, some fell near the road,"
  B ⲞⲨⲞ𝟤 ϧⲈⲚⲠⲬⲒⲚⲞⲢⲈϤⲤⲒⲦ ⲞⲨⲀⲒ ⲘⲈⲚ ⲀϤϨⲈⲒ ϧⲀⲦⲈⲚⲠⲒⲘⲰⲒⲦ "and during the sowing
  (§ 2.6), one, in fact (Greek μέν), it fell near the path" (Luke 8:5)

– ϪⲚ governing a circumstantial form (§ 10.2) or the Second Perfect—"since, from the
  time that": S ϤⲚⲀⲘⲞⲨ𝟤 ⲘⲠⲈⲠ̅Ⲛ̅Ⲁ̅ ⲈⲦⲞⲨⲀⲀⲂ ϪⲒⲚⲈϤϨⲚ𝟤ⲎⲦⲤ ⲚⲦⲈϤⲘⲀⲀⲨ "he will be
  filled with the Holy Spirit from the time that he is in his mother's womb" (Luke 1:15),
  M 𝟤ⲀϤϪⲀⲤ ⲚϬⲒ ⲠⲒⲠⲖⲀⲚⲞⲤ ⲚϪⲒⲚⲈϤⲀⲚϨ "he said, namely that deceiver (Greek πλάνος),
  from the time he was alive" (Matt. 27:63), S ⲞⲨⲚⲞϬ ⲘⲔⲘⲦⲞ ⲈⲦⲈⲘⲠⲈⲞⲨⲞⲚ ⲚⲦⲈϤ𝟤Ⲉ
  ⲰⲰⲠⲈ ϪⲒⲚⲚⲦⲀⲨⲬⲠⲈⲢⲰⲘⲈ 𝟤ⲒϪⲘⲠⲔⲀ𝟤 "a great earthquake, whose like did not happen
  since men were created on the earth" (Rev. 16:18); note also S ⲰⲤⲔ ϪⲒⲚⲦⲀ⸗ with the
  First Perfect—"continue from" = "just": ⲀϤϪⲚⲞⲨϤ ϪⲈⲈⲚⲈⲀϤⲰⲤⲔ ϪⲒⲚⲦⲀϤⲘⲞⲨ "he
  asked him whether he had just died" (Mark 15:44), literally, "that-if-he-continued from-
  he-died"

– ⲘⲚⲚⲤⲀ governing the Causative Infinitive—"after": B ⲘⲈⲚⲈⲚⲤⲀ ⲐⲢⲈϤⲤⲀϪⲒ ⲚⲈⲘⲰⲞⲨ
  ⲀⲨⲞⲖϤ ⲈⲠⲰⲰⲒ ⲈⲦⲪⲈ "after he spoke with them, he was taken up to the sky" (Mark
  16:9).

Greek prepositions are also used as temporal conjunctions, mostly governing circumstantial forms:

– ⲈⲠⲈⲒⲆⲎ (ἐπειδή), with the First and Second Perfect: B ⲈⲠⲈⲒⲆⲎ ⲀϤⲬⲈⲔⲚⲈϤⲰⲀϪⲈ ⲈⲂⲞⲖ
  ⲦⲎⲢⲞⲨ ⲈⲘⲘⲀⲬⲈ ⲘⲠⲖⲀⲞⲤ ⲀϤⲂⲰⲔ ⲈϧⲞⲨⲚ ⲈⲔⲀⲪⲀⲢⲚⲀⲞⲨⲘ "After he completed all
  his words to the ears of the people, he went in to Capernaum" (Luke 7:1)

- ⲌⲞⲤⲞⲚ (ὅσον), ⲈⲠⲌⲞⲤⲞⲚ/ⲈⳜⲞⲤⲞⲚ (ἐφ᾽ ὅσον): M **ϢⲰⲠⲈ ⲈⲔⲂⲎⲖ ⲘⲠⲈⲔⲬⲈⲬⲈ ⲘⲠⲢⲎⲦⲈ ⲌⲞⲤⲞⲚ ⲈⲔⲌⲒⲦⲈⲌⲒⲎ ⲚⲈⲘⲈϤ** "be agreeable with your enemy, likewise, while you are on the road with him" (Matt. 5:25)
- ⲌⲞⲦⲀⲚ (ὅταν): S **ⲌⲞⲦⲀⲚ ⲈⲢⲈⲠⲞⲨⲞⲈⲒⲚ ⲘⲠⲢⲎ ⲚⲂⲞⲖ ϢⲀϤⲌⲰⲂⲤ ⲘⲠⲔⲀⲔⲈ** "when the light of the sun is out, it covers the darkness" (PS 232, 2)
- B ⲌⲞⲦⲈ (ὅτε): **ⲌⲞⲦⲈ ⲈϤⲤⲀϪⲒ ⲒⲤ ⲞⲨϬⲎⲠⲒ Ⲛ̀ⲞⲨⲰⲒⲚⲒ ⲀⲤⲈⲢⳛⲎⲒⲂⲒ ⲈⲬⲰⲞⲨ** "while he was speaking, behold a cloud of light made shade on them" (Matt. 17:5)
- ⲌⲰⲤ (ὥς): S **ⲌⲰⲤ ⲈⲨⲚⲦⲀⲚ ⲘⲘⲀⲨ ⲘⲠⲞⲨⲞⲈⲒϢ ⲘⲀⲢⲚⲈⲒⲢⲈ ⲘⲠⲈⲦⲚⲀⲚⲞⲨϤ Ⲛ̀ⲞⲨⲞⲚ ⲚⲒⲘ** "as long as we have the opportunity, let us do what is good to everyone" (Gal, 6:10)

Oxyrhynchite also uses the Conditional (§ 12.9) with ⲌⲞⲦⲀⲚ: M **ⲤⲈⲚⲚⲎⲞⲨⲖⲈ Ⲛ̄ϬⲒ ⲌⲈⲚⲌⲀⲨ ⲌⲞⲦⲀⲚ ⲀⲨϢⲀⲚϤⲒ ⲘⲠⲀⲦϢⲈⲖⲎⲦ Ⲛ̄ⲦⲀⲦⲞⲨ** "But they are coming, days when the bridegroom shall be taken from them" (Matt. 9:15).

12.7 Content Clauses

Clauses that express the object of a verb are uniformly introduced by **ⲬⲈ**. Examples are, after various verbs:

- A **ⲬⲞⲨ**, BFLMS **ⲬⲰ** "say": M **ⲀⲬⲒⲤ ⲞⲨⲚ ⲚⲈⲚ ⲬⲈⲞⲨ ⲠⲈⲦⲀⲞϬⲒ ⲚⲈⲔ** "Tell us, then (Greek οὖν), what is that which you think (Greek δοκεῖν) for yourself" (Matt. 22:17), B **ⲚⲎ ⲈⲦⲬⲰ Ⲙ̀ⲘⲞⲤ ⲈⲢⲞϤ ⲬⲈϤⲞⲚⳏ̄** "that which said about him that he is alive" (Luke 24:23); also with direct quotations: M **ⲠⲈⲬⲈϤ ⲬⲈⲀⲘⲞⲨ** "He said, 'Come'" (Matt. 14:29)
- AL **Ⲙ̄ⲘⲈ**, B **ⲈⲘⲒ**, F **ⲒⲘⲒ**, MS **ⲈⲒⲘⲈ** "know": B **ⳢⲈⲘⲒ ⲬⲈⲚ̀ⲐⲰⲦⲈⲚ ⲚⲀⲠⲬⲢⲞⲬ Ⲛ̀ⲀⲂⲢⲀⲀⲘ** "I know that you are of the seed of Abraham" (John 8:37)
- AL **ⲤⲀⲨⲚⲈ**, B **ⲤⲰⲞⲨⲚ̄**, FM **ⲤⲀⲞⲨⲚ̄**, S **ⲤⲞⲞⲨⲚ̄** "know": L **ϮⲤⲀⲨⲚⲒ ⲬⲈⲚ̄ⲦⲰⲦⲚ̄ ⲠⲤⲠⲈⲢⲘⲀ Ⲛ̄ⲀⲂⲢⲀⲌⲀⲘ** "I know that you are the seed of Abraham" (John 8:37)
- AL **ⲤⲰⲦⲘⲈ**, BF **ⲤⲰⲦⲈⲘ**, M **ⲤⲞⲦⲘ̄**, S **ⲤⲰⲦⲘ̄** "hear": S **ⲀⲨⲤⲰⲦⲘ̄ ⲬⲈⲒⲤ̄ ⲚⲀⲠⲀⲢⲀⲄⲈ** "they heard that Jesus would pass by (Greek παράγειν)" (Matt. 20:30)
- AL **ⲚⲞ**, BS **ⲚⲀⲨ**, FM **ⲚⲈⲨ** "see": B **ⲈⲦⲀϤⲚⲀⲨ ⲬⲈⲀϤⲖⲞⲬϤ** "when he saw that he was recovered" (Mark 16:4)
- ALS **ⲘⲈⲈⲨⲈ**, B **ⲘⲈⲨⲒ**, F **ⲘⲎⲞⲨⲒ**, M **ⲘⲎⲞⲨⲈ** "think": B **ⲚⲀⲨⲘⲈⲨⲒ ⲬⲈⲦⲘⲈⲦⲞⲨⲢⲞ Ⲛ̄ⲦⲈⳜ̄ ⲚⲀⲞⲨⲰⲚⳏ̄ ⲈⲂⲞⲖ ⲤⲀⲦⲞⲦⲤⲠⲈ** "they were thinking that the kingdom of God was going to be revealed immediately" (Luke 19:11)

12.8 Concessive Clauses

Clauses of concession can be introduced by a number of terms, such as A **ⲈⲒϪⲬⲈ/ⲈⲒⲌⲠⲈ**, B **ⲒⲤⲬⲈ**, FS **ⲈϢⲬⲈ/ⲈϢⲬⲠⲈ**, L **ⲈϢⲠⲈ**, M **ⲈϢⲬⲈ** "if," the preposition **ⲈⲦⲂⲈ/ⲈⲐⲂⲈ ⲬⲈ** "concerning," and B **ⲬⲀⲤ ⲬⲈ**: S **ⲈϢϪⲈ ⲠⲚⲞⲨⲦⲈ Ⲛ̄ϮⲢⲌⲞⲦⲈ Ⲛ̄ϨⲎⲦϤ̄ ⲀⲚ ⲀⲨⲰ Ⲛ̄ⲦϢⲒⲠⲈ ⲀⲚ ϨⲎⲦϤ̄ ⲢⲢⲰⲘⲈ ⲀⲖⲖⲀ ⲈⲦⲂⲈⲦⲈⲒ̈ⲬⲎⲢⲀ ⲞⲨⲈⲌⳢⲒⲤⲈ ⲈⲢⲞⲒ ϮⲚⲀⲢⲠⲈⲤϨⲀⲠ** "Although God, I do not fear him and I do not revere man, but since this widow makes trouble to me, I will make her case," B **ⲬⲀⲤ ⲬⲈⳜ̄ ϮⲈⲢϨⲞϮ ⲀⲚ ⳢⲀⲦⲈϤϨⲎ ⲞⲨⲞϨ Ⲛ̄ⲦϢⲒⲠⲒ ⲀⲚ ⳢⲀⲦϨⲎ Ⲛ̀ⲚⲒⲢⲰⲘⲒ ⲈⲐⲂⲈⲬⲈⲦⲀⲒⲬⲎⲢⲀ ϮϨⲒⲤⲒ** ⲛⲏⲓ ⲧⲛⲁϭⲓ ⲙ̄ⲡⲉⲥⲙ̄ϣⲓϣ "Although God, I do not fear him and I do not revere people, since this widow troubles me, I will avenge her" (Luke 18:4–5). Greek καί τοι is also used: S ⲉⲡⲉⲓⲇⲏ ⲅⲁⲣ ⲛ̄ⲧⲁⲡⲙⲟⲩ ϣⲱⲡⲉ ⲉⲃⲟⲗ ϩⲓⲧⲛ̄ⲟⲩⲣⲱⲙⲉ ⲉⲃⲟⲗ ϩⲓⲧⲛ̄ⲟⲩⲣⲱⲙⲉ ⲟⲛⲡⲉ ⲡⲧⲱⲟⲩⲛ̄ ⲛ̄ⲛⲉⲧⲙⲟⲟⲩⲧ "For since it is from a person that death happened, from a person also is the rising from those who are dead" (1Cor. 15:21), S ⲁⲛⲉⲫⲁⲣⲓⲥⲁⲓⲟⲥ ⲥⲱⲧⲙ̄ ϫⲉⲓ̄ⲥ̄ ⲣ̄ϩⲁϩ ⲙ̄ⲙⲁⲑⲏⲧⲏⲥ ⲁⲩⲱ ϥⲃⲁⲡⲧⲓⲍⲉ ⲉϩⲟⲩⲉⲓ̈ⲱϩⲁⲛⲛⲏⲥ ⲕⲁⲓⲧⲟⲓ ⲓ̄ⲥ̄ ⲁⲛⲡⲉ ⲛⲉϥⲃⲁⲡⲧⲓⲍⲉ "the Pharisees heard that Jesus was making many disciples and baptizing (Greek βαπτίζειν) more than John, even though Jesus was not baptizing" (John 4:1–2).

12.9 Real Conditions

Coptic has a number of means of expressing the protasis of a real condition. The Second Present is often used in this function: M ⲉⲧⲉⲧⲛ̄ⲡⲓⲥⲧⲉⲩⲉ ⲧⲉⲧⲛⲉϫⲓⲧⲟⲩ "if you believe (Greek πιστεύειν), you will receive them" (Matt. 21:22). This form, in turn, is the basis for a dedicated verb form, called the Conditional, which is composed of the Second Present with an infixed AL -ϣⲁ-, BFMS -ϣⲁⲛ-. With a nominal subject the prefix is A ⲁⲣⲉϣⲁ-, BM ⲁⲣⲉϣⲁⲛ-, F ⲁⲗⲉϣⲁⲛ- , L ⲉⲣⲉϣⲁ-, S ⲉⲣⲉϣⲁⲛ- ; pronominal forms are:

1s	A ⲁⲓϣⲁ, BFM ⲁⲓϣⲁⲛ, L ⲉⲓ̈ϣⲁ, S ⲉⲓ̈ϣⲁⲛ	1pl	A ⲁⲛϣⲁ, BFM ⲁⲛϣⲁⲛ, L ⲉⲛϣⲁ, S ⲉⲛϣⲁⲛ	
2ms	A ⲁⲕϣⲁ, BFM ⲁⲕϣⲁⲛ, L ⲉⲕϣⲁ, S ⲉⲕϣⲁⲛ	2pl	A ⲁⲧⲉⲧⲛ̄ϣⲁ, B ⲁⲣⲉⲧⲉⲛϣⲁ, F ⲁⲧⲉⲧⲉⲛϣⲁ, L ⲉⲧⲉⲧⲛ̄ϣⲁ/ ⲉⲣⲉⲧⲛ̄ϣⲁ, M ⲁⲧⲉⲧⲛ̄ϣⲁⲛ, S ⲉⲧⲉⲧⲛ̄ϣⲁⲛ/ⲉⲣⲉⲧⲛ̄ϣⲁⲛ	
2fs	A ⲁⲣⲉϣⲁ, BFM ⲁⲣⲉϣⲁⲛ, L ⲉⲣⲉϣⲁ, S ⲉⲣⲉϣⲁⲛ			
3ms	A ⲁϥϣⲁ, BFM ⲁϥϣⲁⲛ, L ⲉϥϣⲁ, S ⲉϥϣⲁⲛ	3pl	A ⲁⲩϣⲁ, BFM ⲁⲩϣⲁⲛ, L ⲉⲩϣⲁ, FS ⲉⲩϣⲁⲛ	
3fs	A ⲁⲥϣⲁ, BFM ⲁⲥϣⲁⲛ, L ⲉⲥϣⲁ, S ⲉⲥϣⲁⲛ			

The Conditional is specific to the protasis of real conditions: M ⲁⲧⲉⲧⲛ̄ϣⲁⲛϫⲁⲥ ⲙ̄ⲡⲉⲓ̈-ⲕⲉⲧⲁⲩ ϫⲉϥⲓⲧⲕ ϩⲓⲧⲕ ⲉⲑⲁⲗⲁⲥⲥⲁ ⲉⲥⲉϣⲟⲡⲉ "If you say to this mountain also, 'Lift yourself; throw yourself to the sea,' it shall happen" (Matt. 21:21).

The protasis can also be introduced by A ⲉϩⲱⲡⲉ, B ⲉϣⲱⲡ, F ⲉϣⲱⲡⲓ, LS ⲉϣⲱⲡⲉ, M ⲉϣⲟⲡⲉ "happen," and A ⲉⲓϩϫⲉ/ⲉⲓϩⲡⲉ, B ⲓⲥϫⲉ, FS ⲉϣϫⲉ/ⲉϣϫⲡⲉ, L ⲉϣⲡⲉ, M ⲉϣϫⲉ: M ⲉϣⲟⲡⲉ ⲁⲧⲉⲧⲛ̄ϣⲁⲛϭⲓⲛⲉ ⲙ̄ⲙⲁϥ ⲁⲙⲏⲉⲓⲛⲉ ⲙⲁⲧⲁⲙⲁⲓ ϩⲱ "If you happen to find him, come, let me know myself" (Matt. 2:8), L ⲉϣⲡⲉ ⲧⲉⲧⲛ̄ⲣ̄ⲡⲓⲥⲧⲉⲩⲉⲇⲉ ⲉⲛ ⲁⲛ̄ⲥϩⲉⲉⲓ ⲙ̄ⲡⲉⲧⲙ̄ⲙⲉⲩ ⲛ̄ⲉϣ ⲛ̄ϩⲉ ⲉⲧⲉⲧⲛⲁⲣ̄ⲡⲓⲥⲧⲉⲩⲉ ⲁⲛⲁⲥⲉϫⲉ "But if you do not believe the writings of that one, how will you believe my words?" (John 5:47). These can also be introduced by the Greek conjunction ⲕⲁⲛ (κἄν): S ⲕⲁⲛ ⲉⲧⲉⲧⲛ̄ϣⲁⲛϫⲟⲟⲥ ⲙ̄ⲡⲉⲓ̈ⲧⲟⲟⲩ ϫⲉⲧⲱⲟⲩⲛ̄ ⲛ̄ⲅ̄ⲃⲱⲕ ⲉϩⲣⲁⲓ ⲉⲑⲁⲗⲁⲥⲥⲁ ⲥⲛⲁϣⲱⲡⲉ ⲛⲏⲧⲛ̄ "If you say to this mountain, 'Arise and go down to the sea,' it will happen for you" (Matt. 21:21), S ⲕⲁⲛ ⲉϣⲱⲡⲉ ⲁϥⲣ̄ϩⲉⲛⲕⲉⲛⲟⲃⲉ ⲥⲉⲛⲁⲕⲁⲁⲩ ⲛⲁϥ ⲉⲃⲟⲗ

"If he happens to have done any other sins, they will be thrown out for him" (James 5:15). ⲉϣⲱⲡⲉ and ⲉϣϫⲉ also allow for non-verbal protases: A ⲉⲓϣⲡⲉ ⲁⲛⲁⲕ ⲡϫⲁⲉⲓⲥ ⲁⲛⲁⲕ ⲁⲥⲧⲟ ⲧⲁϩⲛⲟⲱϩⲉ "If *I* am the master, where is the fear of me?" (Mal. 1:6), B ⲓⲥϫⲉ ⲛ̄ⲑⲟⲕⲡⲉ ⲡϣⲏⲣⲓ ⲙ̄ⲫϯ ⲁϫⲟⲥ ϩⲓⲛⲁ ⲛ̄ⲧⲉⲛⲁⲓⲱⲛⲓ ⲉⲣⲱⲓⲕ "If *you* are the son of God, speak so that these stones make bread" (Matt. 4:3).

12.10   Unreal Conditions

The proclitic particle ⲉⲛⲉ- is used for protases contrary to fact: L ⲉⲛⲉⲛ̄ⲧⲱⲧⲛ̄ ϩⲉⲛⲃⲗ̄ⲗⲉ ⲛⲉⲙ̄ⲛ̄ⲛⲁⲃⲉ ⲁⲣⲱⲧⲛ̄ "If you were blind, there would be no sin against you" (John 9:41); B ⲉⲛⲉⲫⲁⲓ ⲟⲩⲉⲃⲟⲗ ⲙ̄ⲫϯ ⲁⲛⲡⲉ ⲛⲁϥⲛⲁϣ̄ϫⲉⲙϫⲟⲙ ⲁⲛⲡⲉ ⲉⲉⲣϩⲗⲓ "If this one were not of God, he would not be able to do anything" (John 9:33). The apodosis usually has the past converter, often with the First Future, as these illustrate, but other apodoses also occur: S ⲉⲛⲉⲛ̄ⲧⲁⲛ̄ϭⲟⲙ ⲛ̄ⲧⲁⲩϣⲱⲡⲉ ⲛ̄ϩⲏⲧⲧⲏⲩⲧⲛ̄ ϣⲱⲡⲉ ϩⲛ̄ⲧⲩⲣⲟⲥ ⲙⲛ̄ⲥⲓⲇⲱⲛ ⲉϣⲭⲡⲉ ⲁⲩⲙⲉⲧⲁⲛⲟⲓ ϩⲛ̄ⲟⲩϭⲟⲟⲩⲛⲉ ⲙⲛ̄ⲟⲩⲕ̄ⲣⲙⲉⲥ "If the deeds of power that were among you were in Tyre and Sidon instead, then they would have repented (Greek μετανοεῖν) in sack and ash" (Matt. 11:21).

EXERCISE 12

Translate the following phrases and sentences.

1. L ⲉⲛⲉⲛ̄ⲧⲱⲧⲛ̄ ⲛ̄ϣⲏⲣⲉ ⲛ̄ⲁⲃⲣⲁϩⲁⲙ ⲛⲉⲣⲉⲧⲛ̄ⲁⲣⲛ̄ϩⲃⲏⲩⲉ ⲛ̄ⲁⲃⲣⲁϩⲁⲙ
2. M ⲉϣϫⲉ ⲛ̄ⲧⲁⲕⲡⲉ ⲡϣⲏⲣⲉ ⲙ̄ⲡⲛ̄ϯ ϩⲓⲧⲕ̄ ⲉⲡⲉⲥⲏⲧ
3. S ⲉϣϫⲉ ⲛ̄ⲧⲁϥⲛ̄ⲕⲟⲧⲕ̄ ϥⲛⲁⲧⲱⲟⲩⲛ
4. S ⲉϣⲱⲡⲉ ⲡⲉⲓϣⲟϫⲛⲉ ⲏ ⲡⲉⲓϩⲱⲃ ⲟⲩⲉⲃⲟⲗ ϩⲛ̄ⲛ̄ⲣⲱⲙⲉⲡⲉ ⲉⲓⲉ ϥⲛⲁⲃⲱⲗ ⲉⲃⲟⲗ
5. B ⲓⲥϫⲉ ⲁⲣⲉⲧⲉⲛⲛⲁⲙⲉⲛⲣⲉⲛⲏ ⲉⲑⲙⲉⲓ ⲙ̄ⲙⲱⲧⲉⲛ ⲁϣⲡⲉ ⲡⲉⲧⲉⲛϩⲙⲟⲧ
6. B ⲉϣⲱⲡ ⲁⲣⲉⲧⲉⲛⲛⲁⲉⲣⲡⲉⲑⲛⲁⲛⲉϥ ⲛ̄ⲛⲏ ⲉⲧⲉⲣⲡⲉⲑⲛⲁⲛⲉϥ ⲛⲉⲙⲱⲧⲉⲛ ⲁϣⲡⲉ ⲡⲉⲧⲉⲛϩⲙⲟⲧ
7. B ⲟⲩⲟϩ ⲉⲧⲁϥϭⲓⲛⲓ ⲉⲃⲟⲗ ϩⲁⲫⲓⲟⲙ ⲛ̄ⲧⲉⲧⲅⲁⲗⲓⲗⲉⲁ ⲁϥⲛⲁⲩ ⲉⲥⲓⲙⲱⲛ ⲛⲉⲙⲁⲛⲇⲣⲉⲁⲥ ⲡⲥⲟⲛ ⲛ̄ⲥⲓⲙⲱⲛ ⲉⲩϩⲓⲟⲩⲛⲉ ⲛ̄ⲥⲓϯ ⲉϥⲓⲟⲙ
8. S ⲛⲁⲓ ⲉⲩϣⲁⲛⲥⲁϩⲟⲩ ⲟⲩⲁ ⲟⲩⲁ ϯϫⲱ ⲙ̄ⲡⲕⲟⲥⲙⲟⲥ ⲛⲁϣⲡ̄ⲛ̄ⲭⲱⲱⲙⲉ ⲁⲛ ⲉⲧⲟⲩⲛⲁⲥⲁϩⲟⲩ
9. S ϩⲙ̄ⲡⲧⲣⲉⲩⲕⲁⲧⲟⲓⲅⲟⲣⲉⲓⲇⲉ ⲙ̄ⲙⲟϥ ⲉⲃⲟⲗ ϩⲓⲧⲟⲟⲧⲟⲩ ⲛ̄ⲛⲁⲣⲭⲓⲉⲣⲉⲩⲥ ⲙⲛ̄ⲛⲉⲡⲣⲉⲥⲃⲩⲧⲉⲣⲟⲥ ⲙ̄ⲡⲉϥⲟⲩⲱϣⲃ̄ ⲛ̄ⲗⲁⲩ
10. M ϩⲁϥϣⲛ̄ϩⲧⲏϥ ϩⲁⲣⲁⲩ ϫⲉⲛⲉϩⲁⲩⲥⲕⲩⲗⲗⲉⲡⲉ

Vocabulary

ⲁⲛⲇⲣⲉⲁⲥ B "Andrew"

ⲁⲣⲭⲓⲉⲣⲉⲩⲥ S "high priest" (Greek ἀρχιερεύς)

ⲁϣ B "what?"

ⲂⲰⲖ ⲈⲂⲞⲖ S "disappear" ("loosen out")

ⲄⲀⲖⲒⲖⲈⲀ B "Galilee"

ⲈⲒⲈ S "then"

ⲈⲠⲈⲤⲎⲦ L "down" (Ⲉ-Ⲡ-ⲈⲤⲎⲦ "to-the-ground")

ⲒⲞⲘ B "sea"

ⲔⲀⲦⲞⲒⲅⲞⲢⲈⲒ S "accuse" (Greek κατοιγορεῖν)

ⲔⲞⲤⲘⲞⲤ S "world" (Greek κόσμος)

ⲖⲀⲨ S "anything"

ⲘⲈⲒ, ⲘⲈⲚⲢⲈ- B "love"

ⲚⲀⲚⲈϤ B (see § 6.5)

ⲚⲀⲨ B "see" (with Ⲉ-)

Ⲛ̄ⲔⲞⲦⲔ̄ S "sleep"

ⲞⲨⲀ ⲞⲨⲀ S "one by one"

ⲞⲨⲰϢⲂ̄ S "answer"

ⲠⲢⲈⲤⲂⲨⲦⲈⲢⲞⲤ S "elder" (Greek πρεσβύτερος)

ⲤⲀⲂ꞊ S "write"

ⲤⲒⲘⲰⲚ B "Simon"

ⲤⲒⲚⲒ B "pass" (ⲄⲀ- "by")

ⲤⲒϮ B "throw"

ⲤⲔⲨⲖⲖⲈ M "be troubled" (Greek σκύλλειν)

ⲦⲰⲞⲨⲚ̄ S "arise"

ϢⲚⲈ B "net"

ϢⲚ̄Ⲅ̄ⲦⲎ꞊ M "feel compassion" ("suffer heart," with ⲄⲀ- "for")

ϢⲞϪⲚⲈ S "counsel"

ϢⲠ̄Ⲡ- S "hold, receive"

Ⲅ̄Ⲓ L "throw"

Ⲅ̄ⲘⲞⲦ B "gift"

Ⲅ̄ⲰⲂ S "work," plural Ⲅ̄ⲂⲎⲨⲈ L "works"

ⲬⲰⲰⲘⲈ S "scroll"

Answers to the Exercises

Exercise 2

1. S ⲦⲘⲚⲦⲢ̅Ⲣⲟ Ⲛ̅ⲘⲠⲎⲨⲈ (Matt. 3:2)
   "the kingdom of heaven"

2. B ⲠϢⲎⲢⲒ Ⲙ̀ⲪⲚⲞⲨϮ (Matt. 4:3)
   "the son of God"

3. S ϢⲎⲢⲈ ϢⲎⲘ ⲚⲒⲘ (Matt. 2:16)
   "every small child"

4. S ⲞⲨⲚⲞϬ Ⲙ̅ⲘⲎⲎϢⲈ (Mark 3:7)
   "a big crowd"

5. B ⳈⲀⲚⲢⲈϤⲘⲱⲞⳐⲦ (Matt. 28:4)
   "dead people"

6. B ⲞⲨⲘⲀⲚ̀Ⲙ̀ⲦⲞⲚ (Matt. 11:29)
   "a place of rest"

7. L Ⲛ̅ϢⲎⲢⲈ Ⲛ̀ⲀⲂⲢⲀⳈⲀⲘ (John 8:39)
   "the children of Abraham"

8. F ⲀⲦⲚⲀⲂⲒ (Matt. 12:7)
   "sinless"

9. M ϬⲒⲚⲤⲈⲬⲈ (Matt. 26:73)
   "speech"

10. A ⳈⲱⲂ ⲚⲒⲘ Ⲙ̅ⲘⲎⲈ (Phil. 4:8)
    "everything true"

Exercise 3

1. M ⲚⲀⲠϮ̅ ... ⲚⲀⲚ̀ⲢⲰⲘⲈ (Matt. 16:23)
   "those of God ... those of people"

2. M Ⲛ̅ⲦⲀⲔ ⳈⲰⲔ (Matt. 26:69)
   "you yourself"

3. S ⲦⲈϤⲔⲈⳈⲨⲬⲎ (Luke 14:26)
   "his life also"

4. S Ⲛ̅ⲦⲱⲦⲚ̅ Ⲛ̅ⲦⲈⲦⲚ̅ⳈⲈⲚⲈⲂⲞⲖ Ⳉ̅ⲘⲠⲔⲀⳈ (John 8:23)
   "You, you are from the earth"

5. B ⲚⲒⲘⲠⲈ ⲪⲀⲒ (Matt. 21:10)
   "Who is this?"

6. S ⲁⲛⲅⲟⲩⲁⲅⲁⲑⲟⲥ ⲁⲛⲟⲕ (Matt. 20:15)

   "I myself am a good person"

7. B ⲛⲟⲱⲧⲉⲛ ϩⲱⲧⲉⲛ (Matt. 15:3)

   "you yourselves"

8. L ⲡⲉⲧⲉⲡⲱϥⲡⲉ (John 15:19)

   "the one who is his"

9. B ⲛⲏ ⲉⲧⲉⲛⲟⲩⲓ (Matt. 20:15)

   "those who are mine"

10. S ⲧⲁⲡⲁⲣⲭⲏ ⲙ̅ⲡⲉⲡⲛ̅ⲁ̅ (Rom. 8:23)

    "the first thing of the spirit"

EXERCISE 4

1. S ⲡⲉⲭⲁⲩ ⲛⲁϥ ⲭⲉⲡϣⲟⲣⲡ̅ⲡⲉ (Matt. 21:31)

   "They said to him, 'It is the first'"

2. M ϣⲁⲙⲛ̅ⲧ ⲛ̅ϩⲁⲩ (Matt. 12:40)

   "three days"

3. S ⲡⲉⲭⲁⲩ ⲛⲁϥ ⲭⲉϯⲟⲩ ⲙ̅ⲛ̅ⲧⲃⲧ ⲥⲛⲁⲩ (Mark 6:38)

   "They said to him, 'Five, and two fish'"

4. B ⲫ̅ ⲛ̅ⲥⲁⲑⲉⲣⲓ (Luke 7:41)

   "500 staters"

5. B ⲓ̅ⲃ̅ ⲛ̅ⲣⲟⲙⲡⲓ (Matt. 9:20)

   "12 years"

6. M ϣⲩ ⲛⲉⲥⲁⲩ (Matt. 18:12)

   "a hundred sheep"

7. M ⲡⲙⲉϩⲥⲛⲉⲩ ⲏ ⲡⲙⲉϩϣⲁⲙⲧ̅ ϣⲁⲡⲙⲉϩⲥⲉϣ̅ϥ (Matt. 22:26)

   "the second, or the third, up to the seventh"

8. S ⲧⲙⲉϩϥⲧⲟⲟⲇⲉ ⲛ̅ⲟⲩⲏⲣϣⲉ ⲛ̅ⲧⲉⲩϣⲏ (Matt. 14:25)

   "the fourth watch of the night"

9. B ⲉⲧⲁⲩⲥⲱⲧⲉⲙⲇⲉ ⲛ̅ϫⲉⲡⲓⲕⲉⲓ̈ ⲙ̅ⲙⲁⲑⲏⲧⲏⲥ ⲁⲩⲭⲣⲉⲙⲣⲉⲙ ⲉⲑⲃⲉⲡⲓⲥⲟⲛ ⲃ̅ (Matt. 20:14)

   "And when they heard, namely the other 10 disciples, they grumbled about the 2 brothers"

10. L ⲭⲟⲩⲧⲏ ⲛ̅ⲥⲧⲁⲇⲓⲟⲛ ⲏ ⲙⲁⲁⲃ (John 6:19)

    "twenty-five stadion or thirty"

EXERCISE 5

1. M ϩⲁⲑⲏ ⲉⲙⲡⲁⲧⲟⲩϣⲏ ⲉϩⲟⲩⲛ ⲙ̅ⲛ̅ⲡⲉⲩⲏⲣ ϩⲁϥϭⲛ̅ⲧⲥ̅ ⲉⲥⲏⲧ ⲉⲃⲁⲗ ϩⲛ̅ⲟⲩⲡⲛ̅ⲁ̅ ⲉⲧⲟⲩⲉⲃ (Matt. 1:18)

   "Before they had gone in with each other, he found her pregnant from a holy spirit"

2. M ϩⲁⲩϩⲓⲧⲟⲩ ⲉⲡⲉⲥⲏⲧ (Matt. 2:11)
   "They threw themselves down"

3. B ⲁⲩϣⲉ ⲛⲱⲟⲩ ϧⲉⲛⲟⲩⲅⲟⲓ ϧⲁⲧⲉⲛⲡⲓⲭⲁⲭⲣⲓⲙ ⲉϧⲣⲏⲓ ⲉϕⲓⲟⲙ (Matt. 8:32)
   "They went away in a rush beside the cliff down to the sea"

4. S ⲙ̄ⲡⲣⲥⲱⲟⲩϩ ⲛⲏⲧⲛ̄ ⲉϩⲟⲩⲛ ⲛ̄ϩⲛⲁϩⲟ ϩⲓϫⲙ̄ⲡⲕⲁϩ (Matt. 6:19)
   "Don't gather in for yourselves treasures on earth"

5. M ⲡⲟⲩⲁⲉⲓⲛ ⲉⲧⲛ̄ϩⲏⲧⲕ̄ (Matt. 6:23)
   "the light that is in you"

6. L ⲙⲛ̄ϭⲁⲧⲟⲩⲥ ⲛ̄ⲧⲟⲟⲧⲕ̄ (John 4:11)
   "there is no jar in your hand"

7. L ⲉⲧⲛⲁⲣ̄ⲡⲓⲥⲧⲉⲩⲉ ⲁⲣⲁⲉⲓ ⲁⲃⲁⲗ ϩⲓⲧⲛ̄ⲡⲟⲩⲥⲉϫⲉ (John 17:20)
   "who shall believe in me from your word"

8. S ϥⲣ̄ⲙⲛ̄ⲧⲣⲉ ⲉⲧⲃⲏⲏⲧϥ̄ (John 1:15)
   "he testifies about him"

9. S ⲁϥⲃⲱⲕ ⲉⲃⲟⲗ ϩⲓⲧⲛ̄ⲥⲓⲇⲱⲛ ⲉⲑⲁⲗⲁⲥⲥⲁ ⲛ̄ⲧⲅⲁⲗⲓⲗⲁⲓⲁ (Mark 7:31)
   "He went out of Sidon to the sea of Galilee"

10. B ϧⲉⲛⲛⲓⲉϩⲟⲟⲩ ⲉⲧⲉⲙⲙⲁⲩ (Matt. 3:1)
    "in those days"

EXERCISE 6

1. L ⲁⲛⲁⲕⲡⲉ ⲉⲧⲥⲉϫⲉ ⲛⲙ̄ⲙⲉ (John 4:26)
   "It is I, who speaks with you"

2. M ⲁⲛⲕⲟⲩⲣⲙ̄ⲣⲉϣ (Matt. 11:29)
   "I am a gentle person"

3. S ⲡⲉϥⲣⲁⲛⲡⲉ ⲧⲓⲙⲟⲑⲉⲟⲥ (Acts 16:1)
   "His name was Timothy"

4. S ⲟⲩϣⲗⲟϥⲡⲉ ⲛ̄ⲟⲩⲣⲱⲙⲉ ⲛ̄ⲓⲟⲩⲇⲁⲓ̈ (Acts 10:28)
   "It is a disgrace for a Jewish man"

5. S ⲡⲉϥⲉⲓⲱⲧⲇⲉ ⲛⲉⲟⲩⲉⲓ̈ⲉⲛⲓⲛⲡⲉ (Acts 16:1)
   "but his father was Greek"

6. S ⲧⲡⲩⲗⲏ ⲉⲧⲛⲉⲥⲱⲥ ⲛ̄ⲧⲉⲡⲣⲡⲉ (Acts 3:10)
   "the beautiful gate of the temple"

7. B ⲛⲁⲓⲛⲉ ⲛⲓϣⲏⲣⲓ ⲛ̄ⲧⲉⲧⲙⲉⲧⲟⲩⲣⲟ (Matt. 13:38)
   "those are the children of the kingdom"

8. M ⲧⲉⲓ̈ⲧⲉ ⲧϣⲁⲣⲡⲉ ⲁⲩⲱ ⲧⲛⲁϭ ⲛ̄ⲉⲛⲧⲟⲗⲏ (Matt. 22:38)
   "This is the first and the greatest commandment"

9. S ⲛⲉⲓ̈ⲣⲱⲙⲉ ϩⲉⲛⲓ̈ⲟⲩⲇⲁⲓ̈ⲛⲉ (Acts 16:20)
   "These men are Jews"

10. S ⲡⲁⲓ ⲟⲩⲙⲉⲡⲉ ⲛⲧⲁⲭⲟⲟϥ (John 4:18)

   "This is true, what you said"

EXERCISE 7

1. S ⲙ̄ⲡⲣ̄ⲣ̄ϩⲟⲧⲉ ⲉⲭⲓ ⲙ̄ⲙⲁⲣⲓⲁ ⲧⲉⲕⲥϩⲓⲙⲉ (Matt. 1:20)

   "don't be afraid to take Mary, your wife"

2. B ⲙⲁⲧⲁⲙⲟⲓ (Matt. 2:8)

   "let me know"

3. B ⲙ̄ⲡⲉⲣⲣ̄ⲙⲉⲩⲓ ⲭⲉⲉⲧⲁⲓ̈ ⲉⲃⲉⲗⲡⲓⲛⲟⲙⲟⲥ ⲉⲃⲟⲗ (Matt. 5:17)

   "Don't think that I have come to throw the law out"

4. B ⲛⲉⲧⲁⲓ̈ ⲉⲃⲟⲗⲟⲩ ⲁⲛ ⲁⲗⲗⲁ ⲉⲭⲟⲕⲟⲩ (Matt. 5:17)

   "I have not come to throw them out but to complete them"

5. M ⲥⲁⲗⲡ̄ⲥ ϩⲓⲧⲥ̄ ϩⲁⲃⲁⲗ (Matt. 5:30)

6. L ϥⲓ ⲛⲉⲧⲛ̄ⲃⲉⲗ ⲁϩⲣⲏⲓ̈ (John 4:35)

   "Lift up your eyes"

7. S ⲙ̄ⲡⲣ̄ⲉⲓⲣⲉ ⲙ̄ⲡⲏⲉⲓ ⲙ̄ⲡⲁⲉⲓⲱⲧ ⲙ̄ⲙⲁⲛ̄ⲉϣⲱⲧ (John 2:16)

   "Don't make the house of my father a market"

8. S ⲉⲧⲁϩⲟϥ ⲉⲣⲁⲧ̄ϥ ⲙ̄ⲡϫⲟⲉⲓⲥ (Luke 2:22)

   "to present him to the lord"

9. S ⲡϫⲟⲉⲓⲥ ⲙⲁⲧⲁⲛϩⲟⲛ (Matt. 8:25)

   "Lord, make us live"

10. B ⲁⲙⲱⲓⲛⲓ ⲙⲟϣⲓ ⲛ̀ⲥⲱⲓ (Matt. 4:19)

    "Come, walk behind me"

EXERCISE 8

1. M ⲙ̄ⲙⲛ̄ⲧⲉⲧⲛ̄ ⲃⲉⲕⲏ ⲙ̄ⲙⲉ ⲛ̄ⲧⲛ̄ⲡⲉⲧⲛ̄ⲓⲟⲧ (Matt. 6:1)

   "You have no reward from your father"

2. B ⲛⲉⲟⲩⲟⲛ ⲛ̀ⲧⲉⲟⲩⲁⲓ ⲛ̀ⲟⲩⲃⲱ ⲛ̀ⲕⲉⲛⲧⲉ (Luke 13:6)

   "A certain man had a fig tree"

3. S ⲥⲛⲁϫⲡⲟⲇⲉ ⲛ̄ⲟⲩϣⲏⲣⲉ (Matt. 1:21)

   "And she will give birth to a son"

4. S ⲛⲉⲩⲛⲁⲃⲱⲕ ⲉϩⲣⲁⲓ ⲉⲡⲉⲣⲡⲉ (Acts 3:1)

   "They were going to go up to the temple"

5. L ϩⲉⲱⲥ ϯϩⲛ̄ⲡⲕⲟⲥⲙⲟⲥ ⲁⲛⲁⲕ ⲡⲟⲩⲁⲉⲓⲛ ⲙ̄ⲡⲕⲟⲥⲙⲟⲥ (John 9:5)

   "As long as I am in the world, *I* am the light of the world"

6. M ⲡⲉⲧϩⲓϫⲛ̄ⲡϫⲉⲛⲉⲡⲟⲣ (Matt. 24:17)

   "the one who is on the roof"

7. M ⲡⲉⲧⲅ̄ⲛⲥⲱϣⲉ (Matt. 24:18)

   "the one who is in the field"

8. A ⲛⲁⲣⲉⲓ̈ⲱⲛⲁⲥ ⲛ̄ϩⲏⲧϥ̄ ⲙ̄ⲡⲕⲏⲧⲟⲥ (Jonah 1:17)

   "Jonah was in the belly of the whale"

9. S ⲛⲉϥⲙ̄ⲙⲁⲩⲡⲉ (John 3:22)

   "he was there"

10. B ⲓⲥ ϩⲟⲩⲟ ⲉⲡⲓⲉⲣⲫⲉⲓ̈ ⲙ̄ⲡⲁⲓⲙⲁ (Matt. 12:6)

    "Behold one greater than the temple in this
    place"

EXERCISE 9

1. A ϥⲛⲁⲡⲱⲧ ϩⲓⲭⲛ̄ⲑⲁⲗⲁⲥⲥⲁ ⲛ̄ⲧϩⲉ ⲛ̄ⲟⲩⲙⲟⲩⲓ (AE 25, 14–15)

   "He will run upon the sea like a lion"

2. A ⲁϥϣ̄ⲛϩ̄ⲧⲏϥ ϩⲁⲣⲱⲧⲛⲉ (AE 19, 10)

   "He was merciful to you"

3. A ⲡⲁϩⲉⲡⲭⲁⲉⲓⲥ ϫⲉϯⲛⲁⲥϩⲉⲓ̈ ⲙ̄ⲡⲁⲣⲉⲛ ⲁϫⲛ̄ⲧⲟⲩⲧⲉϩⲛⲉ (AE 20, 17–19)

   "The lord said, 'I will write my name on their forehead'"

4. A ⲛ̄ⲣⲉϥⲣ̄ⲛⲁⲃⲉⲇⲉ ⲛ̄ⲧⲁⲩ ⲥⲉⲛⲁϫⲓϣⲓⲡⲉ (AE 21, 6–7)

   "And the sinners, they will receive shame"

5. A ⲥⲉⲭⲓⲧⲟⲩ ⲁⲧⲙⲏⲧⲣⲟⲡⲟⲗⲓⲥ (AE 26, 17)

   "they take him to the city"

6. F ⲁϥⲉⲝⲟⲙⲟⲗⲟⲅⲓⲛ ⲁⲩⲱ ⲙ̄ⲡⲉϥⲉⲗⲁⲣⲛⲓⲥⲑⲉ (John 1:20)

   "He confessed and did not deny"

7. F ⲁⲛⲁⲕ ϯϫⲱⲕⲉⲙ ⲙ̄ⲙⲱⲧⲉⲛ ϩ̄ⲛⲟⲩⲙⲁⲟⲩ (Matt. 3:11)

   "Me, I baptize you with water"

8. L ⲙ̄ⲡⲣ̄ⲧⲣⲉⲡⲉⲧⲛ̄ϩⲏⲧ ϣⲧⲁⲣⲧⲣ̄ (John 14:1)

   "Let not your heart be troubled"

9. L ⲉⲣⲉⲧⲛ̄ⲛⲁϣⲱⲡⲉ ⲛ̄ϣⲏⲣⲉ ⲙ̄ⲡⲟⲩⲁⲉⲓⲛ (John 12:36)

   "You shall become children of the light"

10. B ⲙⲁⲣⲉⲛϧⲟⲑⲃⲉϥ (Mark 12:7)

    "Let's kill him"

EXERCISE 10

1. S ⲁⲩϩⲉ ⲉⲣⲟϥ ϩ̄ⲙⲡⲉⲣⲡⲉ ⲉϥϩⲙⲟⲟⲥ ⲛ̄ⲧⲙⲏⲧⲉ ⲛ̄ⲛ̄ⲥⲁϩ ⲉϥⲥⲱⲧⲙ̄ ⲉⲣⲟⲟⲩ ⲁⲩⲱ ⲉϥϫⲛⲟⲩ ⲙ̄ⲙⲟⲟⲩ (Luke 2:46)

   "They came upon him in the temple, seated in the midst of the scribes, listening to then
   and questioning them"

2. B ⲁϥⲛⲁⲩ ⲉⲛⲓⲫⲏⲟⲩⲓ ⲉⲁⲩⲫⲱϧ (Mark 1:10)

   "He saw the skies having opened"

3. L ⲚⲦⲀⲢⲉϥⲦⲱⲱⲚⲀⲉ ⲀⲂⲀⲗ ϨⲚⲚⲉⲦⲘⲀⲟⲨⲦ ⲀⲨⲢⲠⲘⲉⲉⲨⲉ ⲭⲓⲚⲉϥⲘⲀⲐⲎⲦⲎⲤ ⲭⲉⲠⲉⲉⲓⲠⲉ ⲉⲚⲉϥⲭⲱ ⲘⲘⲀϥ (John 2:22)

"And when he rose from those who are dead, they remembered, namely his disciples, that this was what he used to say"

4. M ϨⲀϥϭⲱ ⲘⲘⲉ ϢⲀⲚⲦⲉϨⲢⲱⲀⲎⲤ ⲘⲟⲨ (Matt. 2:15)

"He stayed there until Herod died"

5. S ⲦⲱⲱⲂⲉ ⲉⲢⲚⲚⲉⲚⲦⲀⲨⲭⲟⲟⲩ ⲚϬⲓⲚϨⲢⲟⲨⲂⲂⲀⲓ ⲚⲦⲦⲘⲤⲀϨⲟⲨ (Rev. 10:4)

"Seal up what they said, namely the thunders, and don't write them"

6. S Ⲕⲱ ⲉⲂⲟⲗ ⲦⲀⲢⲟⲨⲔⲱ ⲚⲎⲦⲚ ⲉⲂⲟⲗ (Luke 6:37)

"Forgive and you will be forgiven"

7. B ⲠⲓⲭⲱⲚⲦ ⲉⲐⲚⲎⲟⲨ (Matt. 3:7)

"the wrath that is coming"

8. L ⲦⲔⲟⲗⲨⲂⲎⲐⲢⲀ ⲚⲤⲓⲗⲟⲩⲀⲘ Ⲡⲉⲉⲓ ⲉϢⲀⲢⲟⲩⲟⲩⲁϨⲘϥ ⲭⲉⲠⲉⲚⲦⲀⲨⲦⲚⲚⲀⲟⲩϥ (John 9:7)

"the pool of Siloam, the one which is interpreted as 'the one who was sent'"

9. B ⲠⲓⲤⲎⲟⲩ ⲉⲦⲀϥϦⲉⲦϨⲱⲦϥ ⲚⲦⲟⲦⲟⲩ ⲚⲚⲓⲘⲀⲅⲟⲤ (Matt. 2:16)

"the time he learned of from the Magi"

10. L ⲠⲉⲚⲦⲀⲩⲭⲠⲀϥⲀⲉ ⲀⲂⲀⲗ ϨⲚⲦⲤⲀⲢϨ ⲟⲩⲤⲀⲢϨⲠⲉ (John 3:6)

"And he who was created from flesh is flesh"

Exercise 11

1. S ⲀⲓⲤ ⲟⲩⲟⲚϨϥ ⲉⲚⲉϥⲘⲀⲐⲎⲦⲎⲤ ϨⲓⲭⲚⲐⲀⲗⲀⲤⲤⲀ ⲚⲦⲓⲂⲉⲢⲓⲀⲤ ⲚⲦⲀϥⲟⲩⲟⲚϨϥⲀⲉ ⲉⲂⲟⲗ ⲚⲦⲉⲓϨⲉ (John 21:1)

"Jesus revealed himself to his disciples on the sea of Tiberias, and it was in this way that he revealed himself"

2. L ⲚⲦⲀⲚⲉⲉⲓ ⲅⲀⲢ ϢⲱⲠⲉ ⲭⲉⲔⲀⲤⲉ ⲉⲢⲉⲦⲅⲢⲀⲫⲎ ⲚⲀⲭⲱⲔ ⲀⲂⲀⲗ (John 19:36)

"For these happened so that the scripture might be fulfilled"

3. L ⲉⲉⲓⲤⲀⲠⲤⲦ ⲉⲚ ⲭⲉⲉⲔⲀϥⲓⲦⲟⲩ ⲀⲂⲀⲗ ϨⲚⲠⲔⲟⲤⲘⲟⲤ ⲀⲗⲗⲀ ⲭⲉⲔⲀⲤⲉ ⲉⲔⲀⲀⲢⲏϨ ⲀⲢⲀⲩ ⲀⲂⲀⲗ ϨⲚⲠⲠⲟⲚⲎⲢⲟⲤ (John 17:15)

"I pray not that you might lift them from the world, but so that you might guard them from evil"

4. B ⲀⲢⲉⲦⲉⲚⲚⲀⲩ ⲉⲢⲟϥ ⲘⲘⲀⲩ (Matt. 28:7)

"There is where you see him"

5. M ⲘⲉⲩⲭⲭⲉⲢⲀ ⲚⲟⲩϨⲎⲂⲤ ⲚⲤⲉⲔⲉϥ ⲚϨⲟⲩⲚ ϨⲀⲟⲩⲘⲟⲆⲓⲟⲚ ⲀⲗⲗⲀ ⲉϢⲀⲩⲔⲉϥ ϨⲓⲭⲚⲦⲀⲩⲭⲚⲓⲀ ⲚϥⲉⲢⲟⲩⲁⲉⲓⲚ ⲉⲚⲉⲦϨⲚⲠⲎⲓ ⲦⲎⲢⲟⲩ (Matt. 5:15)

"They don't light a lamp and put it in under a bushel, but they put it on the lampstand and it gives light to all those who are in the house"

6. A ⲚⲀⲠϨⲱⲠϢ ⲘⲠⲭⲀⲉⲓⲤ ϭⲱⲗⲦ ⲀⲚⲓⲘ (1Clem. 16:3)

"To whom has the arm of the Lord been revealed?"

7. F ⲈⲨⲦⲰⲚ ⲚⲈⲦⲈⲚⲄⲢⲀⲘⲘⲀⲦⲈⲨⲤ ⲈⲨⲦⲰⲚ ⲚⲈⲦⲈⲚⲬⲒϢⲀⲬⲚⲒ ⲈϤⲦⲰⲚ ⲠⲈⲦⲰⲠ Ⲛ̄ⲚⲈⲤⲒⲞⲨ (Is. 33:18)

   "Where are they, your accountants? Where are they, your advisors? Where is he, the astronomer?" (ⲠⲈⲦⲰⲠ Ⲛ̄ⲚⲈⲤⲒⲞⲨ "the one who reckons the stars")

8. F Ⲛ̄ⲦⲀⲦⲈⲂⲰ ϢⲎⲚϢ̄ Ⲙ̄ⲘⲈⲨ ⲚⲚⲈⲤϢⲎⲢⲒ (Is. 34:15)

   "There is where the snake has given life to her children"

9. F ⲀϪⲚ̄ⲠϬⲞ̄Ⲥ Ⲛ̄ⲦⲀⲚⲒ ⲈⲌⲢⲎⲒ ⲈⲦⲈⲒ̈ⲬⲰⲢⲀ (Is. 36:10)

   "Without the Lord did we come up to this place"

10. B ⲈⲦⲀⲔⲒ ⲈⲘⲚⲀⲒ ⲈⲦⲀⲔⲞⲚ Ⲙ̄ⲠⲀⲦⲈⲠⲈⲚⲤⲚⲞⲨ ϢⲰⲠⲒ (Matt. 8:29)

    "Have you come here to destroy us before our time happens?"

EXERCISE 12

1. L ⲈⲚⲈⲚ̄ⲦⲰⲦⲚ̄ ⲚϢⲎⲢⲈ Ⲛ̄ⲀⲂⲢⲀⲌⲀⲘ ⲚⲈⲢⲈⲦⲚⲀⲢⲠⲚ̄ⲌⲂⲎⲨⲈ Ⲛ̄ⲀⲂⲢⲀⲌⲀⲘ (John 8:39)

   "If you were children of Abraham, you would do the works of Abraham"

2. M ⲈϢϪⲈ Ⲛ̄ⲦⲀⲔⲠⲈ ⲠϢⲎⲢⲈ Ⲙ̄ⲠⲚⲚ̄Ϯ ⲌⲒⲦⲔ̄ ⲈⲠⲈⲤⲎⲦ (Matt. 4:6)

   "If you are the son of God, throw yourself down"

3. S ⲈϢϪⲈ Ⲛ̄ⲦⲀϤⲚ̄ⲔⲞⲦⲔ̄ ϤⲚⲀⲦⲰⲞⲨⲚ̄ (Luke 11:12)

   "If he has *fallen asleep* (§ 11.4), he will arise"

4. S ⲈϢⲰⲠⲈ ⲠⲈⲒ̈ϢⲞϪⲚⲈ Ⲏ ⲠⲈⲒ̈ⲌⲰⲂ ⲞⲨⲈⲂⲞⲖ ⲌⲚ̄Ⲛ̄ⲢⲰⲘⲈⲠⲈ ⲈⲒ̈Ⲉ ϤⲚⲀⲂⲰⲖ ⲈⲂⲞⲖ (Acts 5:38)

   If this counsel or this work happens to be one from people, then it will disappear"

5. B ⲒⲤϪⲈ ⲀⲢⲈⲦⲈⲚⲚⲀⲘⲈⲚⲢⲈⲚⲎ ⲈⲐⲘⲈⲒ̈ Ⲙ̄ⲘⲰⲦⲈⲚ ⲀϢ ⲠⲈ ⲠⲈⲦⲈⲚⲌⲘⲞⲦ (Luke 6:32)

   "If you love only (§ 11.3) those who love you, what is your gift?"

6. B ⲈϢⲰⲠ ⲀⲢⲈⲦⲈⲚⲚⲀⲈⲢⲠⲈⲐⲚⲀⲚⲈϤ Ⲛ̄ⲚⲎ ⲈⲦⲈⲢⲠⲈⲐⲚⲀⲚⲈϤ ⲚⲈⲘⲰⲦⲈⲚ ⲀϢ ⲠⲈ ⲠⲈⲦⲈⲚⲌⲘⲞⲦ (Luke 6:33)

   "If you do what is good only to those who do good with you, what is your gift?"

7. B ⲞⲨⲞⲌ ⲈⲦⲀϤⲤⲒⲚⲒ ⲈⲂⲞⲖ ⲌⲀⲪⲒⲞⲘ Ⲛ̄ⲦⲈⲦⲄⲀⲖⲒⲖⲈⲀ ⲀϤⲚⲀⲨ ⲈⲤⲒⲘⲰⲚ ⲚⲈⲘⲀⲚⲆⲢⲈⲀⲤ ⲠⲤⲞⲚ Ⲛ̄ⲤⲒⲘⲰⲚ ⲈⲨ⌒ⲒⲰⲚⲈ Ⲛ̄ⲤⲒ† ⲈⲪⲒⲞⲘ (Mark 1:16)

   "And when he passed by the sea of Galilee, he saw Simon and Andrew, the brother of Simon, throwing nets of casting into the sea"

8. S ⲚⲀⲒ ⲈⲨϢⲀⲚⲤⲀ⌒ⲞⲨ ⲞⲨⲀ ⲞⲨⲀ †ϪⲰ Ⲙ̄ⲠⲔⲞⲤⲘⲞⲤ ⲚⲀϢⲠ̄Ⲛ̄ϪⲰⲰⲘⲈ ⲀⲚ ⲈⲦⲞⲨⲚⲀⲤⲀ⌒ⲞⲨ (John 21:25)

   "These, if they were written one by one, I say the world will not hold the scrolls that are written"

9. S ⌒Ⲙ̄ⲠⲦⲢⲈⲨⲔⲀⲦⲞⲒⲄⲞⲢⲈⲒⲆⲈ Ⲙ̄ⲘⲞϤ ⲈⲂⲞⲖ ⲌⲒⲦⲞⲞⲦⲞⲨ Ⲛ̄ⲚⲀⲢⲬⲒⲈⲢⲈⲨⲤ Ⲙ̄Ⲛ̄ⲚⲈⲠⲢⲈⲤ-ⲂⲨⲦⲈⲢⲞⲤ Ⲙ̄ⲠⲈϤⲞⲨⲰϢⲂ̄ Ⲛ̄ⲖⲀⲨ (Matt. 27:12)

   "While they were accusing him to the high priest and the elders, he did not answer anything"

10. ⲙ ϩⲁϥϣⲛ̄ϩⲧⲏϥ ϩⲁⲣⲁⲩ ϫⲉⲛⲉϩⲁⲩⲥⲕⲩⲗⲗⲉⲡⲉ (Matt. 9:36)
    "He felt compassion for them, because they had been being (§ 9.5) troubled"

Chrestomathy

Below are readings in each of the six major Coptic dialects. The readings are taken from actual Coptic manuscripts and reproduce the arrangement of the text in the original. Square brackets […] mark restored text.

Akhmimic

The text below is from a 4th or 5th-century copy of the Apocalypse of Elijah (24, 13 – 27, 7).[1] This section contains a retrospective prophecy of the Assyrian invasion of Egypt in the seventh century BC.

ⲉ

ⲧⲃⲉⲛ̄ⲣ̄ⲣⲁⲓ̈ϭⲉⲛ̄ⲁⲥⲥⲩⲣⲓⲟⲥⲙⲛ̄	**ⲣ̄ⲣⲁⲓ̈** "kings"; **ϭⲉ** § 4.6; **ⲁⲥⲥⲩⲣⲓⲟⲥ** "Assyria"
ⲡⲃⲱⲗⲁⲃⲁⲗⲛ̄ⲧⲡⲉⲙⲛ̄ⲡⲕⲁϩ	**ⲃⲱⲗ ⲁⲃⲁⲗ** "dissolution"; **ⲡⲉ** "sky"; **ⲕⲁϩ** "earth"
ⲙⲛ̄ⲛⲉⲧϩⲁⲣⲁϥⲙ̄ⲡⲕⲁϩϯⲛⲟⲩ	**ϯⲛⲟⲩ** "now"
ϭⲉⲥⲉⲛⲁϭⲛ̄ϭⲁⲙⲁⲣⲁⲩⲉⲛⲡⲁϫⲉ	**ϭⲛ̄ϭⲁⲙ** "prevail" (cf. § 9.7); **ⲉⲛ** § 4.6
ⲡϫⲁⲉⲓⲥⲟⲩⲇⲉⲥⲉⲛⲁⲣ̄ϩⲛⲱϩⲉⲉⲛ	**ⲟⲩⲇⲉ** "nor" (Greek οὐδέ); **ϩⲛⲱϩⲉ** "fear"
ϩⲙ̄ⲡⲡⲟⲗⲉⲙⲟⲥϩⲟⲧⲁⲛⲁⲩϣⲁ	**ⲡⲟⲗⲉⲙⲟⲥ** "war" (Greek πόλεμος); **ϩⲟⲧⲁⲛ** § 12.6
[ⲛⲟⲁⲩⲣ̄ⲣⲟⲉϥ]ⲧⲱⲛⲉϩⲙ̄ⲡⲙ̄ϩⲓⲧ	**ⲛⲟ** "see" (with **ⲁ-**); **ⲣ̄ⲣⲟ** "king"; **ⲧⲱⲛⲉ** "rise"; **ⲙ̄ϩⲓⲧ** "north"
[ⲁⲩⲛⲁⲙⲟⲩⲧⲉⲁⲣⲁϥ]ϫⲉⲡⲣ̄ⲣⲟⲛ̄	**ⲙⲟⲩⲧⲉ** "say" (with **ⲁ-** "about" = "call")
[ⲁⲥⲥⲩⲣⲓⲟⲥⲁⲟⲩ]ⲡⲣ̄ⲣⲟⲛ̄ⲧⲁⲇⲓⲕⲓⲁ	**ⲁⲟⲩ** § 7.6; **ⲁⲇⲓⲕⲓⲁ** "injustice" (Greek ἀδικία)
[ϥⲛⲁⲧⲁϣⲟⲛ̄]ⲛⲉϥⲡⲟⲗⲉⲙⲟⲥ	**ⲧⲁϣⲟ** "multiply"
ⲁϫⲛ̄ⲕⲏⲙⲉⲙⲛ̄ⲛⲉϥϩⲧⲁⲣⲧⲣⲉ	**ⲕⲏⲙⲉ** "Egypt"; **ϩⲧⲁⲧⲣⲉ** "trouble"
ⲡⲕⲁϩⲛⲁⲱϣⲉϩⲁⲙϩⲓⲟⲩⲥⲁⲡ	**ⲱϣ** "utter"; **ⲉϩⲁⲙ** "sigh"; **ϩⲓⲟⲩⲥⲁⲡ** "simultaneously"
ϫⲉⲥⲉⲛⲁⲡ̄ϩⲁⲣⲡⲁⲍⲉⲛ̄ⲛⲉⲧⲛ̄	**ϩⲁⲣⲡⲁⲍⲉ** "abduction" (Greek ἁρπάζειν)
ϣⲏⲣⲉⲟⲩⲛ̄ϩⲁϩⲛⲁⲣ̄ⲉ̄ⲡⲓⲑⲩⲙⲉⲓⲁ	**ϩⲁϩ** "many"; **ⲉⲡⲓⲑⲩⲙⲉⲓ** "long" (Greek ἐπιθυμέιν)
ⲡⲙⲟⲩϩⲛ̄ⲛ̄ϩⲟⲟⲩⲉⲉⲧⲙ̄ⲙⲟⲡ	**ⲙⲟⲩ** "death"; **ϩⲟⲟⲩⲉ** "days"; **ⲉⲧⲙ̄ⲙⲟ** § 3.1
ⲙⲟⲩⲇⲉⲛⲁⲡⲱⲧⲁⲃⲁⲗⲙ̄ⲙⲁⲩ	**ⲡⲱⲧ** "run" (**ⲁⲃⲁⲗ ⲙ̄-** "away from")
ⲁⲟⲩϥⲛⲁⲧⲱⲛⲉϭⲉⲟⲩⲣ̄ⲣⲟϩⲛ̄ⲛ̄	**ϩⲛ̄ⲛ̄ⲥⲁ** "afterwards"
ⲥⲁⲙ̄ⲡⲉⲙⲛ̄ⲧⲉⲩⲛⲁⲙⲟⲩⲧⲉⲁⲣⲁϥ	**ⲉⲙⲛ̄ⲧ** "west"
ϫⲉⲡⲣ̄ⲣⲟⲛ̄ϯⲣⲏⲛⲓϥⲛⲁⲡⲱⲧϩⲓϫⲛ̄	**(ⲉ)ⲓⲣⲏⲛⲓ/(ⲉ)ⲓⲣⲏⲛⲏ** "peace" (Greek εἰρήνη)
ⲑⲁⲗⲁⲥⲥⲁⲛ̄ⲧϩⲉⲛ̄ⲟⲩⲙⲟⲩⲓⲉϥϩⲙ̄ϩ	**ⲛ̄ⲧϩⲉ** "in the manner"; **ⲙⲟⲩⲓ** "lion"; **ϩⲙ̄ϩⲙⲉ** "roar"
ⲙⲉϥⲛⲁϩⲱⲧⲃⲉⲙ̄ⲡⲣ̄ⲣⲟⲛ̄ⲧⲁⲇⲓⲕⲓⲁ	**ϩⲱⲧⲃⲉ** "kill"

1 Steindorff 1899.

ϥⲛⲁϫⲓⲙ̅ⲡⲕⲃⲁⲛ̅ⲕⲏⲙⲉϩⲛ̅ϩⲉⲛⲡⲟ	ϫⲓ ⲙ̅ⲡⲕⲃⲁ "take vengeance"
ⲗⲉⲙⲟⲥⲙⲛ̅ϩⲉⲛⲥⲛⲁϥⲉⲩⲁϣ	ⲥⲛⲁϥ "blood(shed)"; ⲁϣ "many"
ⲥⲛⲁϩⲱⲡⲉⲛ̅ⲛ̅ϩⲟⲟⲩⲉⲉⲧⲙ̅ⲙⲟⲁⲧϥ	ϩⲱⲡⲉ "happen" (ⲁ- "for"); ⲧϥⲣ̅ⲕⲉⲗⲉⲩⲉ see §§ 7.21–3
ⲣ̅ⲕⲉⲗⲉⲩⲉⲛ̅ⲟⲩⲉ[ⲓⲣⲏⲛⲏ]ⲁⲃ[ⲁ]ⲗϩⲛ̅ⲕⲏ	
ⲙⲉⲙⲛ̅ⲟⲩⲇⲱⲣⲟ[ⲛⲉϥϣⲟⲩϊⲧϥⲛⲁϯⲛ̅]	ⲇⲱⲣⲟⲛ "gift" (Greek δῶρον); ϣⲟⲩϊⲧ "empty"
ϯⲣⲏⲛⲏⲛ̅ⲛⲉϊⲉⲧⲟ[ⲩⲁⲁⲃⲉⲉϥϫⲱⲙ̅ⲙⲟⲥ]	ⲟⲩⲁⲁⲃⲉ "holy"
ϫⲉⲟⲩⲉⲡⲉⲡⲣⲉⲛⲙ̅[ⲡⲛⲟⲩⲧⲉϥⲛⲁ]	ⲟⲩⲉ see § 4.2; ⲣⲉⲛ "name"
ϯⲛ̅ϩⲉⲛⲧⲁϊⲟⲛ̅ⲛⲉ[ⲧ]ⲟ[ⲩⲁⲁⲃⲉⲙⲛ̅]	ⲧⲁϊⲟ "honor"
ⲟⲩϫⲓⲥⲉⲛ̅ⲛ̅ⲧⲟⲡⲟⲥⲛ̅ⲛⲉⲧⲟⲩⲁⲁⲃⲉ	ϫⲓⲥⲉ "high"; ⲧⲟⲡⲟⲥ "place" (Greek τόπος)
ϥⲛⲁϯϩⲉⲛⲇⲱⲣⲟⲛⲁⲡⲏϊⲙ̅ⲡⲛⲟⲩ	ⲏϊ "house"
ⲧⲉⲉⲩϣⲟⲩϊⲧϥⲛⲁⲕⲁⲧϥⲁⲃⲁⲗϩⲛ̅	ⲕⲁⲧϥ ⲁⲃⲁⲗ "turn from"
ⲙ̅ⲡⲟⲗⲓⲥⲛ̅ⲕⲏⲙⲉϩⲛ̅ⲟⲩⲕⲣⲁϥⲉⲙ	ⲕⲣⲁϥ "guile"
ⲡⲟⲩⲙ̅ⲙⲉϥⲛⲁϫⲓⲏⲡⲉⲛ̅ⲙ̅ⲙⲁⲉⲧⲟⲩ	ⲙ̅ⲙⲉ "know"; ϫⲓⲏⲡⲉ "count"
ⲁⲁⲃⲉϥⲛⲁϩⲓⲛ̅ⲛⲉⲓⲇⲱⲗⲟⲛⲛ̅ⲛ̅ϩⲉ	ϩⲓ "tally"; ⲉⲓⲇⲱⲗⲟⲛ "idol" (Greek εἴδωλον); ϩⲉⲑⲛⲟⲥ
ⲑⲛⲟⲥϥⲛⲁϫⲓⲏⲡⲉⲛ̅ⲟⲩⲭⲣⲏⲙⲁ	"native" (Greek ἔθνος); ⲭⲣⲏⲙⲁ "property" (Greek χρῆμα)
ϥⲛⲁⲥⲉϩⲟⲛ̅ϩⲉⲛⲟⲩϊⲉⲓⲃⲉⲁⲣⲉⲧⲟⲩ	ⲥⲉϩⲟ … ⲁⲣⲉⲧⲟⲩ "set up"; ⲟⲩϊⲉⲓⲃⲉ "priest"
ⲁⲣⲁⲩϥⲛⲁⲣ̅ⲕⲉⲗⲉⲩⲉⲁϭⲱⲡⲉⲛ̅ⲛ̅ⲣⲙ̅	ϭⲱⲡⲉ "seize"; ⲣⲙ̅ⲛ̅ϩⲏⲧ "wise man"
ⲛ̅ϩⲏⲧⲙ̅ⲡⲕⲁϩⲙⲛ̅ⲛ̅ⲛⲁϭⲙ̅ⲡⲗⲁ	ⲛⲁϭ § 2.7; ⲗⲁⲟⲥ "people" (Greek λαός)
ⲟⲥⲥⲉϫⲓⲧⲟⲩⲁⲧⲙⲏⲧⲣⲟⲡⲟⲗⲓⲥⲉⲧ	ϫⲓ "take"; ⲙⲏⲧⲣⲟⲡⲟⲗⲓⲥ "capital" (Greek μητρόπολις)
ϩⲓϫⲛ̅ⲑⲁⲗⲁⲥⲥⲁ …	ⲑⲁⲗⲁⲥⲥⲁ "sea" (Greek θάλασσα)
… ⲙ̅ⲡⲟⲗⲓⲥⲛ̅	ⲡⲟⲗⲓⲥ "city" (Greek πόλις)
ⲕⲏⲙⲉⲛⲁϣϣⲉϩⲁⲙϩⲛ̅ⲛ̅ϩⲟⲟⲩⲉ	
ⲉⲧⲙ̅ⲙⲟⲥⲉⲛⲁⲥⲱⲧⲙⲉⲅⲁⲣⲉⲛⲁⲛϩ	ⲥⲱⲧⲙⲉ "hear"; ϩⲣⲁⲩ "voice"
ⲣⲁⲩⲙ̅ⲡⲉⲧϯⲁⲃⲁⲗⲙⲛ̅ⲡⲉⲧⲧⲁⲩ	ϯ ⲁⲃⲁⲗ "sell"; ⲧⲁⲩ "buy"
ⲛ̅ⲁⲅⲟⲣⲁⲛ̅ⲙ̅ⲡⲟⲗⲓⲥⲛ̅ⲕⲏⲙⲉⲛⲁ	ⲁⲅⲟⲣⲁ "market" (Greek ἀγορά)
ϫⲓϩⲁϊϩⲥⲉⲛⲁⲣⲓⲙⲉϩⲓⲟⲩⲥⲁⲡϭⲉ	ϩⲁϊϩ "dust"; ⲣⲓⲙⲉ "weep"
ⲛⲉⲧϩⲟⲟⲡϩⲛ̅ⲕⲏⲙⲉ	ϩⲟⲟⲡ "exist" (stative of ϩⲱⲡⲉ)

BOHAIRIC

The section below is reproduced from the 4th-century Papyrus Bodmer III.[2] The text is written in an early form of Bohairic, slightly different from the standard form of later centuries. The selection is from the Gospel of John (5:1–18), recounting the story of Jesus's healing of a disabled man at the Pool of Bethsaida.

[ⲙⲙⲉⲛⲉⲥⲁ]ⲛⲁⲓⲇⲉⲛⲉⲡϣⲁⲓⲡⲉⲛⲧⲉ	ⲙⲙⲉⲛⲉⲥⲁ early form of ⲙⲉⲛⲉⲛⲥⲁ (§ 5.4b); ϣⲁⲓ "feast"
[ⲛⲓⲟⲩⲓⲇⲁⲓ] > ⲁϥⲓⲛⲭⲉⲓ̅ⲏ̅ⲥ̅ⲉ2ⲣⲏⲓⲉ̈ⲓⲉ	
[ⲣⲟⲩⲥⲁⲗⲏ]ⲙ > ⲛ2ⲣⲏⲓⲇⲉⲫⲉⲛⲓ̈ⲉⲣⲟⲩⲥⲁ	ï̈ⲉⲣⲟⲩⲥⲁⲗⲏⲙ "Jerusalem"
[ⲗⲏⲙⲛ]ⲉⲟⲩⲟⲛⲟⲩⲕⲟⲗⲩⲙⲃⲏⲧⲣⲁ	ⲕⲟⲗⲩⲙⲃⲏⲧⲏⲣⲁ "bathing pool" (Greek κολυμβήθρα)
[2ⲓⲭⲉⲛⲧⲡⲣ]ⲟⲃⲁⲧⲓⲕⲏⲉⲩⲙⲟⲩ†ⲉⲣⲟⲥ	ⲡⲣⲟⲃⲁⲧⲓⲕⲏ "sheep-gate" (from Greek προβάτειος)
[ⲙⲙⲉⲧ2]ⲉⲃⲣⲉⲟⲥⲭⲉⲃⲏⲧⲥⲁⲓⲇⲁ ⲉⲟⲩ	ⲙⲉⲧ2ⲉⲃⲣⲉⲟⲥ "Hebrew"
[ⲟⲛⲛⲉ̅ⲛ̅ⲥ̅]ⲧⲟⲁⲛⲏⲧⲥ > ⲛⲁⲩⲉⲛⲕⲟⲧ	ⲥⲧⲟⲁ "colonnade" (Greek στοά)
[ⲫⲉⲛⲛⲁ]ⲓⲛⲭⲉⲩⲙⲏϣⲱⲛⲧⲉⲛⲉⲧϣⲱⲛⲓ	ⲙⲏϣⲉ "crowd"; ϣⲱⲛⲓ "suffer"
[2ⲁⲛ6ⲁⲗ]ⲉⲩⲛⲉⲙ2ⲁⲛⲃⲉⲗⲗⲉⲩ > ⲛⲉⲙ	6ⲁⲗⲉⲩ "cripples"; ⲃⲉⲗⲗⲉⲩ "blind" (pl)
[2ⲁⲛⲟⲩⲟ]ⲛⲉ[ⲩϣⲟⲩ]ϣⲟⲩ > ⲛⲉⲟⲩ	ϣⲟⲩϣⲟⲩ "withered"
[ⲟⲛⲟⲩⲣⲱⲙⲓ]ⲇⲉ[ⲙ]ⲙⲁⲡⲉ > ⲉⲁϥⲉⲣ	ⲙⲙⲁ early form of ⲙⲙⲁⲩ (§ 5.1)
ⲗ̅ⲏ̅ ⲛⲣⲟⲙⲡⲓⲫⲉⲛⲡⲉϥϣⲱⲛⲓ > ⲉ	
ⲧⲁϥⲛⲁⲩⲇⲉⲉⲫⲁⲓⲛⲭⲉⲓ̅ⲏ̅ⲥ̅ⲉϥⲉⲛ	
ⲕⲟⲧ ⲁϥⲉⲙⲓⲭⲉⲁϥⲟⲩϣⲉϥⲓⲣⲓⲛⲛⲟⲩ	ⲉⲙⲓ "know"
ⲛⲓϣ†ⲛⲭⲣⲟⲛⲟⲥⲫⲉⲛ[ⲡⲉ]ϥϣⲱⲛⲓ	ⲭⲣⲟⲛⲟⲥ "time" (Greek χρόνος)
ⲡⲉⲭⲁϥⲛⲁϥⲭⲉⲁⲛⲭⲟⲩ[ⲱ]ϣⲉⲟⲩ[ⲭ]ⲁⲓ̈	ⲁⲛ (§ 4.5); ⲟⲩⲱϣ "wish"; ⲟⲩⲭⲁⲓ "become whole"
ⲁϥⲉⲣⲟⲩⲱⲛⲁϥⲛⲭⲉⲡⲉⲧϣⲱⲛⲓ	ⲉⲣⲟⲩⲱ "make reply"
ⲭⲉⲡⲁ6̅ⲥ̅ⲙⲙⲟⲛⲧⲣⲱⲙ[ⲓ]ⲙⲙⲁ	
2ⲓⲛⲁⲁϥϣⲁⲛⲑⲱ2ⲛⲭⲉⲡⲓ	ⲑⲱ2 "become stirred"[3]
ⲙⲱⲟ[ⲩ] > ⲛⲧⲉϥ2ⲓⲧⲉ2ⲣ[ⲏⲓ]ⲉ2ⲣⲏⲓⲉ†	ⲛⲧⲉϥ2ⲓⲧ "and put me" (§§ 10.4, 3.4)
ⲕⲟⲗⲩⲙⲃⲏⲧⲣⲁ > 2ⲟⲥ[ⲇⲉⲉ]ⲓⲛⲁϣⲁ	2ⲟⲥ for 2ⲟⲥⲟⲛ (§ 12.7); ⲛⲁ "go"
ⲣⲉⲕⲉⲟ[ⲩ]ⲁⲓⲉⲣϣⲟⲣⲡⲉ[ⲣⲟ]ⲓ > ⲡⲉ	ⲉⲣϣⲟⲣⲡ "take precedence" ("make first")
ⲭⲁϥⲛⲁϥⲛⲭⲉⲓ̅ⲏ̅ⲥ̅ⲭⲉ[ⲧⲱⲛⲕ]ⲁⲗⲓ	ⲧⲱⲛⲕ "raise yourself"; ⲁⲗⲓⲟⲩⲓ (§ 7.6)
ⲟⲩⲓⲙⲡⲉⲕⲭⲗⲟⲭⲙⲁϣⲉⲛⲁⲕ ⲧⲟⲧⲉ	ⲭⲗⲟⲭ "bed"; ⲙⲁϣⲉ "walk"
ⲁϥⲟⲩⲭⲁⲓⲥⲁⲧⲟⲧϥⲛⲭⲉ[ⲡⲓⲣⲱ]ⲙⲓ	ⲥⲁⲧⲟⲧϥ "immediately"
ⲁϥϣⲱⲗⲓⲙⲡⲉϥⲭⲗⲟⲭⲁϥ[ⲙⲟϣⲓ]	ⲱⲗⲓ "take hold of"; ⲙⲟϣⲓ "walk"
ⲛⲉⲡⲥⲁⲙⲃⲁⲑⲟⲛⲡ[ⲉⲡⲓⲉ2ⲟ]	ⲥⲁⲙⲃⲁⲑⲟⲛ "sabbath"; ⲉ2ⲟⲟⲩ "day"

2   Sharp 2016.

3   Some copies add John 5:4 "for an angel of the Lord went down at certain times into the pool, and stirred the water: whoever stepped in first after the stirring of the water was healed of whatever disease he had."

ογετμμα > ναγχω[ογνμμος]	ογν "therefore" (Greek οὖν)
νχενιογϊΔαι φне[ταγ]θ[ερα]	θεραπεγϊν "heal" (Greek θεραπεύειν)
πεγϊνμμοϥχεπεсαм[в]аθон[πε]	
ογο2ενϣεнакан[ε]ϣλιμπεκ	ογο2ε early form of ογο2 (§ 7.6); ϣε "fitting"
χλοχ νθοϥ[ΔεаϥΕρ]ογϣπε	
χаϥνωογχε[фн]ετаϥτριογχαι	τρι see § 7.3
ν̄θοϥεταϥχος χελλιογιμ	
πεκбλοχογο2εμοϣι > ναγ	бλοχ see χλοχ above
ϣινι[νсω]ϥχενιμπεπιρωμιε	ϣινι "ask" (with νсω⸗)
ταϥτρεκογχαιχοσνακχεϣλι	
μπεκб[λο]χογο2εμοϣι > фн	
Δεεταγερφ[а]ѣριεροϥ > ннаϥсω	ерфаѣρι "do healing"; сωογν "know"
ογнанπεχενιμπεῑн̄сгарне	
аϥ[ε] νϥναпε > εογονογμнϣ	ενϥ "withdraw" ("take himself")
ѣενπιμαετεμа > μμενεсλаϥ	
ναι > аϥχεμμοϥνχεῑн̄с ѣενπι	ναι see να above; χεμμοϥ for χεμϥ "find him"
ερφεϊπεχаϥнаϥχε2нπελκ	ερφεϊ "temple"; 2нπε § 4.5 (εις)
ογχаϊ > [μ]περερνοвιχεχεν	ερνοвι "do sin"; χεχε "so that"
нεπετ[2ω]ογενаϊϣωπιμμοκ	2ωογ ε- "worse than"; ϣωπι "happen"
аϥϣεν[аϥ]Δεнχεπιρωμι > аϥτα	ϣε наϥ "go away"; ταμε- "inform"
μεν[ιογι]Δαιχεῑн̄σπεφнεταϥτ	
[ριογχαι] > εθв[ε]фαιναγχοχιν	χοχι "pursue" (Greek διώκειν)
[χενιογιΔ]αινсаῑн̄с > χεнаϥιρι	
[νν]а[ιενѣεν]πсамваθον > νθοϥ	
[Δ]εаϥερ[ογ]ϣπεχαϥνωογ > χε	
[π]λιωτϣ[λε]ѣογνετνογϥερ2ωв	ϣαε2ογν ετνογ "until now"; ερ2ωв "work"
ογο2εαν[οκ]2ωτερ2ωв > εθвε	2ω § 3.7
фаι[ναγ]κωτνсωϥν	κωτ "go around"; н2ογο "the more"
2̄ογο > νχενιογιΔαϊεѣοτвεϥ	ѣωτεв "kill"
χενκннанχεнаϥвω[λ]μπ[ι]сам	нкнн αν "not only"; вωλ "disregard"
вαθον > αλλαχεϥερπκ[ε]χω[μ]ος	κε see § 3.7; мος for ммос
εϥϯχεπаιωτ > εϥιριμμοϥν2ι	2ιсос "equal" (Greek ἴσος)
соснεμϕ̄ϯ	

FAYUMIC

The text below is from a manuscript originally in the library of the White Monastery, Egypt, and later divided between the Vatican and the French Institute, Cairo.[4] It has not been dated, but is very similar to another Fayumic manuscript dated to the end of the 10th century.[5] This selection contains part of the Prophecy of Isaiah (30:27–33). The lines are short because the original has two columns per page. Supraliteral dots and strokes do not always conform to standard practice (§ 1.4).

ϨⲈⲒⲠⲖⲈ̄	Ϩⲉⲓ § 4.5; ⲗⲉ̄ for ⲗⲉⲛ "name"
ⲘⲠⲞ̄ⲤⲀϥⲚⲎⲞⲨϨⲒ	ⲟ̄ⲥ for B ϭⲟⲉⲓⲥ "lord"; ⲚⲎⲞⲨ "come"; ϨⲒⲦⲈⲚ § 5.4e
ⲦⲈⲚⲞⲨⲚⲀϭⲚⲞⲨⲀⲒⳬ	ⲚⲀϭ "great"; ⲞⲨⲀⲓⳬ "occasion"
ⲞⲨϬⲰⲚⲦⲈϥⲘⲞⲨϨ	ϬⲰⲚⲦ "wrath"; ⲘⲞⲨϨ "burn"
ⲘⲚ̇ⲞⲨⲈⲀⲨⲠⲈⲠ	ⲈⲀⲨ "glory"
ⳬⲈⲬⲒⲚⲚⲈϥⲤⲠⲀⲦⲞⲨ	ⳬⲉⲬⲒ "speech"; ⲤⲠⲀⲦⲞⲨ "lips"
ⲠⲈϥⳬⲈⲬⲒⲀϥⲘⲈϨ	ⲘⲈϨ "full"
ⲚϬⲰⲚⲦ · ⲀⲨⲰ	
ⲦⲞⲢⲄⲎⲘⲠⲈϥϬⲰ	ⲞⲢⲄⲎ "intensity" (Greek ὀργή)
ⲚⲦⲚⲈⲞⲨⲰⲘⲚ̄Ⲧ	ⲞⲨⲰⲘ "consume"
ϨⲎⲚⲞⲨⲔⲰϨⲦ	ϨⲎ "manner"; ⲔⲰϨⲦ "fire"
ⲠⲉϥⲠ̄Ⲛ̄Ⲁ̄ⲚⲎⲞⲨⲚⲦ	ⲠⲚ̄Ⲁ̄ "breath" (Greek πνεῦμα)
ϨⲎⲚⲚⲞⲨⲘⲀⲨⲈϥ	ϨⲎ "front"; ⲘⲀⲨ "water"
ⲤⲰⲔϨⲚⲞⲨϊⲈⲈ⳨Ⲁ	ⲤⲰⲔ "flow"; ⳨ⲉⲉ⳨ "wadi" (desert valley)
ⲠⲘⲀ† · ⲀⲨⲰϥⲚⲈ	ⲘⲀ† "brim"
ⲠⳬⲈⳬⲦⲀⲢ	ⲠⳬⲰ "divide"; ⳳⲦⲀⲢⲦⲈⲢ "trouble"
ⲦⲈⲢⲚⲚⲒⲈⲐⲚⲞⲤ·	ⲈⲐⲚⲞⲤ "nation" (Greek ἔθνος)
ⲈⲬⲈⲚⲦⲈⲨⲠⲖⲀⲚⲎ	ⲠⲖⲀⲚⲎ "go astray" (Greek πλάνη)
ⲈⲦⳳⲞⲨⲒⲦ · ⲀⲨⲰ	ⳳⲞⲨⲒⲦ "empty"
ⲞⲨⲀⲚⲞⲨⲠⲖⲀⲚⲎ	
ⲚⲈⲠⲰⲦⲚⲤⳳⲞⲨ	ⲠⲰⲦ "go (quickly)"; ⲚⲤⳳⲞⲨ § 5.4c
ⲀⲨⲰⲤⲚⲈ̇ⲬⲒⲦⲞⲨⲘ̄	ⲬⲒⲦⲞⲨ "take them"
ⲠⲈⲘⲦⲀⲈⲂⲀⲖⲘⲠⲈⲨ	
ϨⲀ · ⲘⲎϨⲀⲠⲤⲚ	ϨⲀ "face"; ⲘⲎ ϨⲀⲠⲤ "is not (Greek μή) it necessary?"
ⲦⲈⲦⲈⲚⲞⲨⲚⲀϥⲚ	ⲞⲨⲚⲀϥ "rejoice, rejoicing"

4   Chassinat 1902.
5   Yelenskaya 1969.

ⲛⲟⲩⲁⲓⲱⲛⲓⲙ : ⲁⲩⲱ	ⲟⲩⲁⲓⲱ "occasion"
ⲉⲡⲱⲧⲉϩⲟⲩⲛⲉⲛⲁ	ⲛⲁ § 3.3
ⲡⲉⲧⲟⲩⲉⲉⲃⲛ̄ⲟⲩⲁⲓⲱ	ⲟⲩⲉⲉⲃ "holy"
ⲛⲓⲃⲓⲛⲧϩⲏⲛⲛⲉ	ⲛⲓⲃⲓ for ⲛⲓⲙ (§ 2.7)
ⲧⲉⲗⲱⲉⲉⲓⲙⲛⲛⲉⲧ	ⲉⲗⲱⲉⲉⲓ "make (ⲉⲗ-) festival"
ⲟⲩⲛⲁϥⲙⲙⲁⲩ	
ⲁⲩⲱⲉⲡⲱⲧⲉϩⲟ̄ⲩ	ⲉϩⲟ̄ⲩ for ⲉϩⲟⲩⲛ
ⲙⲛϩⲉⲛⲥ̄ϩⲓⲛ	ⲥ̄ϩⲓ ⲛ̄ϫⲱ "flute" ("reed for singing")
ϫⲱⲉⲡⲧⲁⲩⲙⲫ̄ⲧ̄	ⲧⲁⲩ "mountain"; ⲫ̄ⲧ̄ for ⲃ ⲫⲛⲟⲩⲧ "God"
ⲁⲗⲉⲧϥⲙⲫ̄ⲧ̄ⲉⲧ	ⲁⲗⲉⲧϥ "to his foot"
ϫⲁⲁⲣ · ⲁⲩⲱⲡⲡⲉ	ϫⲁⲁⲣ "strong"; ⲡⲉⲧⲟⲩⲉⲃ "holy one"
ⲧⲟⲩⲉⲃⲙⲡⲓⲥ̄ⲣ̄ⲁ	ⲓⲥ̄ⲣ̄ⲁ for ⲓⲥⲣⲁⲏⲗ "Israel"
ⲁⲩⲱϥ̄ⲧ̄ⲛⲉⲧⲣⲉⲩ	ⲛⲏ § 3.3; ϫⲁⲁⲥ "say it"
ⲥⲱⲧⲉⲙⲉⲡⲉⲁⲩ	ⲉⲁⲩ "glory"
ⲛⲧⲉϥⲥⲙⲏ · ⲁⲩⲱ	ⲥⲙⲏ "voice"
ϥⲛⲉⲟⲩⲱⲛⲁϩⲉⲃⲁⲗ	ⲟⲩⲱⲛⲁϩ "reveal"
ⲙⲡϭⲱⲛ̄ⲧⲙⲡⲉϥ	
ϭⲃⲁⲓ · ϩⲛⲟⲩⲟⲣⲅⲏ	ϭⲃⲁⲓ "arm"
ⲙⲛⲟⲩϭⲱⲛⲧⲙ̄ⲛ	
ⲟⲩϣⲉϩⲉϥⲟⲩⲱⲙ	ϣⲉϩ "fire"; ⲟⲩⲱⲙ "consume"
ⲛϥϣⲁⲗⲟⲩⲛⲛⲁⲙⲧ·	ϣⲁⲗⲟⲩ "destroy them"; ⲛⲁⲙⲧ "power"
ⲁⲩⲱⲛⲧϩⲏⲛⲛⲟⲩ	
ⲙⲁⲩⲙⲛⲛⲟⲩⲁⲗⲉⲙ	ⲙⲁⲩ "water"; ⲁⲗⲉⲙⲡⲏ "hailstone" ("stone of sky")
ⲡⲏⲉⲩⲛⲏⲟⲩⲉⲡⲉ	
ⲥⲏⲧϩⲓⲟⲩⲥⲁⲡⲛⲛⲁⲙⲧ	ϩⲓⲟⲩⲥⲁⲡ "together" ("at a time")
ϩⲓⲧⲉⲛⲡⲉϩⲗⲁⲩⲅⲁⲣ	ϩⲗⲁⲩ "voice"
ⲙⲡϭ̄ⲥ̄ⲛⲉⲁⲥⲥⲩⲣⲓⲟⲥ	ⲁⲥⲥⲩⲣⲓⲟⲥ "Assyrian"
ⲛⲉϭⲱⲡⲧϩⲛⲧⲉⲡ	ϭⲱⲡⲧ "be defeated"; ⲡⲗⲏⲅⲏ "blow" (Greek πληγή)
ⲗⲩⲅⲏⲉⲧⲉϥⲛⲉⲣⲉϩ	ⲣⲉϩⲧⲟⲩ "strike them"
ⲧⲟⲩⲙⲙⲁⲥ · ⲁⲩⲱ	
ⲥⲉⲛⲉϣⲱ̄ⲡⲓⲛⲏϥ	ⲛⲏϥ for ⲛⲉϥ (§ 5.3)
ⲙⲡⲉϥⲕⲱⲧ	

LYCOPOLITAN

This text comes from a 4th-century codex with papyrus pages.[6] Now in London, it was discovered during excavations south of Asyut in 1923. This section records the miracle of the loaves and fishes (John 6:1–15).

ⲙ̄ⲛ̄ⲛ̄ⲥⲁⲛⲉⲉⲓⲁⲓ̄ⲏ̄ⲥ̄ⲃⲱⲕⲁ	ⲃⲱⲕ "go"
ⲡⲕⲣⲟⲛ̄ⲑⲁⲗⲁⲥⲥⲁⲛ̄ⲧⲅⲁ	ⲕⲣⲟ "far side"; ⲑⲁⲗⲁⲥⲥⲁ "sea" (for ⲑⲉⲗⲁⲥⲥⲁ)
ⲗⲓⲗⲁⲓⲁⲛ̄ⲧⲓⲃⲉⲣⲓⲁⲥ· ⲛⲉⲩⲛ̄	ⲅⲁⲗⲓⲗⲁⲓⲁ "Galilee"; ⲧⲓⲃⲉⲣⲓⲁⲥ "Tiberias"
ⲟⲩⲙⲏϣⲉⲉⲛⲁϣⲱϥⲟⲩⲏ2	ⲛⲁϣⲱ= § 6.5; ⲟⲩⲏ2 "set" (stative of ⲟⲩⲱ2)
ⲛ̄ⲥⲱϥϫⲉⲛⲉⲩⲛⲉⲩⲁⲛⲙⲁ	ⲛⲉⲩ ⲁ- "see"; ⲙⲁⲉⲓⲛ "miracle"
ⲉⲓⲛⲉⲧϥⲓⲣⲉⲙ̄ⲙⲁⲩⲁ2ⲛ̄ⲛⲉ	
ⲧⲱⲛⲉ· ⲓ̄ⲏ̄ⲥ̄ⲇⲉⲁϥⲃⲱⲕ	ϣⲱⲛⲉ "ill"
ⲁ2ⲣⲏ̈ⲁ2ⲛ̄ⲧⲁⲩⲁϥ2ⲙⲉⲥⲧ'	ⲧⲁⲩ "hill"; 2ⲙⲉⲥⲧ "sit"
ⲟⲩⲁⲉⲉⲧϥⲙ̄ⲛⲛⲉϥⲙⲁⲑⲏ	ⲟⲩⲁⲉⲉⲧϥ "by himself"; ⲙⲁⲑⲏⲧⲏⲥ "disciple"
ⲧⲏⲥ· ⲛⲉϥ2ⲏⲛⲇⲉⲁ2ⲟⲩⲛ	2ⲏⲛ "near" (stative of 2ⲱⲛ "approach")
ϫⲓⲡⲡⲁⲥⲭⲁⲛ̄ϣⲁⲉⲓⲉⲛ̄ⲛⲓⲟⲩ	ⲡⲁⲥⲭⲁ "Passover"; ϣⲁⲉⲓⲉ "festival"; ⲓⲟⲩⲧⲁⲉⲓ "Jew"
ⲧⲁⲉⲓ· ⲓ̄ⲏ̄ⲥ̄ⲇⲉⲁϥϥⲓⲛⲉϥⲃⲉⲗ	ϥⲓ "lift"; ⲃⲉⲗ "eye"
ⲁ2ⲣⲏ̈ⲁϥⲛⲉⲩϫⲉⲟⲩⲛⲟⲩ	
ⲙⲏϣⲉⲛ̄ⲛⲏϣⲁⲁⲣⲁϥ· ⲡⲁ	ⲛⲏⲩ "coming"
ϫⲉϥⲙ̄ⲫⲓⲗⲓⲡⲡⲟⲥϫⲉⲉⲛⲁ	ⲫⲓⲗⲓⲡⲡⲟⲥ "Phillip"
ⲧⲁⲩⲁⲉⲓⲕ'ⲧⲟⲭⲉⲉⲣⲉⲛⲉⲉⲓ	ⲧⲁⲩ "buy"; ⲧⲟ "where?"
ⲛⲁⲟⲩⲱⲙ'ⲛ̄ⲧⲁϥϫⲉⲡⲉⲉⲓ	ⲟⲩⲱⲙ "eat"; ϫⲉ- "say"
ⲇⲉⲉϥⲣ̄ⲡⲓⲣⲁⲍⲉⲙ̄ⲙⲁϥ· ⲛ̄ⲧⲁϥ	ⲣ̄ⲡⲓⲣⲁⲍⲉ "test" (ⲣ̄ "do" plus Greek πειράζειν)
ⲅⲁⲣⲛⲉϥⲥⲁⲩⲛⲉⲇⲉⲉⲩⲡⲉⲧᶜⲛⲁ	ⲥⲁⲩⲛⲉ "know"; ⲡⲉⲧᶜⲛⲁ – ϥ added secondarily
ⲉⲉϥ· ⲗⲟⲩⲟϣⲱ̄ⲃ̄ϫⲓⲫⲓⲗⲓⲡⲡⲟⲥ	ⲉⲉϥ "do it"; ⲟⲩⲱϣⲱ̄ⲃ̄ "answer"
ϫⲉⲙ̄ⲛ̄ϣⲏⲧⲛ̄ⲥᵀⲁⲧⲉⲉⲣⲉⲛⲁ	ⲙ̄ⲛ̄ § 8.8; ϣⲏⲧ § 4.2; ⲥⲧⲁⲧⲉⲉⲣⲉ "stater" (a coin)
ⲉⲓⲕ'ⲣⲱϣⲉⲁⲣⲁⲩⲭⲉⲉⲣⲉⲡⲟⲩⲉ	ⲣⲱϣⲉ "suffice"; ⲡⲟⲩⲉⲉ ⲡⲟⲩⲉⲉ "each one"
ⲉⲡⲟⲩⲉⲉϫⲓⲛ̄ⲟⲩϣⲏⲙ'ⲡⲁ	ϫⲓ "take"; ϣⲏⲙ "little"
ϫⲉⲟⲩⲉⲉⲛⲉϥⲁⲃⲁⲗ2ⲛ̄ⲛⲉϥⲙⲁ	ⲟⲩⲉⲉ ... ⲁⲃⲁⲗ 2ⲛ̄ "one of"
ⲑⲏⲧⲏⲥⲁⲛⲇⲣⲉⲁⲥⲡⲥⲁⲛⲛ̄ⲥⲓ	ⲁⲛⲇⲣⲉⲁⲥ "Andrew"; ⲥⲁⲛ "brother"; ⲥⲓⲙⲱⲛ "Simon"
ⲙⲱ[ⲛ]ⲡⲉⲧⲣⲟⲥϫⲉⲟⲩⲛⲟⲩϣⲏ	ⲡⲉⲧⲣⲟⲥ "Peter"; ϣⲏⲣⲉ "boy"
ⲣⲉ[ϣⲏ]ⲙ̄ⲙ̄'ⲡⲉⲉⲓⲙⲁⲉⲩⲛ̄ⲧⲟⲩ	ⲙⲁ "place"; ϯⲟⲩ § 4.2
[ⲛ̄ⲧⲟⲟ]ⲧϥ̄ⲛⲁⲉⲓⲕ'ⲛ̄ⲉⲓⲱⲧ'ⲙ̄ⲛ̄	ⲉⲓⲱⲧ "barley"
[ⲧⲃⲧ]ⲥⲛⲉⲩ· ⲁⲗⲗⲁⲛⲉⲉⲓⲉⲩⲛⲁ	ⲧⲃⲧ "fish"; ⲥⲛⲉⲩ § 4.2

6   Thompson 1924.

[ⲣ̄]ⲉⲩⲙ̄ⲡⲉⲉⲓⲙⲏⲏϣⲉ· ⲡⲁϫⲉ	ⲣ̄ⲉⲩ for ⲣⲉ ⲟⲩ "do what?"
ⲓ̄ⲏ̄ⲥ ⲛⲉⲩⲭⲉⲙⲁⲣⲉⲛ̄ⲣⲱⲙⲉ ⲛⲁ	ⲛⲁⲭⲟⲩ "set themselves"
ⲭⲟ ⲁ2ⲣⲏⲓ̈· ⲛⲉⲩⲛ ⲟⲩⲭⲟⲣⲧⲟⲥ	ⲭⲟⲣⲧⲟⲥ "pasture" (Greek χόρτος)
ⲉⲛⲁϣⲱϥ 2ⲛ̄ⲡⲙⲁ ⲉⲧⲙ̄ⲙⲉⲩ·	ⲛⲁϣⲱ⸗ § 6.5
ⲁ ⲛⲣⲱⲙⲉ 6ⲉ ⲛⲁ ⲭⲟⲩ ⲉⲩ ⲛⲁ	
ⲣ̄ ⲧ ⲟⲩ ⲛ̄ϣⲟ· ⲓ̄ⲏ̄ⲥ 6ⲉ ⲁϥ ϫⲓ ⲛ̄ⲛ̄	ⲧ ⲟⲩ ⲛ̄ϣⲟ § 4.2
ⲁⲉⲓⲕ'ⲁⲩ ⲱ ⲁϥ ϣⲡ 2ⲙⲁⲧ'ⲁϥ ⲧ̄	ϣ ⲡ 2ⲙⲁⲧ "give thanks" ("take grace")
ⲛ̄ⲛⲉϥ ⲙⲁⲑⲏⲧⲏⲥ· ⲙ̄ⲙⲁⲑⲏ	
ⲧⲏⲥ ⲇⲉ ⲁⲩ ⲧ̄ ⲛ̄ⲛ ⲉⲧⲛⲏ ϫ'ⲁⲩ	ⲛⲏ ϫ "seated"
ϣⲁⲛⲡⲉⲛⲧⲁⲩ ϫⲓⲧϥ ⲁⲣⲁⲩ	ⲁⲛ § 5.1; ϫⲓⲧϥ "take it"
ⲁⲃⲁⲗ'2ⲛ̄ ⲛ̄ⲧⲃⲧ· ⲛ̄ⲧⲁⲣⲟⲩ ⲥⲓ	ⲥⲓ "sate"
ⲇⲉ ⲡⲁ ϫⲉϥ ⲛ̄ⲛⲉϥ ⲙⲁⲑⲏⲧⲥ	
ϫⲉ ⲥⲱⲟⲩ2 ⲁ2ⲟⲩⲛ ⲛ̄ⲛ̄ⲗⲉ	ⲥⲱⲟⲩ2 "gather"; ⲗⲉ ⲕⲙ "piece"
ⲕⲙ ⲉⲛⲧⲁⲩ ⲥⲉⲉⲡⲉ ϫⲉ ⲕⲁ ⲥⲉ	ⲥⲉⲉⲡⲉ "leave over"
ⲛⲉ ⲗⲁⲅⲉ 2ⲁⲉⲓⲉ ⲁⲃⲁⲗ'· ⲁⲩ ⲥⲁⲩ	ⲗⲁⲅⲉ "nothing"; 2ⲁⲉⲓⲉ ⲁⲃⲁⲗ "be wasted" ("fall out")
2ⲟⲩ 6ⲉ ⲁⲩⲙⲁ2 ⲙ̄ⲛ̄ⲧⲥⲛⲁⲟⲩⲥ	ⲙⲁ2 "fill"; ⲙ̄ⲛ̄ⲧⲥⲛⲁⲟⲩⲥ § 4.2
ⲛ̄ⲃⲓⲣ ⲛ̄ⲛ̄ⲗⲉ ⲕⲙ ⲉⲛⲧⲁⲩ ⲥⲉ	ⲃⲓⲣ "basket"
ⲉ ⲡⲉⲁⲛⲉⲧ ⲟⲩ ⲱⲙ'ⲁⲃⲁⲗ'2ⲛ̄	
ⲡ ⲧ ⲟⲩ ⲛ̄ⲁⲉⲓⲕ'ⲛ̄ⲉⲓⲱⲧ'· ⲛ̄	
ⲣⲱⲙⲉ 6ⲉ ⲛ̄ⲧⲁⲣⲟⲩⲛⲉⲩ ⲁ	
ⲡⲙⲁⲉⲓⲛ ⲛ̄ⲧⲁϥⲉⲉϥ ⲛⲉⲩ ⲭⲱ	
ⲙ̄ⲙⲁⲥ ϫⲉ ⲡⲉⲉⲓ ⲁ ⲙⲁⲙⲏ ⲡⲉ	ⲙⲁⲙⲏⲉ "truly"
ⲡ̄ ⲡⲣⲟⲫⲏⲧⲏⲥ ⲉⲧⲛ̄ⲛⲏⲩ ⲁ	ⲡⲣⲟⲫⲏⲧⲏⲥ "prophet" (Greek προφήτης)
ⲡⲕⲟⲥⲙⲟⲥ· ⲓ̄ⲏ̄ⲥ 6ⲉ ⲛ̄ⲧⲁⲣⲉϥ	ⲕⲟⲥⲙⲟⲥ "world" (Greek κόσμος)
ⲙ̄ⲙⲉ ϫⲉ ⲥⲉ ⲛ̄ⲛⲏ ⲩ ⲛ̄ⲥⲉ ⲧⲁ	ⲙ̄ⲙⲉ "realize"; ⲧⲁⲣⲉⲡ⸗ "seize"
ⲣⲉ ⲡϥ ϫⲉ ⲕⲁ ⲥⲉ ⲉⲩ ⲛⲁ ⲉⲉ ϥ ⲛ̄	
ⲣ̄ ⲣⲟ ⲁϥ ⲥⲉ2ⲧ ϥ ⲁⲛⲁ 2ⲣⲏ ⲓ̈ ⲁ ⲭ ⲛ̄	ⲣ̄ⲣⲟ "king"; ⲥⲉ2ⲧ⸗ "remove"
ⲡⲧⲁ ⲟⲩ ⲗⲁ ⲉⲉ ⲧϥ·	

OXYRHYNCHITE

The Scheide Library of the University of Princeton contains a codex of the 5th century, of unknown provenance.[7] The selection from it below is Matt. 2:1–15.

ⲓ̄ⲥ̄Ⲇⲉ2ⲁⲓ̈ⲭⲡⲁϥ2ⲛ̄	ⲭⲡⲁ= "create, give birth to"
ⲧⲃⲏⲑⲗⲉⲉⲙⲛ̄ⲧⲉϯ	ⲃⲏⲑⲗⲉⲉⲙ "Bethlehem"; ϯⲟⲩⲆⲁⲓⲁ "Judea"
ⲟⲩⲆⲁⲓⲁ2ⲛ̄ⲛⲉ2ⲁⲩⲛ̄	ⲉ2ⲁⲩ "days"
2ⲏⲣⲱⲆⲏⲥⲡⲉⲣⲁ · 2ⲉⲓ̈	2ⲏⲣⲟⲆⲏⲥ "Herod"; ⲉⲣⲁ "king"; 2ⲉⲓ̈ⲡⲉ § 4.5
ⲡⲉ2ⲁⲅⲉⲓ̄ⲛ̄ⲟ̄2ⲉⲛ	ⲉⲓ "come"; ⲛ̄ⲟ̄ⲏ § 4.5
ⲙⲁⲅⲟⲥⲉⲃⲁⲗ'2ⲓⲣⲁⲫⲉ	ⲙⲁⲅⲟⲥ Persian sage; ⲣⲁⲫⲉⲉ̄ "east" ("rising side")
ⲉ̄ⲉ̄2ⲣⲏⲓ̈ⲉ̄ⲧ2ⲓⲉⲣⲟ	2ⲓⲉ̄ⲣⲟⲥⲟⲗⲩⲙⲁ "Jerusalem"
ⲗⲩⲙⲁⲉⲩⲭⲱⲙ̄ⲙⲁⲥ·	
ⲭⲉⲁϥⲧⲟⲛⲡⲉⲣⲁⲛ̄ⲛ̄	ⲧⲟⲛ § 5.1
ⲓ̈ⲟⲩⲆⲁⲓⲉⲓⲉ̄ⲑⲁⲩⲭⲡⲁϥ·	ⲓ̈ⲟⲩⲆⲁⲓⲉⲓ "Jew"
2ⲁⲛⲛⲉⲅⲁⲣⲉ̄ⲡⲉϥⲥⲓ	ⲛⲉ ⲉ̄- "see"; ⲥⲓⲟⲩ "star"
ⲟⲩ2ⲓⲣⲁⲫⲉⲉ̄2ⲁⲛⲉⲓ	
ⲉ̄ⲟⲩⲱϣⲧⲛⲉϥ· >>>—	ⲟⲩⲱϣⲧ "pay respects"
2ⲁϥⲥⲟⲧⲙⲆⲉⲛ̄ⲟ̄ⲏ	ⲥⲟⲧⲙ "hear"
2ⲏⲣⲱⲆⲏⲥ	
2ⲁϥϣⲧⲁⲣⲧⲣ̄ⲉ̄ⲙⲁϣⲁ	ϣⲧⲁⲣⲧⲣ "be disturbed"; ⲉ̄ⲙⲁϣⲁ "greatly"
ⲙ̄ⲛⲛⲁⲧ2ⲓⲉ̄ⲣⲟⲥⲟⲗⲩ	ⲛⲁ- § 3.3
ⲙⲁⲧⲏⲣⲟⲩⲛⲉⲙⲉϥ·	ⲧⲏⲣ= § 3.7; ⲛⲉⲙⲉ= § 5.3
ⲁⲩⲱ2ⲁϥⲧⲁⲩⲧⲉⲛ̄	ⲧⲁⲩⲧⲉ "gather"
ⲛⲁⲣⲭⲓⲉⲣⲉⲩⲥⲧⲏⲣⲟⲩ	ⲁⲣⲭⲓⲉⲣⲉⲩⲥ for ⲁⲣⲭⲓⲉⲣⲉⲩⲥ "high priest" (Greek ἀρχιερεύς)
ⲙ̄ⲛⲛⲉⲅⲣⲁⲙⲙⲁⲧⲉⲩⲥ	ⲅⲣⲁⲙⲙⲁⲧⲉⲩⲥ "record-keeper" (Greek γραμματεύς)
ⲙ̄ⲡⲗⲁⲟⲥ· 2ⲁϥϣⲓⲛⲉ	ⲗⲁⲟⲥ "people" (Greek λαός); ϣⲓⲛⲉ "ask"
ⲉ̄ⲃⲁⲗ2ⲓⲧⲁⲧⲟⲩⲭⲉⲁⲩ	
ⲛⲉⲭⲡⲁⲙ̄ⲡⲉⲭⲣ̄ⲥ̄ⲧⲟⲛ·	ⲭⲡⲁ- see above
ⲛ̄ⲧⲁⲩⲆⲉⲡⲉⲭⲉⲩⲛⲉϥ·	
ⲭⲉ2̄ⲛ̄ⲧⲃⲏⲑⲗⲉⲉⲙ	
ⲛ̄ⲧⲉϯⲟⲩⲆⲁⲓⲁ· ⲁϥⲥ2ⲏ	ⲥ2ⲟⲩⲧ "written" (stative)
ⲟⲩⲧⲅⲁⲣⲉ̄ⲧⲃⲏⲧϥ̄ⲛ̄	
ⲧⲉⲓ̈2ⲏⲉ̄ⲃⲁⲗ2ⲓⲧⲁ	2ⲏ "manner"
ⲧϥ̄ⲙ̄ⲡⲉⲡⲣⲟⲫⲏⲧⲏⲥ	ⲡⲣⲟⲫⲏⲧⲏⲥ "prophet" (Greek προφήτης)

7 Schenke 1981.

ⲬⲉⲚⲦⲀϨⲰⲦⲉⲂⲎⲞⲗⲉ	ⲚⲦⲀ ϨⲰⲦⲉ § 3.5, 3.7
ⲉⲘⲠⲔⲉϨⲉⲚⲒ̈ⲞⲨⲆⲀ·	ⲉⲘⲠⲔⲉϨⲉ for ⲉⲘⲘ̄ⲠⲔⲉϨⲉ; ⲔⲉϨⲉ "country"
Ⲛ̄ⲦⲉⲞⲅⲉⲗⲀⲬⲒⲤⲦⲞⲤ	ⲉⲗⲀⲬⲒⲤⲦⲞⲤ for ⲉⲗⲀⲬⲒⲤⲦⲞⲤ "least" (Greek ἐλάχιστος)
ⲉⲚⲚ̄ⲚⲒⲚⲎⲒ̈Ϩ̄ⲚⲚ̄Ϩ2Ⲏ	ϨⲎⲅⲉⲘⲀⲚ "ruler" (Greek ἡγεμών)
ⲙⲀⲚⲚⲒ̈ⲞⲨⲆⲀ· ⲉ́	
ⲢⲉⲞⲨϨⲎⲅⲞⲨⲘⲉⲚⲞⲤ	ϨⲎⲅⲞⲨⲘⲉⲚⲞⲤ "leader" (Greek ἡγούμενος)
ⲉ́ⲉⲒⲉ́ⲂⲀⲗⲚ̄ϨⲎⲦⲉⲉⲋ	
ⲚⲉⲘⲀⲚⲉⲘ̄ⲠⲀⲗⲞⲤⲠ̄ⲒⲀ̄ >>>–	ⲙⲀⲚⲉ "shepherd"; Ⲡ̄ⲒⲀ̄ for ⲠⲒⲤⲢⲀⲎⲗ "Israel"
ⲦⲞⲦⲉϨⲎⲢⲰⲆⲎⲤϨⲀ̄ϥ	
ⲙⲞⲨⲦⲉⲉⲘⲘⲀⲅⲞⲤ	ⲙⲞⲨⲦⲉ "call"
ϨⲚⲞⲨϨⲞⲠ· ϨⲀ̄ϥϣⲒⲚⲉ	ϨⲚⲞⲨϨⲞⲠ "in secret"
ⲉⲂⲀⲗϨⲒⲦⲀⲦⲞⲨⲚ̄ⲤⲀ	
ⲠⲞⲨⲀⲒ̈ϣⲘ̄ⲠⲤⲒⲞⲨ	ⲞⲨⲀⲒ̈ϣ "time"
ⲉ́ⲑⲀϥⲞⲨⲞⲚϨⲉ́ⲂⲀⲗ·	ⲞⲨⲞⲚϨ "be revealed"
ⲀⲨⲰϨⲀ̄ϥⲭⲚⲉⲨⲉⲦⲂⲎ	ⲭⲚⲉ꞊ "send"
ⲑⲗⲉⲉⲘ· Ⲡⲉⲭⲉϥ· ⲭⲉ	
ⲙⲉϣⲉⲚⲎⲦⲚ̄ϣⲒⲚⲉ	ⲙⲉϣⲉ "go"
Ϩ̄ⲚⲞⲨⲭⲭⲢⲀⲉⲦⲂⲉ	ⲭⲭⲢⲀ "diligent"
ⲠⲉⲒ̈Ⲁ́ⲗⲞⲨ· ⲉ́ϣⲞⲠⲉ	Ⲁ́ⲗⲞⲨ "child"
Ⲁ́ⲦⲉⲦⲚϣⲀⲚϬⲒⲚⲉ	ϬⲒⲚⲉ "find"
Ⲙ̄ⲙⲀϥⲀ́ⲘⲎⲉⲒⲚⲉⲘⲀ	Ⲁ́ⲘⲎⲉⲒⲚⲉ § 7.6; ⲙⲀⲦⲀⲘⲀⲒ̈ "let me know"
ⲦⲀⲙⲀⲒ̈ϨⲰ· ⲭⲉⲔⲉⲤⲉⲒ̈	Ϩⲱ § 3.7
ⲉ́ⲉⲒⲚ̄ⲦⲀⲞⲨⲞϣⲦⲚⲉϥ >>>–	
Ⲛ̄ⲦⲀⲨϨⲀⲨⲤⲞⲦⲘ̄Ⲛ	
ⲤⲀⲠⲉⲢⲀϨⲀⲨϣⲉⲚⲉⲨ·	ϣⲉ Ⲛⲉ꞊ "go away"
ⲀⲨⲰϨⲉⲒ̈ⲠⲉϨⲒⲠⲤⲒⲞⲨ	ϨⲉⲒⲠⲉ 21 § 4.5
ⲉⲑⲀⲨⲚⲉⲉ́ⲢⲀϥϨⲒⲢⲀ	
ϣⲉ́ⲉⲚⲀϥⲤⲞⲔϨⲀⲭⲞ	ⲤⲞⲔ "glide"
ⲞⲨϣⲀⲚⲦ̄ϥⲉⲒⲚϥⲞ	ⲞϨⲉⲢⲀⲦ꞊ "stand"
ϨⲉⲢⲉⲦϥϨⲒⲭⲚ̄ⲠⲘⲉ	ⲙⲉ "place"
ⲉ́ⲦⲚⲀⲢⲉⲠⲀⲗⲞⲨⲘ̄	
ⲙⲀϥ· ϨⲀⲨⲚⲉⲆⲉⲉ́ⲠⲤⲒ	
ⲞⲨ· ϨⲀⲨⲢⲉϣⲉϨⲚⲞⲨ	Ⲣⲉϣⲉ "rejoice"
ⲚⲀϬⲚ̄Ⲣⲉϣⲉⲉ́ⲙⲀϣⲀ·	
ϨⲀⲨⲉⲒⲉ́ϨⲞⲨⲚⲉ́ⲠⲎⲒ̈	ⲎⲒ̈ "house"
ϨⲀⲨⲚⲉⲉ́ⲠⲀⲗⲞⲨⲘ̄Ⲛ	

ⲦⲈϤⲘⲀⲨⲘⲀⲢⲒⲀ· ⲌⲀⲨ	ⲘⲀⲨ "mother"
ⲌⲒⲦⲞⲨⲈⲠⲈⲤⲎⲦⲌⲀⲨ	ⲌⲒⲦ⸗ "set"
ⲞⲨⲞⲰⲦⲚⲈϤ· ⲀⲨⲰ	
ⲌⲀⲨⲞⲨⲞⲚⲈⲚⲈⲨⲀⲌⲰⲢ	ⲞⲨⲞⲚ "open"; ⲁ̀Ⲍⲱ "treasure"; ⲢⲌⲀⲨⲈⲒⲚⲈ § 10.9
ⲌⲀⲨⲈⲒⲚⲈⲚⲈϤⲚ̄ⲌⲈⲚ	
ⲆⲰⲢⲞⲚ· ⲞⲨⲚⲞⲨⲂ'·	ⲆⲰⲢⲞⲚ "gift" (Greek δῶρον); ⲚⲞⲨⲂ "gold"
ⲞⲨⲖⲒⲂⲀⲚⲞⲤ· ⲞⲨϢⲈⲖ·	ⲖⲒⲂⲀⲚⲞⲤ "incense" (Greek λίβανος); ϢⲈⲖ "myrrh"
ⲀⲨⲰⲌⲀⲨⲦⲞⲨⲚⲈⲈⲒⲈ̀	ⲦⲞⲨⲚⲈⲈⲒⲈ̀Ⲧ⸗ "warn" ("raise eye")
ⲦⲞⲨⲈⲂⲀⲖ'ⲌⲚ̄ⲞⲨⲢⲈⲤⲞⲨⲈ̀	ⲢⲈⲤⲞⲨⲈ̀ "dream"
ⲬⲈⲚ̀ⲚⲈⲨⲔⲀⲦⲦⲞⲨ	ⲔⲀⲦⲦ⸗ "return" ("turn self")
Ⲉ̀ⲢⲈⲦϤⲚ̀ⲌⲎⲢⲰⲆⲎⲤ·	Ⲉ̀ⲢⲈⲦϤ "to" ("to his foot")
Ⲛ̄ⲦⲀⲨⲆⲈⲌⲀⲨϢⲈⲚⲈⲨ	
Ⲉ̀ⲂⲀⲖⲌⲒⲔⲈⲌⲒⲎⲈⲌⲢⲎ	ⲌⲒⲎ "way"
Ⲓ̈Ⲉ̀ⲦⲈⲨⲬⲰⲢⲀ· Ⲉ̀ⲐⲀⲨ	ⲬⲰⲢⲀ "country" (Greek χώρα)
ϢⲈⲚⲈⲨⲆⲈ· ⲌⲒⲠⲀⲅ	ⲌⲒ § 4.5; ⲀⲅⲅⲈⲖⲞⲤ "messenger" (Greek ἄγγελος)
ⲄⲈⲖⲞⲤⲘ̀ⲠⲬⲤ̅ⲌⲀϤ	ⲬⲤ̅ abbreviation for ⲬⲖⲈⲒⲤ "lord"
ⲞⲨⲞⲚⲌⲈ̀Ⲓ̈ⲰⲤⲎⲪ	Ⲓ̈ⲰⲤⲎⲪ "Joseph"
Ⲍ̄ⲚⲞⲨⲢⲈⲤⲞⲨⲈ̀ⲈϤⲬⲰ	
Ⲙ̀ⲘⲀⲤ· ⲬⲈⲦⲞⲨⲚⲔ	ⲦⲞⲨⲚ⸗ "raise"
ϤⲒⲘ̀ⲠⲈⲒ̈Ⲁ̀ⲖⲞⲨⲘⲚ	ϤⲒ "carry"
ⲦⲈϤⲘⲈⲨⲠⲞⲦⲈ̀ⲌⲢⲎ	ⲠⲞⲦ "run"
Ⲓ̈Ⲉ̀ⲔⲎⲘⲈϢⲞⲠⲈⲘ̀	ϢⲞⲠⲈ "exist"
ⲘⲈϢⲀⲚⲦϪⲈⲤⲚⲈⲔ·	Ⲭ̇Ⲉ⸗ "say"
ⲌⲎⲢⲰⲆⲎⲤⲄⲀⲢⲚⲈ	
ϢⲒⲚⲈⲚ̀ⲤⲀⲠⲈⲒ̈ⲔⲞⲨⲒ̈	ⲔⲞⲨⲒ̈ "little"
Ⲛ̀Ⲁ̀ⲖⲞⲨⲈ̀ⲦⲀⲔⲀϤ· Ⲛ̀	ⲦⲀⲔⲀ "destroy"
ⲦⲀϤⲆⲈⲌⲀϤⲦⲞⲨⲚⲚ̄ϥ	
Ⲍ̄Ⲛ̄ⲦⲈⲨϢⲎⲌⲀϤⲬⲒⲘ̀	ⲦⲈⲨϢⲎ "night"
ⲠⲀⲖⲞⲨⲘⲚ̄ⲦⲈϤⲘⲈⲨ	
ⲌⲀϤⲒⲈ̀ⲌⲢⲎⲒ̈Ⲉ̀ⲔⲎⲘⲈ	
ⲌⲀϤϬⲰⲘ̀ⲘⲈϢⲀⲚⲦⲈ	
ⲌⲎⲢⲰⲆⲎⲤⲘⲞⲨ·	ⲘⲞⲨ "die"

SAIDIC

The Chicago manuscript of the Proverbs of Solomon is an unprovenanced codex on vellum, dated to the 6th century.[8] The section below is Prov. 2:1–10.

ϢⲎⲢⲈⲈⲔϢⲀⲚⲬⲒⲚ̄Ⲛ̄	ⲬⲒ "accept"
ϢⲀⲬⲈⲚ̄ⲦⲀⲈⲚⲦⲞⲖⲎ	ϢⲀⲬⲈ "word"; ⲈⲚⲦⲞⲖⲎ "advice" (Greek ἐντολή)
Ⲛ̄Ⲅ̄ⲂⲞⲠⲞⲨⲂⲀⲦⲎⲔ ·	ⲂⲞⲠꞋ "hide"; ⲂⲀⲂⲦⲎⲔ for ⲂⲀⲂⲦⲎⲔ (ⲂⲦⲎꞋ "heart")
ⲠⲈⲘⲀⲬⲈⲚⲀⲤⲰⲦⲘ̄	ⲠⲈⲘⲀⲬⲈ for ⲠⲈⲔⲘⲀⲬⲈ; ⲘⲀⲬⲈ "ear"; ⲤⲰⲦⲘ̄ "listen"
[Ⲛ]ⲤⲀⲦⲤⲞⲪⲒⲀⲠⲈ · ⲀⲨ	ⲤⲞⲪⲒⲀ "wisdom" (Greek σοφία); ⲠⲈ supefluous
[Ⲱ]ⲔⲚⲀϯⲘ̄ⲠⲈⲔⲂⲎⲦ	ⲂⲎⲦ "heart"
ⲈⲨⲘ̄ⲚⲦⲤⲀⲂⲈ · Ⲛ̄Ⲅ̄	Ⲙ̄ⲚⲦ § 2.6; ⲤⲀⲂⲈ "learned"
ⲦⲀⲀⲤⲆⲈⲘ̄ⲠⲈⲔϢⲎ	ⲦⲀⲀⲤ "give it"
ⲢⲈⲚ̄ⲤⲂⲰ · ⲈϢⲰⲠⲈ	ⲤⲂⲰ "teaching"
ⲄⲀⲢⲈⲔϢⲀⲚⲘⲞⲨⲦⲈ	ⲘⲞⲨⲦⲈ "call"
ⲞⲨⲂⲈⲦⲤⲞⲪⲎⲒⲀ · Ⲛ̄Ⲅ̄	
ⲘⲞⲨⲦⲈⲆⲈⲈⲦⲀⲒⲤⲐⲎ	ⲀⲒⲤⲐⲎⲤⲒⲤ "perception" (Greek αἴσθησις)
ⲤⲒⲤⲂ̄ⲚⲞⲨⲚⲞϬⲚ̄Ⲥ	ⲤⲘⲎ "voice"
ⲘⲎ · Ⲛ̄Ⲅ̄ϢⲒⲚⲈⲆⲈⲚ̄	ϢⲒⲚⲈ "search"
ⲤⲰⲤⲚ̄ⲐⲈⲚ̄ⲂⲈⲚⲀⲂⲞ	ⲀⲂⲞ "treasure"
Ⲛ̄ⲂⲀⲦꞋⲚ̄[Ⲅ̄]ⲂⲞⲦⲂ̱̄Ⲧ̄Ⲛ̄	ⲂⲀⲦ "silver"; ⲂⲞⲦⲂ̄Ⲧ "inquire"
Ⲛ̄ⲤⲰⲤⲂ̄ⲚⲞⲨⲢⲞⲦ ·	ⲞⲨⲢⲞⲦ "eagerness"
ⲦⲞⲦⲈⲔⲚⲀ[Ⲛ]ⲞⲒ̈Ⲛ̄ⲦⲘ̄Ⲛ̄[Ⲧ]	ⲦⲞⲦⲈ "then" (Greek τότε); ⲚⲞⲒ̈ "understand" (Greek νοεῖν)
ⲘⲀⲒ̈ⲚⲞⲨⲦⲈ · Ⲛ̄Ⲅ̄Ⲃ̄Ⲉ	ⲘⲀⲒ̈ⲚⲞⲨⲦⲈ "God-loving" (§§ 2.6, 7.5); Ⲃ̄Ⲉ Ⲉ- "find" ("fall on")
ⲈⲦⲀⲒⲤⲐⲎⲤⲒⲤⲈⲦⲞⲨⲀ	ⲞⲨⲀⲀⲂ "holy"
ⲀⲂ̄Ⲛ̄ⲦⲈⲦⲈⲔⲞⲨⲈⲢⲎ	ⲞⲨⲈⲢⲎⲦⲈ "foot"
ⲦⲈⲦⲘ̄ⲬⲒⲬⲢⲞⲠ · ⲠⲚ[ⲞⲨ]	Ⲧ̄Ⲙ § 7.8; ⲬⲒⲬⲢⲞⲠ "stumble" (ⲬⲒ- "take"; ⲬⲢⲞⲠ "obstacle")
ⲦⲈⲄⲀⲢⲚⲀϯⲚⲀⲔⲚ̄Ⲧ[ⲤⲞ]	
ⲪⲒⲀⲈⲂⲞⲖⲂ̄Ⲛ̄ⲢⲰϥⲘ̄Ⲛ̄	ⲢⲰϥ "his mouth"
ⲞⲨⲀⲒⲤⲐⲎⲤⲒⲤⲘ̄ⲚⲞⲨ	
Ⲙ̄ⲚⲦⲢ̄Ⲙ̄Ⲛ̄ⲂⲎⲦ · ⲀⲨⲰ	Ⲣ̄Ⲙ̄Ⲛ̄ⲂⲎⲦ "wise man" ("man of heart")
ϢⲀϥⲤⲈⲨⲂⲂⲞⲎⲐⲒⲀⲈ	ⲤⲈⲨⲂ- "collect"; ⲂⲞⲎⲐⲒⲀ "help" (Greek βοήθεια)
ⲂⲞⲨⲚⲚ̄Ⲛ̄ⲆⲒⲔⲀⲒⲞⲤ ·	ⲆⲒⲔⲀⲒⲞⲤ "righteous" (Greek δίκαιος)
ⲈϥⲢ̄ⲚⲀϢⲦⲈⲈⲚⲈⲨ[ⲂⲒ]Ⲟ	Ⲣ̄ⲚⲀϢⲦⲈ "do (Ⲣ̄) protection"; ⲂⲒⲞⲞⲨⲈ "paths"
ⲞⲨⲈ · ⲈϥⲂⲀⲢⲈⲂⲈⲚ[Ⲉ]	ⲂⲀⲢⲈⲂ "guard"

8　Worrell 1931.

ⲀⲢⲞⲞⲨⲄⲈⲚ̄ⲦⲘⲈ · ⲰⲀϥ   ⲘⲈ "truth"

ⲦⲤⲦⲎⲀⲈⲈⲚⲈϨⲒⲞⲞⲨ   ⲦϨⲦⲎ for ⲦϨⲎⲦ "pay heed" ("give heart")

ⲈⲚ̄ⲚⲚⲀⲎⲦˈⲦⲀⲒⲞ̈Ⲉ   ⲚⲀⲎⲦ "compassionate" (ⲚⲀ "merciful" of (Ϩ)ⲎⲦ "heart")

ⲦⲈⲐⲈⲚ̄ϨⲞⲨⲞ[Ⲉ]ⲔⲚⲀ   Ⲛ̄ϨⲞⲨⲞ "even more"

ⲚⲞⲒ̈ⲚⲦⲀⲒⲔⲀⲒⲞⳝⲨⲚⲎ   ⲀⲒⲔⲀⲒⲞⳝⲨⲚⲎ "justice" (Greek δικαιοσύνη)

Ⲙ̄ⲚⲦⲘⲈ · ⲞⲨⲚⲦⲈⲦⲘⲈ   ⲞⲨⲚⲦⲈ- § 8.8

ⲄⲀⲢϨⲈⲚϨⲒⲞⲞⲨⲈⲈⲨⲤⲞⲨ   ⲤⲞⲨⲦⲰⲚ "straight" (stative)

ⲦⲰⲚ · ⲀⲄ[Ⲱ]ϢⲀⲢⲈⲚⲈ

ⲀⲢⲞⲞⲨⲄⲈⲘ̄Ⲡ̄ⲠⲈⲦⲚⲀ   ⲚⲀⲚⲞⲨϥ § 6.5

ⲚⲞⲨϥⲤⲞⲞⲨⲚⲦ̄Ⲛ̄ · ⲈⲢ   ⲤⲞⲞⲨⲚⲦ̄Ⲛ̄ for ⲤⲞⲞⲨⲦ̄Ⲛ̄ "be straight"

ϢⲀⲚⲦⲤⲞⲪⲒⲀⲄⲀⲢⲈⲒ

ⲈⲠⲈⲔϨⲎⲦˈⲀⲨⲰⲚ̄Ⲅ̄

ⲘⲈⲈⲨⲈⲈⲦⲀⲒⳜⲐⲎⲤⲒⳜ   ⲘⲈⲈⲨⲈ "think"

ⲬⲈⲚⲀⲚⲞⲨⳜⲚ̄ⲦⲈⲔⲮⲨ   ⲪⲨⲬⲎ "spirit" (Greek ψυχή)

ⲬⲎ ·

DICTIONARY

The Coptic entries below are listed in the alphabetical order of § 1.4, with the following exceptions: ⲉⲓ is treated as ⲓ but ⲟⲩ as ⲟ + ⲩ rather than as ⲩ; ⲑ, ⲭ, and ⲫ are treated as ⲧ, ⲕ, and ⲡ, respectively, unless they are monograms for ⲧⲝ, ⲕⲝ, and ⲡⲝ, respectively; ⲝ and ⲫ are treated as the same letter; ⲧ is alphabetized as ⲧⲓ. Greek loanwords, in Greek alphabetical order, are listed at the end.

COPTIC

ⲁ̄ 1 (§ 4.1)

ⲁ̄ 1,000 (§ 4.1)

ⲁ- /a/ § 5.1, 9.4

ⲁ-, ⲁ⸗ /a/ § 9.2

ⲁ⸗ /a/ § 11.2

ⲁ⸗ⲉ- /a ... ε/ § 9.4

ⲁ⸗ⲯⲁ-, ⲁ⸗ⲯⲁⲛ- /a ... ša(n)/ § 12.9

ⲁⲃⲁⲗ /a-bal'/ out, § 5.4a

ⲁⲃⲣⲁⲅⲁⲙ /ab-ra-ḥam'/ Abraham

ⲁⲗⲉ- /a-lε/ § 11.2

ⲁⲗⲉⲙⲡⲏ /al-ɛm-pe'/ hailstone (stone of sky)

ⲁⲗⲉⲯⲁⲛ- /a-lε-šan/ § 12.9

ⲁⲗⲏⲩ /a-le'-u/ perhaps, § 5.3

ⲁⲗⲓ-, ⲁⲗⲓⲧ⸗ /a-li/, /a-lit'/ do, § 7.6

ⲁⲗⲓⲟⲩⲓ /a-li'-ui/ § 7.6

ⲁⲗⲟⲕ, ⲁⲗⲟ, ⲁⲗⲱⲧⲛ̄ /a-lɔk'/, /a-lɔ'/, /a-lo'-tn/ stop, § 7.6

ⲁ́ⲗⲟⲩ /a'-lu/ child

ⲁⲗⲫⲁ /al'-fa/ § 1.4

ⲁⲙⲉⲩ /a-mεu'/ to there, § 5.4a

ⲁⲙⲏ /a-me'/ come, § 7.6

ⲁ́ⲙⲏⲉⲓⲛⲉ, ⲁⲙⲱⲓⲛⲉ, ⲁⲙⲱⲓⲛⲓ /a-me'-i-ne/, /amo'-i-nε/, /amo'-i-ni/ come, § 7.6

ⲁⲙⲏⲉⲓⲧⲛ̄, ⲁⲙⲏⲏⲧⲛ̄ /a-me'-i-tn/, /a-me'-e-tn/ come, § 7.6

ⲁⲙⲟ /a-mɔ'/ to there, § 5.4a

ⲁⲙⲟⲩ /a-mu'/ come, § 7.6

ⲁⲛ /an/ § 4.5, 5.3

ⲁⲛ /an/ not, § 4.6, 6.6, 8.7, 11.5

ⲁⲛ /an/ again, also, still, § 5.3

ⲁⲛⲁⲕ, ⲁⲛⲟⲕ; ⲁⲛⲧ̄, ⲁⲛⲕ̄ /a-nak'/, /a-ng/, /a-nk/ § 3.5

ⲁⲛⲁⲛ, ⲁⲛⲟⲛ /a-nan'/, /a-nɔn'/ § 3.5

ⲁⲛⲁⲩ, ⲁⲛⲉⲩ /a-nau'/, /a-nεu'/ see, § 7.6

ⲁⲛⲇⲣⲉⲁⲥ /an-drε'-as/ Andrew

ⲁⲛⲓ-; ⲁⲛⲓ⸗, ⲁⲛⲓⲧ⸗, ⲉⲛⲓ /a-ni/, /a-ni(t)'/, /ε-ni'/ get, § 7.6

ⲁⲛⲓⲟⲩⲓ, ⲁⲛⲉⲓⲛⲉ /a-ni'-ui/, /a-ni'-nε/ come, § 7.6

ⲁⲛⲏⲅⲉ /a-ne'-ḥe/ ever, § 5.4a

ⲁⲟⲩ /a-u'/ and, § 4.5

ⲁⲡⲁⲅⲟⲩ /a-paḥ'-u/ backward, § 5.4a

ⲁⲡⲉⲥⲏⲧ /a-pε-set'/ down(ward), § 5.4a

ⲁⲣⲁ⸗ /a-ra'/ § 5.1

ⲁⲣⲉ- /a-rε/ § 11.2

ⲁⲣⲉⲧ⸗ /a-ret'/ § 5.2a

ⲁⲣⲉⲯⲁ-, ⲁⲣⲉⲯⲁⲛ- /a-rε-ša(n)/ § 12.9

ⲁⲣⲏⲟⲩ, ⲁⲣⲏⲩ /a-re'-u/ perhaps, § 5.3

ⲁⲣⲏⲅ /a-reḥ'/ guard (with ⲁ-)

ⲁⲣⲓ-, ⲉⲣⲓ-; ⲁⲣⲓ⸗, ⲁⲣⲓⲧ⸗ /a-ri/, /ε-ri/, /a-ri(t)'/ do, § 7.6

ⲁⲣⲓⲟⲩⲓ, ⲁⲣⲓⲣⲉ /a-ri'-ui/, /a-ri'-rε/ do, § 7.6

-ⲁⲥⲉ /as'-ε/ six, § 4.2

ⲁⲥⲥⲩⲣⲓⲟⲥ /as-sy-ri'-ɔs/ Assyria

ⲁⲧⲛ̄- /a-tn/ § 5.2a

ⲁⲧⲟ /a-tɔ'/ to where, § 5.4a

ⲁⲧⲟⲟⲧ⸗ /a-tɔ:t'/ § 5.2a

ⲁⲧⲉⲅⲏ, ⲁⲧⲅⲓ /a-tε-ḥe'/, /a-tḥi'/ beforehand, § 5.4a

ⲁⲧⲟ́ⲛⲉ-, ⲁⲧⲟ́ⲛⲟⲩ⸗ /at-ṭnε/, /at-ṭnu'/ § 5.1

ⲁⲩ, ⲁⲅⲉ, ⲁⲅⲉⲓ, ⲁⲅⲉⲓⲥ, ⲁⲅⲉⲉⲓ /au/, /a-ue'/, /a-
    ui'/, /a-uis'/, /a-uei'/ give, come, § 7.6

ⲁⲅⲱ /a-uɔ'/ and § 4.5

ⲁⲟⲩⲱⲛ, ⲁⲟⲩⲟⲛ; ⲁⲟⲩⲛ̄-, ⲟⲩⲛ̄- /a-uon'/, /a-
    uɔn'/, /au-n/, /u-n/ open, § 7.6

ⲁϩⲟ, ⲁ̇ϩⲱⲣ /a-hɔ'/, /a-hor'/ treasure

ⲁϩⲟⲩⲟ /a-ḥuɔ'/ more, § 5.4a

ⲁⲭⲛ̄-, ⲁⲭⲉⲛ-, ⲁⲭⲭⲛ̄-; ⲁⲭⲛ̄ⲧ⸗, ⲁⲭⲉⲛⲧ⸗ /a-d̲n/,
    /a-d̲ɛn/, /ad̲-d̲n/, /a-d̲nt'/, /a-d̲ɛnt'/ § 5.1

ⲁϣ /aš/ many

ⲁϣ /aš/ § 3.2

-ⲁϥⲧⲉ /af'-tɛ/ four, § 4.2

ⲁϩⲟⲩⲛ, ⲁϩⲟⲩⲛ /a-ḥun'/, /a-xun'/ in(ward),
    § 5.4a

ⲁϩⲣⲏ, ⲁϩⲣⲏⲉⲓ /a-ḥre'/, /a-ḥrei'/ up(ward), § 5.4a

ⲁϩⲣⲏⲓ /a-xrei'/ down(ward), § 5.4a

ⲁϩⲣⲛ̄, ⲁϩⲣⲉ⸗ /aḥ-rn/, /a-ḥrɛ'/ § 5.2a

ⲁϩⲁⲣⲉ-, ⲁϩⲁⲣ⸗ /a-xa-rɛ/, /a-xar'/ § 11.2

ⲁⲭⲉ-, ⲁⲭⲓ-; ⲁⲭⲓ⸗, ⲁⲭⲟ⸗, ⲁⲭⲟⲧ⸗, ⲉⲭⲓ⸗ /a-d̲ɛ/, /a-
    d̲i/, /a-d̲i'/, /a-d̲ɔ'/, /ad̲ɔt'/, /ɛ-d̲i/ say, § 7.6

ⲁⲭⲛ̄-, ⲁⲭⲱ⸗ /a-d̲n/, /a-d̲o'/ § 5.2a

ⲁⲭⲱ /a-d̲o'/ say, § 7.6

ⲁϭⲛⲉ-, ⲁϭⲛⲟⲩ⸗ see ⲁⲧϭⲛⲉ-

ⲃ̄ 2 (§ 4.1)

ⲃ̄ 2,000 (§ 4.1)

ⲃⲁⲗ /bal/ out, § 5.3

ⲃⲉⲕⲏ /bɛ-ke'/ reward

ⲃⲉⲗ /bel/ eye

ⲃⲉⲗⲗⲉⲩ /bɛl-lɛu'/ blind (pl)

ⲃⲏⲧⲁ, ⲃⲓⲇⲁ /bi'-ta/ § 1.4

ⲃⲏⲑⲗⲉⲉⲙ /betʰ-lɛ'-ɛm/ Bethlehem

ⲃⲓⲣ /bir/ basket

ⲃⲱ ⲛ̀ⲕⲉⲛⲧⲉ /bo n-kɛn'-tɛ/ fig tree

ⲃⲱⲕ /bok/ go

ⲃⲱⲗ /bol/ disregard

ⲃⲱⲗ ⲁⲃⲁⲗ /bol a-bal'/ dissolution

ⲃⲱⲗ ⲉⲃⲟⲗ /bol ɛ-bɔl'/ throw out, disappear
    (loosen out)

ⲅ̄ 3 (§ 4.1)

ⲅ̄ 3,000 (§ 4.1)

ⲅⲁⲗⲓⲗⲁⲓⲁ, ⲅⲁⲗⲓⲗⲉⲁ /ga-li-lɛ'-a/ Galilee

ⲅⲁⲙⲙⲁ /gam'-ma/ § 1.4

ⲇ̄ 4 (§ 4.1)

ⲇ̄ 4,000 (§ 4.1)

ⲇⲁⲗⲇⲁ /dal'-da/ § 1.4

ⲉ̄ 5 (§ 4.1)

ⲉ̄ 5,000 (§ 4.1)

ⲉ- /ɛ/ § 5.1, 10.9, 11.2

ⲉ⸗ /ɛ/ § 10.2, 10.7, 11.2

ⲉ⸗ⲁ-, ⲉ⸗ⲉ- /ɛ ... a/, /ɛ ... ɛ/ § 9.4

ⲉ⸗ϣⲁ-, ⲉ⸗ϣⲁⲛ- /ɛ-ša(n)/ § 12.9

ⲉⲁⲩ /ɛ-au'/ glory

ⲉⲃⲁⲗ, ⲉⲃⲟⲗ /ɛ-bal'/, /ɛ-bɔl'/ out, § 5.4a

ⲉⲃⲟⲗ ϩ̄ⲙ- /ɛ-bɔl' ḥm/ from

ⲉⲉ⸗ /ɛ'-ɛ/ do

ⲉⲓⲁ, ⲉⲓ̈ⲉ, ⲉⲉⲓⲉ /ɛ-ia'/, /ɛ-iɛ'/ then, § 4.5

ⲉⲗ- /ɛl/ make, do

ⲉⲗⲁ⸗ /ɛ-la'/ § 5.1

ⲉⲗⲉ- /ɛ-lɛ/ § 10.2, 10.7

ⲉⲗⲉ ... ⲉ- /ɛ-lɛ ... ɛ/ § 9.4

ⲉⲙⲁⲧⲉ, ⲉⲙⲁⲧ̇ /ɛ-mat'-ɛ/, /ɛ-mat'-i/ greatly,
    § 5.4a

ⲉⲙⲁⲩ /ɛ-maw'/ to there, § 5.4a

ⲉ̇ⲙⲁϣⲁ, ⲉⲙⲁϣⲱ /ɛ-ma-ša'/, /ɛ-ma-šo'/ greatly,
    5.4a

ⲉⲙⲓ , /ɛ'-mi/ know

ⲉⲙⲛⲁⲓ /ɛm-nai'/ here, § 5.3

ⲉⲙⲛ̄ⲧ /ɛ-mnt'/ west

ⲉⲛ- /ɛn/ § 5.1

ⲉⲛ /ɛn/ not, § 4.6, 6.6, 8.7, 11.5

ⲉⲛ, ⲉⲛⲉ /ɛn, ɛn'-ɛ/ § 4.5

ⲉⲛⲉ- /ɛ-nɛ/ § 12.10

ⲉⲛⲉϩ /ɛ-nɛḥ'/ ever, § 5.4a

ⲉⲛⲟ /ɛ-nɔ'/ see, § 7.6

ⲉⲛϥ /ɛn'-f/ withdraw (take himself)

ⲉⲡⲁϩⲟⲩ, ⲉⲫⲁϩⲟⲩ, ⲉⲡⲉϩⲟⲩ /ɛ-pah'-u/, /ɛ-pʰaḥ'-
    u/, /ɛ-pɛḥ'-u/ backward, § 5.4a

ⲉⲡⲉⲥⲏⲧ /ɛ-pɛ-set'/ down(ward), § 5.4a

ⲉⲣⲁ⸗, ⲉⲣⲟ⸗ /ɛ-ra'/, /ɛ-rɔ'/ § 5.1

ⲉⲣⲁ /ɛ-ra'/ king

ⲉⲣⲁⲧ⸗, ⲉⲣⲉⲧ⸗ /ɛ-rat', ɛ-ret'/ § 5.2a

ⲉⲣⲉ- /ɛ-rɛ/ § 10.2, 10.7. 11.2

ⲉⲣⲉ ... ⲁ, ⲉ- /ɛ-rɛ ... a/. /ɛ-rɛ ... ɛ// § 9.4

ⲉⲣⲛⲟⲃⲓ /ɛr-nɔb'-i/ do sin

ⲉⲣⲟⲩⲁⲉⲓⲛ /ɛr-uain/ give light (construct of ⲉⲓⲡⲉ make plus ⲟⲩⲁⲉⲓⲛ light)

ⲉⲣⲟⲩⲱ /ɛr-uo'/ make reply

ⲉⲣⲫⲁⲡⲣⲓ /ɛr-pʰax'-ri/ do healing

ⲉⲣⲫⲉⲓ /ɛr-pʰei'/ temple

ⲉⲣϣⲟⲣⲡ /ɛr-šɔr'-p/ take precedence (make first)

ⲉⲣϩⲱⲃ /ɛr-ħob'/ work

ⲉⲥⲁⲩ /ɛ-sau'/ sheep

-ⲉⲥⲉ /ɛs'-ɛ/ six, § 4.2

ⲉⲥⲏⲧ /ɛ-set'/ pregnant

ⲉⲥⲧⲉ /ɛs'-tɛ/ behold, § 4.5

ⲉⲧ-, ⲉⲧⲉ- /ɛt/, /ɛ-tɛ/ § 3.1, 10.8

ⲉⲧ⸗ /ɛt/ § 10.8

ⲉⲧⲁ-, ⲉⲧⲁ⸗ /ɛ-ta/, /ɛ-ta'/ § 11.2

ⲉⲧⲁⲧ⸗, ⲉⲧⲟⲧ⸗, ⲉⲧⲟⲟⲧ⸗ /ɛ-tat'/, /ɛ-tɔt'/, /ɛ-tɔːt'/ § 5.2a

ⲉⲧⲃⲉ-, ⲉⲑⲃⲉ-; ⲉⲧⲃⲏⲏⲧ⸗, ⲉⲧⲃⲏⲧ, ⸗ⲉⲑⲃⲏⲧ⸗ /ɛ-tbɛ/, /ɛ-tʰbɛ'/, /ɛ-tbet', ɛ-tʰbeːt'/ § 5.2a

ⲉⲧⲉⲗⲉ-, ⲉⲧⲉⲣⲉ- /ɛ-tɛ-lɛ/, /ɛ-tɛ-rɛ/ § 10.8

ⲉⲧⲙ̄ⲙⲁⲩ, ⲉⲧⲙ̄ⲙⲉ, ⲉⲧⲙ̄ⲙⲉⲩ, ⲉⲧⲙ̄ⲙⲟ /ɛt-m-mau'/, /ɛt-m-mɛ'/, /ɛt-m-mɛu'/, /ɛt-m-mɔ'/ § 3.1

ⲉⲧⲛ̄-, ⲉⲧⲉⲛ- /ɛ-tn/, /ɛ-tɛn/ § 5.2a

ⲉⲧⲟⲛ, ⲉⲧⲱⲛ, ⲉⲑⲱⲛ /ɛ-tɔn'/, /ɛ-ton'/, /ɛ-tʰon'/ to where, § 5.4a

ⲉⲧⲟⲩⲛ-, ⲉⲧⲟⲩⲱ⸗ /ɛ-tun/, /ɛ-tuo'/ § 5.2a

ⲉⲩ /ɛu/ § 3.2

ⲉⲩⲉⲛ /ɛ-uɛn'/ open, § 7.6

ⲉϣ- /ɛš/ § 9.7

ⲉϣ /ɛš/ § 3.2

ⲉϣⲁⲣⲉ-, ⲉϣⲁ⸗ /ɛ-ša-rɛ/, /ɛ-ša'/ § 11.2

ⲉϣⲱⲡ, ⲉϣⲱⲡⲓ, ⲉϣⲱⲡⲉ, ⲉϣⲟⲡⲉ /ɛ-šop'/, /ɛ-šo'-pi/, /ɛ-šo'-pɛ/, /ɛ-šɔ'-pɛ/ § 12.9

ⲉϣⲡⲉ, ⲉϣⲭⲉ, ⲉϣⲭⲡⲉ /ɛš'-pɛ/, /ɛš'-ḏɛ/, /ɛš'-ḏpɛ/ if, § 4.5, 12.8, 12.9

-ⲉϥⲧⲉ /ɛf'-tɛ/ four, § 4.2

ⲉϩⲁ-, ⲉϩⲁ⸗ /ɛ-ḥa/, /ɛ-ḥa'/ § 11.2

ⲉϩⲁⲙ /ɛ-ḥam'/ sigh

ⲉϩⲁⲩ /ɛ-ḥau'/ days

ⲉϩⲛⲉ-, ⲉϩⲛⲁ⸗ /ɛ-ḥnɛ/, /ɛ-ḥna'/ willing, § 6.5

ⲉϩⲟⲟⲩ /ɛ-ḥou'/ day

ⲉϩⲟⲩⲁ, ⲉϩⲟⲩⲟ /ɛ-ḥua'/, /ɛ-ḥuɔ'/ more, § 5.4a

ⲉϩⲟⲩⲛ, ⲉⲡⲟⲩⲛ /ɛ-ḥun'/, /ɛ-xun'/ in(ward), § 5.4a

ⲉϩⲗⲉ⸗ /ɛ-ḫlɛ'/ § 5.2a

ⲉϩⲗⲏⲉⲓ, ⲉϩⲗⲏⲓ /ɛ-ḫlei'/ up(ward), down(ward), § 5.4a

ⲉϩⲣⲁ⸗, ⲉϩⲣⲉ⸗ /ɛ-ḥra'/, /ɛ-ḥrɛ'/ § 5.2a

ⲉϩⲣⲁⲓ, ⲉϩⲣⲏ /ɛ-ḥrai'/, /ɛ-ḥre'/ down(ward), § 5.4a

ⲉϩⲣⲛ̄-, ⲉϩⲣⲉⲛ- /ɛḫ-rn/, /ɛḫ-rɛn/ § 5.2a

ⲉϩⲣⲏⲓ /ɛ-ḥrei'/ up(ward), down(ward), § 5.4a

ⲉϩ /ex/ § 3.2

ⲉϩⲱⲡⲉ /ɛ-xo'-pɛ/ § 12.9

ⲉⲡⲣⲏⲓ /ɛ-xrei'/ down(ward), § 5.4a

ⲉⲝⲛ̄-, ⲉⲝⲉⲛ-; ⲉⲝⲟ⸗, ⲉⲝⲱ⸗ /ɛ-ḏn/, /ɛ-ḏen/, /ɛ-ḏɔ'/, /ɛ-ḏo'/ § 5.2a

ⲍ̄ 6 (§ 4.1)

ⲍ̅ 6,000 (§ 4.1)

ⲍ̄ 7 (§ 4.1)

ⲍ̅ 7,000 (§ 4.1)

ⲍⲏⲧⲁ, ⲍⲓⲧⲁ /zi'-ta/ § 1.4

ⲏ̄ 8 (§ 4.1)

ⲏ̅ 8,000 (§ 4.1)

ⲏⲓ , ⲏ̈ⲓ , ⲏⲉⲓ /ei/ house

ⲏⲣ /er/ union

ⲏⲧⲁ, ϩⲏⲧⲁ /e'-ta/, /ḥe'-ta/ § 1.4

ⲑ̄ 9 (§ 4.1)

ⲑ̅ 9,000 (§ 4.1)

ⲑⲏⲧⲁ, ⲑⲓⲧⲁ /tʰe'-ta/ § 1.4

ⲓ 10 (§ 4.1)

ī 10,000 (§ 4.1)

ι, ει /i/ come

ιλ /i-a′/ then, § 4.5

ει, ειε /i/, /i′-ε/ § 1.4

ϊεει /i-εi′/ wadi (desert valley)

ϊερογϲαλημ /iε-ru-sa-lem′/ Jerusalem

ιομ /i-ɔm′/ sea

ιοτ, ειωτ /i-ɔt′/, /i-ot′/ father

ϊογδαιει, ϊογδαϊ, ιογταει /iu-dai′/ Jew

ειρε /i′-rε/ make

ειϲ, ιϲ /is/ behold, § 4.5

ιϲραηλ /is-ra-el′/ Israel

ειϲτε /is′-tε/ behold, § 4.5

ιϲχε-, ιϲχεκ- /is-dε/, /is-dεk/ if, § 4.5

ιϲχεν- /is-dεn/ § 5.4

ιωτα, ιοτα, ιαγδα /io′-ta/, /iɔ′-ta/, /iau′-ta/ § 1.4

ιωναϲ /io′-nas/ Jonas

ϊωϲηφ /io-sep^hʳ/ Joseph

ειωτ /i-ot′/ barley; father (see ιοτ)

ειϩπε ειϩχε /ix′-pε/, /ix′-dε/ if, § 4.5, 12.8, 12.0

κ̄ 20 (§ 4.1)

κ-, χ- /k, kʰ/ § 3.6

και- /kai/ §3.7

καππα /kap′-pa/ § 1.4

κατ⸗ αβαλ /kat a-bal′/ turn from; καττ⸗ return (turn self)

καϩ /kaḥ/ earth

κε, κε- /kε/ § 3.7

κεχωογνι /kε-kʰou′-ni/ §3.7

κετ, χετ /kεt, kʰεt/ §3.7

κετε, κητε, χετ /kεt′-ε/, /ket′-e/, /kʰεt′-i/ §3.7

κεϩε /kεḥ′-ε/ earth, country

κη, ϭη, κη- /ke/, /ke̠/ §3.7

κημε /ke′-mε/ Egypt

κογ /ku/ §3.7

κογϊ /ku-i′/ little § 2.7

κοογε /kɔ′-uε/ §3.7

κραϥ /kraf/ guile

χρεμρεμ /kʰrεm′-rεm/ grumble

κρο /krɔ/ far side

κ̄ϲ- /ks/ half § 4.4

κω /ko/ put, throw; with εβολ out = forgive

κωτ /ko′-ti/ go around

κωϩτ /ko′-ḥt/ fire

λ̄ 30 (§ 4.1)

λε- /lε/ § 4.4

λαγδα /lau′-da/ § 1.4

λαγε /la′-uε/ anything, nothing

λεκμ /lεk′-m/ piece

λεν /lεn/ name

λετ⸗ /lεt/ foot

λεϥ- /lεf/ § 2.6

μ̄ 40 (§ 4.1)

μ̄- /m/ § 2.4

μα- /ma/ give, make, § 7.6

μα⸗ /ma/ § 9.3

μα /ma/ place

μααβ, μααβε, μαβ; μαβ- /maːb/, /maː′-bε/, /mab/ thirty, § 4.2

μαειν /ma′-in/ miracle

μαγοϲ /ma′-gɔs/ sage

μαϊνογτε /mai-nu′-tε/ God-loving (§ 2.6, 7.5)

μαλε-, μαλ⸗ /ma-lε/ § 9.4

μαμηε /ma-me′-ε/ truly

μαν̄- /ma-n/ § 2.6

μανε /ma′-nε/ shepherd

μαν̄εϣωτ /ma-n-ε-šot′/ market (place of merchant)

μαογ, μαγ /mau/ water

μαογτ /ma′-ut/ dead (stative)

μαρε-, μαρ⸗ /ma-rε/ § 9.4

ματαμαϊ /ma-ta-mai′/ let me know

ματ /ma′-ti/ brim

μαγ /ma′-u/ mother

μαϣε /ma′-šε/ walk

μαϩ- /maḥ/, § 4.3

μαϩ /maḥ/ fill

μαχε /ma′-d̠ε/ ear

ⲘⲂⲈⲢⲒ /m-bɛr'-i/ recently, § 5.4b

ⲘⲈⳂ /mɛ/ § 9.3

ⲘⲈ /mɛ/ place

ⲘⲈ /mɛ/ true, truth

ⲘⲈⲂ /mɛb/ thirty, § 4.2

ⲘⲈⲈⲨⲈ /mɛ:'-uɛ/ think

ⲘⲈⲒ, ⲘⲈⲚⲢⲈ- /mɛ'-i/, /mɛn-rɛ/ love

ⲘⲈⲒ- /mɛ-i/ § 2.6

ⲘⲈⲖⲈ- /mɛ-lɛ/ § 9.3

ⲘⲈⲚⲈⲚⲤⲀ-, ⲘⲚⲚ̄ⲤⲀ-; ⲘⲈⲚⲈⲤⲰⳂ, ⲘⲚⲚ̄ⲤⲰⳂ /mɛn-ɛn-sa/, /mn-n-sa/, /mɛn-ɛn-so'/, /mn-n-so'/ § 5.2b

ⲘⲈⲢⲈ- /mɛ-rɛ/ § 9.3

ⲘⲈⲦ- /mɛt/ § 2.6

ⲘⲈⲦ- /mɛt/ ten, § 4.2

ⲘⲈⲦⲞⲨⲢⲞ /mɛt-u-rɔ'/ kingdom

ⲘⲈⲦⲞⲨⲢⲞ ⲘⲈⲦⲌⲈⲂⲢⲈⲞⲤ /mɛt-ḥɛ-brɛ'-ɔs/ Hebrew

ⲘⲈϢⲀⲔ /mɛ-šak'/ perhaps, § 5.3

ⲘⲈϢⲈ /me'-šɛ/ go

ⲘⲈⲌ- /mɛḥ/, § 4.3

ⲘⲈⲌ /mɛḥ/ full

ⲘⲈⲌⲈⲔ /mɛ-xɛk'/ perhaps, § 5.3

ⲘⲎⲈ /mɛ'-ɛ/ truth

ⲘⲎⲦ; ⲘⲎⲦⲈ, ⲘⲎⳀ /met/, /me'-tɛ/, /me'-ti/ ten, § 4.2

ⲘⲎⲦⲈ /me'-tɛ/ midst

ⲘⲎϢⲈ, ⲘⲎⲎϢⲈ /me(:)'-šɛ/ crowd, multitude

ⲘⲒ, ⲘⲎ, ⲘⲈ /mi/, /me/, /mɛ/ § 1.4

Ⲙ̄ⲘⲀⳂ, Ⲙ̄ⲘⲞⳂ, Ⲙ̄ⲘⲰⳂ /m-ma'/, /m-mɔ'/, /m-mo'/ § 5.1, 8.3

Ⲙ̄ⲘⲀ /m-ma'/ early form of Ⲙ̄ⲘⲀⲨ

Ⲙ̄ⲘⲀⲨ /m-ma'-u/ there, § 5.3, 5.4b, 8.8

Ⲙ̄ⲘⲀϢⲰ /m-ma-šo'/ greatly, § 5.4b

Ⲙ̄ⲘⲈ /m'-mɛ/ know, realize

Ⲙ̄ⲘⲈ, Ⲙ̄ⲘⲈⲞⲨ /m-me'/, /m-me'-u/ there, § 5.3, 5.4b, 8.8

Ⲙ̄ⲘⲈⲚⲈⲤⲀ /m-mɛn-ɛ-sa'/ early form of ⲘⲈⲚⲈⲚⲤⲀ (§ 5.2b)

Ⲙ̄ⲘⲈⲦⲈ, Ⲙ̄ⲘⲈⳀ /m-mɛt'-ɛ/, /m-mɛt'-i/ only, § 4.6

Ⲙ̄ⲘⲎⲈⲒⲦⲚ̄ /m-me'-i-tn/ here, § 4.5

Ⲙ̄ⲘⲎⲚⲈ, Ⲙ̄ⲘⲎⲚⲒ /m-me'-nɛ/, /m-me'-ni/ daily, § 5.4b

Ⲙ̄ⲘⲒⲚ /m-min'/ proper, § 4.6

Ⲙ̄ⲘⲚ̄- /m-mn/ there is not, § 8.8

Ⲙ̄ⲘⲞⲚⲦⳂ /m-mɔnt'/ § 8.5

Ⲙ̄ⲘⲚ̄ⲦⲈⳂ, Ⲙ̄ⲘⲚ̄Ⲧ /m-mn-tɛ'/m-mnt'/ § 8.5

Ⲙ̄ⲘⲞ /m-mɔ'/ there, § 4.5, 5.3, 5.4b, 8.8

Ⲙ̄Ⲛ̄- /mn/ § 5.1

Ⲙ̄Ⲛ̄- /mn/ there is not, § 8.8

Ⲙ̄Ⲛ̄- /mn/ and

Ⲙ̄ⲚⲚ̄ⲤⲀ- /mn-n-sa/ § 12.6

Ⲙ̄ⲚⲠⲈⲨⲎⲢ /mn-pɛu-er'/ together (literally, with their union)

Ⲙ̄ⲚⲦ- /mnt/ § 2.6

Ⲙ̄ⲚⲦ- /mnt/ ten, § 4.2

Ⲙ̄ⲚⲦⲈⳂ, Ⲙ̄ⲚⲦ /mn-tɛ'/, /mnt/ § 8.8

Ⲙ̄ⲚⲦⲢⲈ /mn-trɛ'/ testify

Ⲙ̄ⲚⲦⲢ̄ⲢⲞ /mnt-r-rɔ'/ kingdom

Ⲙ̄ⲚⲦⲤⲚⲀⲞⲨⲤ /mnt-snaus'/ § 4.2

ⲘⲞ /mɔ/ here, § 4.5

ⲘⲞⲤ /mɔs/ for ⲘⲘⲞⲤ

ⲘⲞⲨ /mu/ die, death

ⲘⲞⲨⲒ /mu'-i/ lion

ⲘⲞⲨⲦⲈ /mu'-tɛ/ say, call

ⲘⲞⲨⲌ /muḥ/ burn

ⲘⲞϢⲒ /mɔ'-ši/ walk

Ⲙ̄ⲠⲈ-, Ⲙ̄Ⲡ /m-pɛ/, /mp/ § 9.2

Ⲙ̄ⲠⲀⲢⲈ-, Ⲙ̄ⲠⲀⳂ /m-pa-rɛ/, /m-pa'/ § 9.3

Ⲙ̄ⲠⲀⲦⲈ-, Ⲙ̄ⲠⲀⲦⳂ /m-pat'-ɛ/, /m-pat'/ § 9.2

Ⲙ̄ⲠⲈⲖ- /m-pɛl/ don't, § 7.8

Ⲙ̄ⲠⲈⲘⲦⲀ, Ⲙ̄ⲠⲈⲘⲦⲞ, Ⲙ̄ⲠⲈⲘⲐⲞ /m-pɛm-ta'/, /m-pɛm-tɔ'/, /m-pɛm-tʰɔ'/ § 5.2c

Ⲙ̄ⲠⲈⲢ-, Ⲙ̄Ⲙ̄Ⲣ- /m-pɛr/, /m-pr/ don't, § 7.8, 9.4

Ⲙ̄ⲠⲎⲨⲈ /m-pe'-uɛ/ heaven (the-skies)

Ⲙ̄ⲠⲰⲢ, Ⲙ̄ⲪⲰⲢ, Ⲙ̄ⲠⲞⲢ /m-por'/, /m-pʰor'/, /m-pɔr'/ don't, § 7.8

Ⲙ̄ⲦⲞⲚ /m-tɔn'/ rest

ⲘⲰⲒⲚⲒ /mo'-i-ni/ here, § 4.5

ⲘⲰⲞⲨⲦ /mo'-ut/ dead (stative)

Ⲙ̄ⲌⲒⲦ /m-ḥit'/ north

N̄ 50 (§ 4.1)

N̄- /n/ § 2.4, 5.1, 6.6, 8.3, 8.7, 10.9, 11.2, 11.5

N⸗ /n/ § 9.4

NA, NAI /na/, /nai/ go

NA- /na/ § 3.3, 3.4

NA-, NE- /na/, /nɛ/ § 8.6, 9.5

NA⸗, NE⸗ /na/, /nɛ/ § 8.5, 9.5

NA⸗, NE⸗, NH⸗, NⲰ⸗ /na/, /nɛ/, /ne/, /no/ § 5.1

NAA-, NAE-; NA(A)A⸗, NAE⸗, NEE⸗ /na:/, /na-ɛ/, /na(:)-a'/, /na-ɛ'/, /nɛ-ɛ'/ great, § 6.5

NAHT /na-et'/ compassionate (NA merciful of (ϩ)HT heart)

NAI /nai/ § 3.3

NAIAT⸗, NAIET⸗, NAIHT⸗, NEIET⸗ /na-iat'/, /na-iet'/, /na-iet'/, /nɛ-iet'/ blessed, § 6.5

NAX⸗ /nad̲/ set

NAME, NAMIE /na-mɛ'/, /na-mi'-ɛ/ truly, § 5.4b

NAM⳦ /nam'-ti/ power

NANE-, NANOY-; NANE⸗, NANOY⸗ /na-nɛ/, /na-nu/, /na-nɛ'/, /na-nu'/ good, § 6.5

NAPE-, NAAE-, NEAE- /na-rɛ/, /na-lɛ/, /nɛ-lɛ/ § 8.5, 9.5

NAY ⲉ- /nau ɛ/ see

NAϢE-; NAϢO⸗, NAϢⲰ⸗ /na-šɛ/, /na-šɔ'/, /na-šo'/ many, § 6.5

NAϨAOϬ⸗, NAϨAⲰϬ⸗ /na-ḥlɔk̲'/, /na-ḥlok̲'/ pleasant, § 6.5

NAϨP̄N-, NAϨPEN-; NAϨPA⸗, NAϨPE⸗, NAϨAE⸗ /naḥ-rn/, /naḥ-ren/, /na-ḥra'/, /na-ḥrɛ'/, /na-ḥlɛ'/ § 5.2c

NAϬ /nak̲/ great

N̄B̄PPE /n-br'-rɛ/ recently, § 5.4b

N̄Ⳓ- /ng/ § 10.4

NE /nɛ/ § 1.4

NE- /nɛ/ § 2.4

NE⸗ /nɛ/ § 3.4

-NE /nɛ/ § 3.3, 6.3

NE- /nɛ/ § 9.4

NE /nɛ/ § 4.5

NE ⲉ́- /nɛ ɛ/ see

NE, NEEI /nɛ-i/ § 3.3

NEM-; NEMA⸗, NEME⸗, N̄MMA⸗ /nɛm/, /nɛ-ma'/, /nɛ-me'/, /nm-ma'/ § 5.1

NECBⲰⲰ /ne-sbo:'/ wise, § 6.5

NECE-; NECO⸗, NECⲰ⸗ /nɛ-sɛ/, /nɛ-sɔ'/, /nɛ-so'/ beautiful, § 6.5

NEY A- /neu ɛ/ see

NEϤP- /nɛf-r/ good, § 6.5

NEϬⲰ⸗, NEϬⲰⲰ⸗ /nɛ-k̲o'/, /nɛ-k̲o:'/ ugly, § 6.5

NH /ne/ § 3.3

NHϤ /nef/ for NEϤ (§ 5.1)

NHOY, NHY /ne-u/ come, coming (stative)

NHX /ned̲/ seated

NI- /ni/ § 2.4

NIBEN /ni'-bɛn/ § 2.7

NIBI /ni'-bi/ for NIM

NIM /nim/ § 2.7, 3.2

N̄K- /ng/ 10.4

N̄KA, ǸXAI, N̄KE, N̄KEEN, N̄KEI /n-ka'/, /n-kʰai'/, /n-kɛ'/, /n-kɛ'-ɛn/, /n-kɛ-i'/ thing, § 2.7

N̄KAICATⲠ, N̄KECATⲠ, N̄KECOTⲠ /n-kai-sap'/, /n-kɛ-sap'/, /n-kɛ-sɔp'/ again, § 5.4b

NKHN AN /n-ken' an/ not only

N̄KOT̄K /n-kot'-k/ sleep

N̄MME /nm-mɛ'/ § 3.4, 5.1

N̄NE-, N̄N⸗ /n-nɛ/ § 9.4

NO A- /nɔ a/ see

NOY⸗ /nu/ § 3.3, 3.4

NOYB /nub/ gold

N̄C- /ns/ 10.4

N̄CA-, N̄CE-, N̄CⲰ⸗ /n-sa/, /n-sɛ/, /n-so'/ § 5.2c

N̄CAOYCA /n-sau-sa'/ apart, § 5.4c

N̄CACANIM, N̄CACENIM /n-sa-sa-nim'/, /n-sa-sɛ-nim'/ everywhere, § 5.4c

N̄CE-, N̄COY- /n-sɛ/, /n-su/ 10.4

N̄T- /nt/ § 10.9

N̄T⸗ /nt/ § 10.4

ǸTA ϨⲰTE /n-ta' ḥo'-tɛ/ § 3.5, 3.7

N̄TA-, N̄TA⸗ /n-ta/ § 11.2

N̄TA⸗, ǸⲐO⸗, N̄TO⸗ /n-ta'/, /n-tʰɔ'/, /n-tɔ'/ § 3.5

N̄TAAE⸗ /n-ta-lɛ/ § 10.5

N̄TAP⸗ /n-tar'/ § 10.3, 10.5

Ⲛ̄ⲦⲀⲢⲈ- /n-tar-ɛ/ § 10.3

ⲚⲦⲀϥ, Ⲛ̄ⲐⲞⲞϥ, Ⲛ̄ⲦⲞϥ /n-taf′/, /n-tʰɔf′/, /n-tɔf′/ but, § 4.6

Ⲛ̄ⲦⲈ- /n-tɛ/ § 5.1, 10.4

Ⲛ̄ⲦⲈⲖⲈ-, Ⲛ̄ⲦⲈⲢⲈ- /n-tɛ-lɛ/, /n-tɛ-rɛ/ § 10.3

Ⲛ̄ⲦⲈⲢ⸗ /n-ter′/ § 10.3

Ⲛ̄ⲦⲚ̄-, Ⲛ̄ⲦⲈⲚ-; Ⲛ̄ⲦⲀⲦ⸗, Ⲛ̄ⲦⲞⲦ⸗, Ⲛ̄ⲦⲞⲞⲦ⸗ /n-tn/, /n-tɛn/, /n-tat/, /n-tɔ′t/, /n-tɔ:t′/ § 5.2c

Ⲛ̀ⲐⲰⲞⲨ /n-tʰo′-u/ § 3.5

Ⲛ̄ⲦⲰⲦⲚⲈ, Ⲛ̀ⲐⲰⲦⲈⲚ, Ⲛ̄ⲦⲀⲦⲈⲚ, Ⲛ̄ⲦⲰⲦⲚ̄ /n-tot′-nɛ/, /n-tʰo′-tɛn/, /n-ta′-tɛn/, /n-to′-tn/ § 3.5

Ⲛ̄ⲦⲀⲈ /n-tʰɛ′/ in the manner

Ⲛ̄ϢⲀⲢⲈ-, Ⲛ̄ϢⲀ⸗ /n-ša′-(rɛ)/ § 11.2

Ⲛ̄ϥ- /nf/ 10.4

Ⲛ̄Ⲁ̄ⲎⲦ⸗, Ⲛ̄Ⲁ̄ⲎⲦ, Ⲛ̄ⲂⲎⲦ⸗ /n-het/, /n-xet′/ § 5.1

Ⲛ̄Ⲁ̄ⲞⲨⲞ /n-huɔ′/ the more

Ⲛ̀ⲬⲈ- /n-d̠ɛ/ namely, § 4.5

Ⲛ̄ⲬⲈ- /n-d̠ɛ/ that, § 4.5

Ⲛ̄ⲬⲒⲚ- /n-d̠in/ § 5.1

Ⲛ̀ϬⲎ, Ⲛ̄ϬⲒ /n-k̠e′/, /n-k̠i′/ namely, § 4.5

Ⲍ̄ 60 (§ 4.1)

Ⲟ̄ 70 (§ 4.1)

Ⲟ /ɔ/ § 3.2

Ⲟ, ⲞⲨ /ɔ/, /u/ § 1.4

ⲞⲚ /ɔn/ again, also, still, § 5.3

ⲞⲨ- /u/ § 2.4

ⲞⲨ /u/ § 3.2

ⲞⲨⲀ, ⲞⲨⲀⲒ /ua/, /uai/ one, a certain person § 4.2

ⲞⲨⲀ ⲞⲨⲀ /ua ua/ one by one

ⲞⲨⲀⲀⲂ, ⲞⲨⲀⲀⲂⲈ, ⲞⲨⲈⲂ, ⲞⲨⲈⲈⲂ /ua:b/, /ua:′-bɛ/, /uɛb/, /uɛ:b′/ holy

ⲞⲨⲀⲈⲈⲦϥ /ua-ɛ:t′-f/ by himself

ⲞⲨⲀⲈⲒⲚ /uain/, /ua′-in/ light

ⲞⲨⲀⲒϢ, ⲞⲨⲀⲒϢ̄ /uaiš/, /ua′-iš/ occasion, time

ⲞⲨⲀⲚⲦⲀ-, ⲞⲨⲞⲚⲦⲈ-, ⲞⲨ̄ⲚⲦⲈ- /uan-ta′/, /uɔn-tɛ′/, /un-te′/ 8.8

ⲞⲨⲀⲚ /uan/ § 2.7, 8.2, 8.8

ⲞⲨⲀⲦ-, ⲞⲨⲈⲦ- /uat, uet/ § 6.5

ⲞⲨⲂⲈ-; ⲞⲨⲂⲎ⸗ /u-bɛ/, /u-be′/ § 5.1

ⲞⲨⲈ-; ⲞⲨⲎ⸗ /uɛ, ue/ § 5.1

ⲞⲨⲈ, ⲞⲨⲈⲈⲒ /uɛ/, /uɛi/ one, § 4.2

ⲞⲨⲈⲈ ... ⲀⲂⲀⲖ Ⲁ̄Ⲛ /uɛ′-ɛ ... a-bal′ hn/ one of

ⲞⲨⲈⲒ̈ⲈⲚⲒⲚ /uɛ-iɛ-nin′/ Greek

ⲞⲨⲈⲢⲎⲦⲈ /uɛ-re′-tɛ/ foot

ⲞⲨⲎⲢϢⲈ /uer′-šɛ/ watch

ⲞⲨⲎⲀ̄ /ueh/ set (Stative)

ⲞⲨⲒ, ⲞⲨⲒⲈ /ui/, /ui′-ɛ/ one, § 4.2

ⲞⲨⲒ̈ⲈⲒⲂⲈ /ui:′-bɛ/ priest

ⲞⲨⲚ̄- /un/ § 3.2, 8.2, 8.8

ⲞⲨⲚⲀϥ /u-naf′/ rejoice, rejoicing

ⲞⲨ̄ⲚⲦ⸗, ⲞⲨ̄ⲚⲦⲈ⸗, ⲞⲨⲞⲚⲦⲀ⸗, ⲞⲨⲞⲚⲦⲎ⸗ /unt/, /un-tɛ′/, /uɔn-ta′/, /uɔn-te′/ § 8.8

ⲞⲨⲞⲒ /uɔi/ rush

ⲞⲨⲞⲚ /ɔɔn/ § 2.7, 8.2, 8.8

ⲞⲨⲞⲚ /uɔn/ open

ⲞⲨⲞⲚⲀ̄ /uɔn′-h/ be revealed

ⲞⲨⲞⲀ̄ /uɔh/ and, § 4.4

ⲞⲨⲞⲀ̄Ⲉ /uɔh′-ɛ/ early form of ⲞⲨⲞⲀ̄ (§ 4.4)

ⲞⲨⲢⲞⲦ /u-rɔt′/ eagerness

ⲞⲨⲦⲈ-; ⲞⲨⲦⲞ⸗ⲞⲨⲦⲰ⸗ /u-tɛ/, /u-tɔ′/, u-to′/ § 5.1

ⲞⲨⲰⲘ /uom/ consume, eat

ⲞⲨⲰⲚⲀ̄, ⲞⲨⲰⲚⲀ̄Ⲁ̄ /uo′-nah, uo′-nh/ reveal

ⲞⲨⲰⲦ /uot/ § 6.5

ⲞⲨⲰϢ /uoš/ wish

ⲞⲨⲰϢ̄Ⲃ /uo′-šb/ answer

ⲞⲨⲰϢ̄Ⲧ /uo′-št/ pay respects, worship

ⲞⲨⲰϨⲘ̄ /uo′-hm/ interpret

ⲞⲨⲬⲀⲒ̈ /u-d̠ai′/ become whole

Ⲟ̄Ⲁ̄ⲈⲢⲀⲦ⸗ /ɔh-ɛ-rat′/ stand

Ⲡ̄ 80 (§ 4.1)

Ⲡ, Ⲫ- /p/, /pʰ/ § 2.4

ⲠⲀ-, ⲪⲀ- /pa/, /pʰa/ § 3.3, 3.4

ⲠⲀⲒ, ⲪⲀⲒ /pai/, /pʰai/ § 3.3

ⲠⲀⲒⲢⲎ† /pai-re′-ti/ then, so, § 4.5

ⲠⲀⲤⲬⲀ /pas′-xa/ Passover

ⲠⲀϢⲈ, ⲪⲀϢⲒ /paš′-ɛ/, /pʰaš′-i/ half, § 4.4

ⲠⲀⲀ̄ⲞⲨ, ⲪⲀⲀ̄ⲞⲨ /pah′-u/, /pʰah′-u/ end, behind, § 5.3

ⲡⲁϫⲉ-, ⲡⲉϫⲉ-; ⲡⲉϫⲁ⸗, ⲡⲉϫⲉ⸗, ⲡⲉϫⲏ⸗ /pa-ḏε/, /pε-ḏε/, /pε-ḏa′/, /pε-ḏε′/, /pε-ḏe′/ say, said, § 9.2

ⲡⲉ /pε/ sky

ⲡⲉ- /pε/ § 2.4

ⲡⲉ⸗ /pε/ § 3.4

-ⲡⲉ /pε/ § 3.3, 6.3, 8.5

ⲡⲉⲓ̈, ⲡⲉⲉⲓ /pε-i/ § 3.3

ⲡⲉⲧⲣⲟⲥ /pεt′-rɔs/ Peter

ⲡⲉϣⲉ, ⲡⲉϣⲓ /peš′-ε/, /peš′-i/ half § 4.4

ⲡⲉϩⲟⲩ /peḥ′-u/ end, behind, § 5.3

ⲡⲏ, ⲫⲏ /pe/, /pʰe/ § 3.3

ⲫⲏⲟⲩⲓ /pʰe′-ui/ skies

ⲫⲓⲗⲓⲡⲡⲟⲥ /pʰi-lip′-pɔs/ Phillip

ⲡⲓ /pi/ § 1.4

ⲡⲓ- /pi/ § 2.4

ⲡⲓⲥⲣⲁⲏⲗ, ⲡ̄ⲓ̄ⲗ̄ /pis-ra-el′/ Israel

ⲡⲓⲥⲧⲁⲓⲟⲩ, ⲡⲓⲥⲧⲉⲟⲩⲓ /pis-tai′-u/, /pis-tε′-ui/ ninety, § 4.2

ⲡⲛⲟⲩϯ, ⲫⲛⲟⲩϯ, ⲡ̄ϯ̄, ⲫ̄ϯ̄ /pnu′-ti/, /pʰnu′-ti/ God

ⲡⲟⲧ /pɔt/ run

ⲡⲟⲩ- /pu/ § 3.4

ⲡⲟⲩⲉⲉ ⲡⲟⲩⲉⲉ /puε′-ε puε′-ε/ each one

ⲫⲓⲥ, ⲫⲓⲧ, ⲫⲓⲧⲉ /psis/, /psit/, /psi′-tε/ nine, § 4.2

ⲡⲱ⸗, ⲫⲱ⸗, ⲡⲟ⸗ /po/, /pʰo/, /pɔ/ § 3.3

ⲡⲱⲧ /pot/ run, go (ⲁⲃⲁⲗ ⲙ̄- away from)

ⲡⲱϣ /poš/ divide

ⲫⲱⳉ /pʰox/ burst open

ⲣ̄ 100 (§ 4.1)

ⲣ̄ 900 (§ 4.1)

ⲣ̄- /r/ § 10.9

ⲣⲁ- /ra/ § 4.4

ⲣⲁⲛ /ran/ name

ⲣⲁϣⲉⲉ̀ /ra-šε′-ε/ east (rising side)

ⲣⲉ- /rε/ § 4.4

ⲣⲉϩⲧ⸗ /reḥt/ strike

ⲣⲉⲛ /rεn/ name

ⲣⲉⲥⲟⲩⲉ̀ /rεs′-u-ε/ dream

ⲣ̄ⲉⲩ /r-εu′/ do what?

ⲣⲉϣⲉ /reš′-ε/ rejoice

ⲣⲉϥ- /rεf/ § 2.6

ⲣⲓⲙⲉ /ri′-mε/ weep

ⲣ̀ⲙⲉⲩⲓ /r-mε′-ui/ think

ⲣ̄ⲙ̄ⲛ̄ϩⲏⲧ /rm-n-ḥet′/ wise man (man of heart)

ⲣ̄ⲙⲣⲉϣ /rm-reš′/ gentle person

ⲣ̄ⲛⲁⲃⲉ/ⲣ̄ⲛⲁⲃⲓ /r-nab′-ε/, r-nab′-i/ sin (§ 2.6)

ⲣ̄ⲛⲁϣⲧⲉ /r-naš′-tε/ do protection

ⲣⲟ, ⲣⲱ, ϩⲣⲱ /rɔ/, /ro/, /ḥro/ § 1.4

ⲣⲟⲙⲉ /rɔ′-mε/ person

ⲣⲟⲙⲡⲓ /rɔm′-pi/ year

ⲣ̄ⲡⲉ /r-pε′/ temple

ⲣ̄ⲡⲙⲉⲉⲩⲉ /r-pme:′-uε/ remember (do the thought)

ⲣ̄ⲣⲁⲓ̈ /r-rai′/ kings

ⲣ̄ⲣⲟ /r-rɔ′/ king

ⲣⲱ⸗ /ro/ mouth

ⲣⲱϣⲉ /ro′-šε/ suffice

ⲣ̄ϩⲁⲩⲉⲓⲛⲉ /r-ḥau-i′-nε/ § 10.9

ⲣ̄ϩⲟⲧⲉ /r-ḥɔt′-ε/ fear, be afraid

ⲥ̄ 200 (§ 4.1)

ⲥ- /s/ § 3.6, 10.4

ⲥⲁⲃⲁⲗ, ⲥⲁⲃⲟⲗ /sa-bal′/, /sa-bɔl′/ away, § 5.4c

ⲥⲁⲃⲉ /sab′-ε/ learned

ⲥⲁⲙⲃⲁⲑⲟⲛ /sam-ba′-tʰɔn/ sabbath

ⲥⲁⲛ /san/ brother

ⲥⲁⲟⲩⲥⲁ /sa-u-sa′/ apart, § 5.4c

ⲥⲁⲡ /sap/ time, sometimes, § 5.3

ⲥⲁⲡⲥⲁ /sa-psa′/ part, 5.4c

ⲥⲁⲡⲥⲛ̄ /sap′-sp/ pray

ⲥⲁⲥⲁⲛⲓⲃⲉⲛ, ⲥⲁⲥⲁⲛⲓⲙ /sa-sa-ni′-bεn/, /sa-sa-nim′/ everywhere, § 5.4c

ⲥⲁⲧⲟⲧϥ /sa-tɔt′-f/ immediately

ⲥⲁⲩ, ⲥⲁ /sau/, /sa/ six, § 4.2

ⲥⲁⲩⲛⲉ /sau′-nε/ know

ⲥⲁϣϥ̄, ⲥⲁϣϥⲉ, -ⲥⲁϣϥⲉ /saš′-f/, /saš′-fε/ seven, § 4.2

ⲥⲁϩ /saḥ/ scribe; see also ⲥϩⲁⲓ̈

ⲥⲁϩ⸗ /saḥ/ write

ⲥⲁϩⲣⲁⲓ /sa-ḥrai′/ up, § 5.4c

ⲥⲁϣϥ̄; ⲥⲁϣϥⲉ, -ⲥⲁϣⲃⲉ /sax'-f/, /sax'-fɛ/, /sax'-bɛ/ seven, § 4.2

ⲥⲃⲱ /sbo/ teaching

ⲥⲉ- /sɛ/ § 3.6, 10.4

ⲥⲉ /sɛ/ sixty, § 4.2

ⲥⲉⲉⲡⲉ /sɛ:'-pɛ/ leave over

ⲥⲉϣϥ̄ /seš'-f/ seven, § 4.2

ⲥⲉⲩⲋ- /sɛuḥ/ collect

ⲥⲉⲋⲟ ... ⲁⲣⲉⲧⲟⲩ /se-ḥɔ' ... a-rɛt'-u/ set up

ⲥⲉⲋⲧ⸗ /sɛḥt/ remove

ⲥⲉⲭⲉ /sɛd'-ɛ/ speak, word

ⲥⲏ /se/ sixty, § 4.2

ⲥⲏⲙⲙⲁ, ⲥⲩⲙⲙⲁ /sem'-ma/, /sym'-ma/ § 1.4

ⲥⲏⲟⲩ /seu/ time

ⲥⲏϭⲓ ⲛ̄ϫⲱ /se'-fi n-ḏo'/ flute (reed for singing)

ⲥⲓ /si/ sate

ⲥⲓⲇⲱⲛ /si-don'/ Sidon

ⲥⲓⲗⲟⲩⲁⲙ /si-lu-am'/ Siloam

ⲥⲓⲙⲱⲛ /si'-mon/ Simon

ⲥⲓⲛⲓ /si'-ni/ pass (ⲋⲁ- by)

ⲥⲓⲟⲩ /si'-u/ star

ⲥⲓϯ /si'-ti/ throw

ⲥⲙⲏ /sme/ voice

ⲥⲛⲁⲩ; -ⲥⲛⲁ(ⲟ)ⲩⲥ, -ⲥⲛⲁⲟⲩⲥⲉ /snau/, /snaus/, /snau'-sɛ/ two, § 4.2

ⲥⲛⲁϥ /snaf/ blood(shed)

ⲥⲛⲉⲩ /sneu/ § 4.2

ⲥⲛⲏϯ /sne'-ti/ two, § 4.2

ⲥⲛⲟ; -ⲥⲛⲟⲟⲩⲥ, -ⲥⲛⲟⲟⲩⲥⲉ /snɔ/, /snɔus/, /snɔu'-sɛ/ two, § 4.2

ⲥⲛⲟⲩϯ /snu'-ti/ two, § 4.2

ⲥ̄ⲛⲧⲉ /sn'-tɛ/ two, § 4.2

ⲥⲟⲕ /sɔk/ glide

ⲥⲟⲗⲡ̄ /sɔl'-p/ cut off

ⲥⲟⲛⲉ /sɔ'-nɛ/ sister

ⲥⲟⲟⲩ, ⲥⲟⲉ /sɔ'-u/, /sɔ'-ɛ/ six, § 4.2

ⲥⲟⲟⲩⲧⲛ̄ /sɔu'-tn/ be straight

ⲥⲟⲡ /sɔp/ time, sometimes, § 5.3

ⲥⲟϣⲉ /sɔš'-ɛ/ field

ⲥⲟⲧⲙ̄ /sɔt'-m/ hear

ⲥⲟⲩ- /su/ § 3.6, 10.4

ⲥⲟⲩⲧⲱⲛ /su-ton'/ straight (stative)

ⲥⲡⲁⲧⲟⲩ /spat'-u/ lips

ⲥⲱϥ /sof/ abomination

ⲥⲱⲕ /sok/ flow

ⲥⲱⲟⲩⲛ̄ /so'-un/ know

ⲥⲱⲟⲩⲋ̄ /so'-uḥ/ gather

ⲥⲱⲧⲙ̄, ⲥⲱⲧⲙⲉ /so'-tm/, /so'-tmɛ/ listen, hear

ⲥϋⲁⲓ, ⲥϋⲉⲓ /shai/, /sxɛi/ write

ⲥϋⲏⲟⲩⲧ /she'-ut/ written (stative)

ⲥϋⲓⲙⲉ /shi'-mɛ/ wife

ⲥϋⲃⲉ /sx-bɛ'/ seventy, § 4.2

ⲧ̄ 300 (§ 4.1)

ⲧ, ⲑ- /t/, /tʰ/ § 2.4

ⲧⲁ- /ta/ § 7.3, 10.4

ⲧⲁ-, ⲑⲁ- /ta/, /tʰa/ § 3.3, 3.4

ⲧⲁⲁ⸗ /ta:'/ give

ⲧⲁⲉⲓⲟⲩ, ⲧⲁⲓⲟⲩ /tai'-u/ fifty, § 4.2

ⲧⲁⲕⲁ, ⲧⲁⲕⲟ /ta-ka'/, /ta-kɔ'/ destroy

ⲧⲁⲓ, ⲑⲁⲓ /tai/, /tʰai/ § 3.3

ⲧⲁⲓ /tai/ here, § 5.3

ⲧⲁⲓⲟ /ta-iɔ'/ honor

ⲧⲁⲗⲉ- /ta-lɛ/ § 10.5

ⲧⲁⲙⲟ, ⲧⲁⲙⲉ- /ta-mɔ'/, /ta-mɛ/ inform

ⲧⲁⲛⲋⲟ /tan-ḥɔ'/ make live

ⲧⲁⲣ⸗ /tar/ § 10.3, 10.5

ⲧⲁⲣⲉ- /ta-rɛ/ § 10.3, 10.5

ⲧⲁⲣⲉⲡ⸗ /ta'-rɛp/ seize

-ⲧⲁⲥⲉ /tas'-ɛ/ six, § 4.2

ⲧⲁⲩ /tau/ § 1.4

ⲧⲁⲩ, ⲧⲟⲟⲩ /tau/, /tɔu/ buy, § 7.2

ⲧⲁⲩ /tau/ hill, mountain

ⲧⲁⲩⲧⲉ /tau'-tɛ/ gather

ⲧⲁϣⲟ /ta-šɔ'/ multiply

-ⲧⲁϥⲧⲉ /taf'-tɛ/ four, § 4.2

ⲧⲁⲋⲟ ⲉⲣⲁⲧ⸗ /ta-ḥɔ' ɛ-rat'/ present (make stand to foot)

ⲧⲃⲁ, ⲧⲃⲉ, ⲑⲃⲟ /tba/, /tbɛ/, /tʰbɔ/ ten thousand, § 4.2

ⲧ̄ⲃⲧ /tbt/ fish

ⲧⲉ- /tɛ/ § 2.4, 7.3, 10.4

ⲧⲉ⸗ /tɛ/ § 3.4

ⲧⲉ-, ⲧⲉⲗ- /tɛ/, /tɛl/ § 3.6

-ⲧⲉ /tɛ/ § 3.3, 6.3

ⲧⲉⲓⲟⲩ, ⲧⲉⲓ̈ⲟⲩⲉ, ⲧⲉⲟⲩⲉ /tɛ'-iu/, /tɛi'-uɛ/, /tɛ'-uɛ/ fifty, § 4.2

ⲧⲉⲛⲟⲩ /tɛ-nu'/ now, § 5.3

-ⲧⲉⲥⲉ /tɛs'-ɛ/ six, § 4.2

ⲧⲉⲧⲛ̅-, ⲧⲉⲧⲉⲛ- /tɛ-tn/, /tɛ-tɛn/ § 3.6, 10.4

-ⲧⲉ ϥ ⲧⲉ /tɛf'-tɛ/ four, § 4.2

ⲧⲉ ϩ ⲛⲉ /tɛh'-nɛ/ forehead

ⲧⲉⲩ ϣ ⲏ /tɛ-u-šɛ'/ night

ⲧⲏ, ⲑⲏ /te/, /tʰe/ § 3.3

ⲧⲏ /te/ five, § 4.2

ⲧⲏⲣ⸗ /ter/ § 3.7

ϯ- /ti/ § 2.4, 3.6

ϯ, -ϯ /ti/ five, § 4.2

ϯ ⲁⲃⲁⲗ /ti a-bal'/ sell

ϯ ϩ ⲏⲧ /ti ḥet/ pay heed (give heart)

ⲧⲓⲃⲉⲣⲓⲁⲥ /ti-bɛ-ri-as'/ Tiberias

ϯⲙⲉ, ϯⲙⲓ /ti'-mɛ/, /ti'-mi/ village

ϯⲛⲟⲩ /ti-nu'/ now, § 5.3

ϯⲟⲩ, ϯⲉ /ti'-u/, /ti'-ɛ/ five, § 4.2

ϯⲟⲩⲇⲁⲓⲁ /ti-u-da'-ia/ Judea

ⲧⲕ̅- /tk/ § 7.3

ⲧⲙ̅ /tm/ § 7.8

ⲧⲛ̅- /tn/ § 7.3

ⲧⲛ̅-, ⲧⲉⲛ- /tn/, /tɛn/ § 3.6, 10.4

ⲧⲛ̅ⲛⲁⲩ, ⲧⲉⲛⲛⲁⲩ, ⲧⲛ̅ⲛⲟⲟⲩ /tn-nau'/, /tɛn-nau'/, /tn-nɔu'/ send, § 7.2k

ⲧⲟ, ⲧⲟⲛ /tɔ/, /tɔn/ where, § 5.3

ⲧⲟⲩ- /tu/ § 3.4, 7.3

ⲧⲟⲩⲛ⸗ /tun/ raise

ⲧⲟⲩⲛⲉⲉⲓⲉ̇ⲧ⸗ /tu-nɛ-i-ɛt'/ warn (raise eye)

ⲧⲟⲩⲛⲟⲩⲥ, ⲧⲟⲩⲛⲟⲥ, ⲧⲧⲟⲩⲛⲉⲥ /tu-nus'/, /tu-nɔs'/, /ttu'-nɛs/ wake, § 7.2k

ⲧⲣ⸗, ⲑⲣ⸗ /tr/, /tʰr/ § 7.3

ⲧⲥ̅- /ts/ § 7.3

ⲧⲱ⸗, ⲑⲱ⸗, ⲧⲟ⸗ /to/, /tʰo/, /tɔ/ § 3.3

ⲧⲱⲛ, ⲑⲱⲛ /ton/, /tʰon/ where, § 5.3

ⲧⲱⲛ /ton/ raise (oneself)

ⲧⲱⲛⲉ /to'-nɛ/ rise

ⲧⲱⲟⲩⲛ̅ /tou'-n/ arise

ⲧⲱⲱⲃⲉ /to:'-bɛ/ put a seal, with ⲉⲣ- to the mouth = seal up

ⲧⲱⲱⲛ /to:n/ rise

ⲑⲱ ϩ /tʰoḥ/ become stirred

ⲧ ϥ̅- /tf/ § 7.3

ⲅ̅ 400 (§ 4.1)

ⲫ̅ 500 (§ 4.1)

ⲫⲓ /fi/ § 1.4

ⲭ̅ 600 (§ 4.1)

ⲭⲓ /kʰi/ § 1.4

ⲯ̅ 700 (§ 4.1)

ⲯⲓ /psi/ § 1.4

ⲱ̅ 800 (§ 4.1)

ⲱ /o/ § 1.4

ⲱ /o/ oh, § 7.7

ⲱⲗⲓ /o'-li/ take hold of

ⲱⲡ /op/ reckon

ⲱ ϣ /oš/ utter

ϣ- /š/ § 9.7

ϣⲁ-, ϣⲁⲁ- /ša(:)/ § 5.1

ϣⲁ⸗ /ša/ § 9.3

ϣⲁ /ša/ one thousand, § 4.2

ϣⲁⲃⲁⲗ, ϣⲁⲃⲟⲗ /ša-bal'/, /ša-bɔl'/ outward, § 5.4d

ϣⲁⲉ ϩ ⲟⲩⲛ ⲉⲧⲛⲟⲩ /ša-ɛ-ḥun' ɛ-ti-nu'/ until now

ϣⲁⲉ ϩ ⲣⲏⲓ /ša-ɛ-ḥrei'/ upward, § 5.4d

ϣⲁⲓ, ϣⲉⲓ /šai/, /šɛi/ § 1.4

ϣⲁⲓ̈, ϣⲁⲉⲓⲉ /šai/, /ša'-iɛ/ feast, festival

ϣⲁⲗ⸗ /šal/ destroy

ϣⲁⲗⲁ⸗ /ša-la'/ § 5.1

ϣⲁⲗⲉ- /ša-lɛ/ § 9.3

ϣⲁⲙⲧ̅, ϣⲁⲙⲛ̅ⲧ, ϣⲁⲙⲧⲉ /šam'-t/, /šam'-nt/, /šam'-tɛ/ three, § 4.2

ϣⲁⲛⲧⲉ-, ϣⲁⲛⲧ⸗ /šan-tɛ/, /šant/ § 10.3

ϣⲁⲣⲁ⸗, ϣⲁⲣⲟ⸗ /ša-ra'/, /ša-rɔ'/ § 5.1

ϣⲁⲣⲉ-, ϣⲁⲣ⸗ /ša-rɛ/, /šar/ § 9.3

ϢⲀⲢⲠ̄, ϢⲀⲢⲠⲈ, ϢⲀⲢⲠⲒ /šar'-p/, /šar'-pɛ/, /šar'-pi/ first, § 4.3

ϢⲀⲦⲈ-, ϢⲀⲦ⸗ /ša-tɛ/, /šat/ § 10.3

ϢⲀϢ̄ϥ, ϢⲀϢϥⲒ /šaš'-f/, /šaš'-fi/ seven, § 4.2

ϢⲀϨⲞⲨⲚ, ϢⲀϨⲞⲨⲚ, ϢⲀⲃⲞⲨⲚ /ša-ḥun'/, /ša-xun'/ inward, § 5.4d

ϢⲀϨⲢⲀⲒ, ϢⲀϨⲢⲎⲈⲒ /ša-ḥrai'/, /ša-ḥrei'/ upward, § 5.4d

ϢⲀϪⲈ /šad̲'-ɛ/ word

ϢⲂⲎ /šbe/ seventy, § 4.2

ϢⲈ /še/ fitting

ϢⲈ /še/ one hundred, § 4.2

ϢⲈ ⲚⲀ⸗, ϢⲈ ⲚⲈ⸗ /še na/, /še nɛ/ go away

ϢⲈⲈⲒ /šɛi/ festival

ϢⲈⲖ /šɛl/ myrrh

ϢⲈϨ /šɛḥ/ fire

ϢⲈϪⲒ /šɛd̲'-i/ speech

ϢⲎ /še/ one hundred, § 4.2

ϢⲎⲘ /šem/ little, § 2.7

ϢⲎⲚϢ /še'-nš/ give life

ϢⲎⲢⲈ, ϢⲎⲢⲒ /še'-rɛ/, /še'-ri/ male child

ϢⲎⲦ /šet/ two hundred, § 4.2

ϢⲒⲚⲈ, ϢⲒⲚⲒ /ši'-nɛ/, /ši'-ni/ ask, search

ϢⲒⲠⲈ /ši'-pɛ/ shame

ϢⲖⲞϥ /šlɔf/ disgrace

ϢⲘⲎⲚ, ϢⲘⲎⲚⲒ; -ϢⲘⲎⲚⲈ /šmen/, /šmen'-i/, /šmen'-ɛ/ eight, § 4.2

ϢⲘ̄Ⲧ-, ϢⲘ̄ⲚⲦ- /šmt/, /šm'-nt/ three, § 4.2

ϢⲘⲞⲨⲚ, ϢⲘⲞⲨⲚⲈ /šmun/, /šmu'-nɛ/ eight, § 4.2

ϢⲚⲈ /šnɛ/ net

ϢⲚ̄ⲦⲤⲚ̄ⲦⲈ /šnt-sn'-tɛ/ two hundred, § 4.2

ϢⲚ̄Ϩ̄ⲦⲎ⸗ /šn-ḥte'/ feel compassion, be merciful (suffer heart, with ϨⲀ- for)

ϢⲞ /šɔ/ one thousand, § 4.2

ϢⲞⲘ̄Ⲧ, ϢⲞⲘ̄ⲚⲦ; ϢⲞⲘⲦⲈ, ϢⲞⲘϮ; -ϢⲞⲘⲦⲈ /šɔm'-t/, /šɔm'-nt/, /šom'-tɛ/, /šɔm'-ti/, /šom'-tɛ/ three, § 4.2

ϢⲞⲠⲈ /šɔ'-pɛ/ exist

ϢⲞⲢⲠ̄, ϢⲞⲢⲠⲈ, ϢⲞⲢⲠⲒ /šɔr'-p/, /šɔr'-pɛ/, /šɔr'-pi/ first, § 4.3

ϢⲞⲨⲒ̈Ⲧ/ϢⲞⲨⲒⲦ /šu-it'/ empty

ϢⲞⲨϢⲞⲨ /šu-ou'/ withered

ϢⲞϪⲚⲈ /šɔd̲'-nɛ/ counsel

ϢⲠ̄- /šp/ hold, receive

ϢⲠ̄ϨⲘⲀⲦ /šp-ḥmat'/ give thanks (take grace)

ϢⲦⲀⲢⲦⲈⲢ, ϢⲦⲀⲢⲦⲢ̄ /štar'-tɛr/, /štar'-tr/ be troubled, be disturbed

ϢⲦⲘ̄-, ϢⲦⲈⲘ- /štm/, /štɛm/ § 7.8

ϢⲨ /šy/ one hundred, § 4.2

ϢⲰⲚⲈ, ϢⲰⲚⲒ /šo'-nɛ/, /šo'-ni/ suffer, ill

ϢⲰⲠⲈ/ϢⲰⲠⲒ /šo'-pɛ/, /šo'-pi/ become

ϢϥⲈ /šfɛ/ seventy, § 4.2

ϢϪⲈⲘϪⲞⲘ /šd̲ɛm-d̲ɔm'/ be able, § 9.7

ϢϬⲘϬⲀⲘ, ϢϬⲘϬⲞⲘ /šk̲m-kam'/, /šk̲m-kɔm'/ be able, § 9.7

q̄ 90 (§ 4.1)

ϥ- /f/ § 3.6

ϥⲀⲒ, ϥⲈⲒ /fai/, /fɛi/ § 1.4

ϥⲒ /fi/ lift, carry

ϥⲦⲀⲨ, ϥⲦⲰⲞⲨ, ϥⲦⲞⲨ, ϥⲦⲞⲈ, ϥⲦⲞⲨ-, ϥⲦⲈⲨ- /ftau/, /ftou/, /ftu/, /ftɔ'-ɛ/, /ftu/, /ftɛu/ four, § 4.2

ϥⲦⲞⲨϪⲞⲨⲰⲦ /ftu-d̲uot'/ eighty, § 4.2

Ϩⲁ- /ḥa/ § 5.1

Ϩⲁ-, Ϩⲁ⸗ /ḥa/ § 9.2

Ϩⲁ /ḥa/ face

ϨⲀⲂⲀⲖ /ḥa-bal'/ out

ϨⲀⲈⲒⲈ ⲀⲂⲀⲖ /ḥa'-iɛ a-bal'/ be wasted (fall out)

ϨⲀⲖⲀ⸗ /ḥa-la'/ § 5.1

ϨⲀⲚ- /ḥan/ § 2.4

ϨⲀⲠⲤ /ḥap'-s/ it is necessary

ϨⲀⲢⲈϨ /ḥa-rɛḥ'/ guard

ϨⲀⲢⲀ⸗, ϨⲀⲢⲞ⸗ /ḥa-ra'/, /ḥa-rɔ'/ § 5.1

ϨⲀⲢⲀⲦ⸗, ϨⲀⲢⲈⲦ⸗, ϨⲀⲖⲀⲦ⸗ /ḥa-rat'/, /ḥa-rɛt'/, /ḥa-lat'/ § 5.2f

ϨⲀⲢⲎⲨ /ḥa-re'-u/ perhaps, § 5.3

ϨⲀⲢⲚ̄-, ϨⲀⲢⲰ⸗ /ḥa-rn/, /ḥa-rɔ'/ § 5.2f

ϨⲀⲦ /ḥad/ silver

ϨⲀⲦⲈ⸗Ϩ̄ /ḥa-tɛ⸗ḥe'/ § 5.2f

ϨΑⲦⲚ̄-; ϨΑⲦΑⲦ⸗, ϨΑⲦΟΟⲦ⸗ /ḥa-tn/, /ḥa-tat'/,
/ḥa-tɔ:t'/ § 5.2f

ϨΑΘⲎ-, ϨΑΘⲎ⸗ /ḥa-the'/ § 5.2d

ϨΑⲨ /ḥau/ day

ϨΑϨ /ḥah/ many

ϨΑϨⲦⲚ̄-; ϨΑϨⲦⲎ⸗, ϨΑⲦⲎ⸗ /ḥah-tn/, /ḥa-(ḥ)te'/
§ 5.2f

ϨΑⲬⲚ̄-, ϨΑⲬⲈⲚ-; ϨΑⲬΟ⸗, ϨΑⲬⲰ⸗ /ḥa-ḏn/, /ḥa-
ḏen/, /ḥa-ḏɔ'/, /ḥa-ḏo'/ § 5.2f

ϨⲂⲎⲨⲈ /ḥbe'-ue/ works (plural of ϨⲰⲂ)

ϨⲂⲰ /ḥbo/ snake

ϨⲈ /ḥε/ § 1.4

ϨⲈ /ḥε/ way, manner

ϨⲈ /ḥε/ fall; with Ⲉ- come upon

ϨⲈⲒⲈ, ϨⲈⲒⲠⲈ /ḥεi'-ε/, /ḥεi'-pε/ behold § 4.5

ϨⲈⲚ- /ḥεn/ § 2.4

ϨⲎ /ḥe/ front

ϨⲎ /ḥe/ manner

ϨⲎⲂⲤ̄ /ḥe'-bs/ lamp

ϨⲎⲎⲠⲈ, ϨⲎⲠⲈ, ϨⲎⲎⲦⲈ /ḥe(:)'-pε/, /ḥe:'-tε/ behold, § 4.5

ϨⲎⲚ /ḥεn/ near (stative of ϨⲰⲚ approach)

ϨⲎⲢⲰⲆⲎⲤ /ḥe-ro'-des/ Herod

ϨⲎⲦ /ḥet/ heart

ϨⲎⲦ⸗ /ḥet/ belly (with obligatory pronominal
suffix)

ϨⲒ-; ϨⲒⲰⲰ⸗, ϨⲒⲰⲦ⸗ /ḥi/, /ḥi-o:'/, /ḥi-ot'/ § 5.1

ϨⲒ, ϨⲈⲒ /ḥi/ behold § 4.5

ϨⲒ, ϨⲒ⸗ /ḥi/ throw, put

ϨⲒⲂⲀⲖ, ϨⲒⲂΟⲖ /ḥi-bal/, /ḥi-bɔl'/ outside, § 5.4e

ϨⲒⲉⲢΟⲤΟⲖⲨⲘⲀ /ḥi-ε-rɔ-sɔ'-ly-ma/ Jerusalem

ϨⲒⲚⲀⲒ, ϨⲒⲚⲈⲈⲒ, ϨⲒⲚⲈⲒ̈ /ḥi-nai'/, /ḥi-nεi'/ thus,
§ 5.4e

ϨⲒⲎ /ḥi-e'/ way

ϨⲒΟΟⲨⲈ /ḥi-ɔ'-uε/ paths (plural of ϨⲒⲎ)

ϨⲒΟⲨⲈ /ḥi'-uε/ throw

ϨⲒΟⲨⲤⲀⲠ, ϨⲒΟⲨⲤΟⲠ /ḥi-u-sap'/, /ḥi-u-sɔp'/ sim-
ultaneously, together (at a time), § 5.4e

ϨⲒⲠⲀϨΟⲨ, ϨⲒⲫⲀϨΟⲨ /ḥi-paḥ'-u/, /ḥi-pʰaḥ'-u/ behind, § 5.4e

ϨⲒⲠⲈⲤⲎⲦ /ḥi-pε-set'/ below, § 5.4e

ϨⲒⲢⲀⲦ⸗, ϨⲒⲢⲈⲦ⸗ /ḥi-rat'/, /ḥi-rεt'/ § 5.2e

ϨⲒⲦ⸗ /ḥit/ set, throw

ϨⲒⲦⲚ̄-, ϨⲒⲦⲈⲚ-; ϨⲒⲦΑⲦ⸗, ϨⲒⲦΟⲦ⸗, ϨⲒⲦΟΟⲦ⸗ /ḥi-
tn/, /ḥi-tεn/, /ḥi-tat'/, /ḥi-tɔ(:)t'/ § 5.2e

ϨⲒⲦΟⲨⲚ̄-; ϨⲒⲦΟⲨΟ⸗, ϨⲒⲦΟⲨⲰ⸗, ϨⲒΘΟⲨⲰ⸗ /ḥi-tu-
n/, /ḥi-tuɔ'/, /ḥi-tuo/, /ḥi-tʰuo'/ § 5.2e

ϨⲒϨΟⲨⲚ, ϨⲒϨΟⲨⲚ, ϨⲒϧΟⲨⲚ /ḥi-ḥun'/, /ḥi-xun'/ inside, § 5.4e

ϨⲒϨⲢⲀⲒ, ϨⲒϨⲢⲈⲒ, ϨⲒϨⲢⲒ /ḥi-ḥrai'/, /ḥi-ḥrεi'/ upward, § 5.4e

ϨⲒⲬⲚ̄-, ϨⲒⲬⲈⲚ-; ϨⲒⲬΟ⸗, ϨⲒⲬⲰ⸗ /ḥi-ḏn/, /ḥi-ḏen/,
/ḥi-ḏɔ'/, /ḥi-ḏo'/ § 5.2e

ϨⲖⲀⲨ /ḥlau/ voice

ϨⲖⲎⲒ, ϨⲖⲎⲈⲒ /ḥlei/ up, down § 5.3

ϨⲘⲈ /ḥmε/ forty, § 4.2

ϨⲘⲈⲚⲈ /ḥmεn'-ε/ eighty, § 4.2

ϨⲘⲈⲤⲦ /ḥmεst/ sit

ϨⲘⲎ /ḥme/ forty, § 4.2

ϨⲘΟΟⲤ /ḥmɔ:s/ seated (stative)

ϨⲘΟⲦ /ḥmɔt/ gift

ϨⲘ̄Π- /ḥmp/ § 12.6

ϨⲘ̄ΠⲀΟⲨ, ϨⲘ̄ΠΟΟⲨ /ḥm-pau'/, /ḥm-pɔu'/ today,
§ 5.4f

ϨⲘ̄ϨⲘⲈ /ḥm'-ḥmε/ roar

ϨⲚ̄-, ϨⲈⲚ- /ḥn/, /ḥεn/ § 5.1

ϨⲚⲈ-; ϨⲚΑ⸗, ϨⲚⲈ⸗, ϨⲚⲈ /ḥnε/, /ḥna/, ḥnε/
willing, § 6.5

ϨⲚ̄Ⲛ̄ⲤⲀ /ḥn-n-sa'/ afterwards

ϨⲚ̄ΟⲨⲘⲈ, ϨⲚ̄ΟⲨⲘⲈⲈ, ϨⲚ̄ΟⲨⲘⲈⲒ̈, ϨⲚ̄ΟⲨⲘⲎⲈ /ḥn-
u-mε(:)'/, /ḥn-u-mei'/, /ḥn-u-me'-ε/ truly,
§ 5.4f

ϨⲚ̄ΟⲨϨΟⲠ /ḥn-u-ḥɔp'/ in secret

ϨⲚ̄ΟⲨϬⲈⲠⲎ /ḥn-u-ḵε-pe'/ quickly, § 5.4f

ϨⲚⲰϨⲈ /ḥno'-ḥε/ fear

ϨΟⲂ /ḥɔb/ thing, § 2.7

ϨΟΟⲨⲈ /ḥou'-ε/ days

ϨΟⲠ⸗ /ḥɔp/ hide

ϨΟⲢⲒ /ḥɔr'-i/ § 1.4

ϨΟⲦϨⲦ̄ /ḥɔt'-ḥt/ inquire

ϨΟⲨⲚ /ḥun/ interior, inside, § 5.3

ϨΟⲨΟ /ḥuɔ/ one great

ⲍⲟⲩϥ, ⲍⲟⲩⲟⲩϥ /ḥuf/, /ḥu:f/ also, § 4.6

ⲍⲣⲁⲓ /ḥrai/ up, down § 5.3

ⲍⲣⲁⲩ /ḥrau/ voice

ⲍⲣⲏⲓ, ⲍⲣⲏⲉⲓ /ḥrei/ up, down § 5.3

ⲍⲣⲟⲩⲃⲃⲁⲓ /ḥrub-bai'/ thunder

ⲍⲧⲏ⸗ /ḥte/ heart

ⲍⲱⲱ⸗, ⲍⲱ⸗, ⲍⲟⲩⲟⲩ⸗ /ḥo(:)/, /ḥu:/ § 3.7

ⲍⲱⲃ /ḥob/ thing, § 2.7

ⲍⲱⲃ /ḥob/ work

ⲍⲱⲟⲩ ⲉ- /ḥou ɛ/ worse than

ⲍⲱϥ, ⲍⲱⲱϥ /ḥof/, /ḥo:f/ also, § 4.6

ⲍ- /x/ § 9.7

ⲍⲁ-, ϧⲁ- /xa/ § 5.1

ⲍⲁⲓ, , ϧⲁⲓ /xai/ § 1.4

ⲍⲁⲓⲍ /xaix/ dust

ⲍⲁⲙⲧ̄, ⲍⲁⲙⲧⲉ /xam'-t/, /xam'-tɛ/ three, § 4.2

ⲍⲁⲣⲁ⸗, ϧⲁⲣⲟ⸗ /xa-ra'/, /xa-rɔ'/ § 5.1

ⲍⲁⲣⲁⲧ⸗, ϧⲁⲣⲁⲧ⸗ /xa-rad'/ § 5.2f

ⲍⲁⲣⲉ-, ⲍⲁⲣ⸗ /xa-rɛ/ § 9.3

ϧⲁⲣⲉⲛ-, ϧⲁⲣⲱ⸗ /xa-rn/, /ḥa-ro'/ § 5.2f

ⲍⲁⲣⲡ̄ /xar'-p/ first, § 4.3

ⲍⲁⲧⲉ⸗ⲍⲏ, ϧⲁⲧⲉ-ⲍⲏ /xa-tɛ⸗ḥe'/ § 5.2f

ϧⲁⲧⲉⲛ-, ϧⲁⲧⲟⲧ⸗ /xa-tɛn/, /xa-tɔt'/ § 5.2f

ⲍⲁⲍⲧⲉ-, ⲍⲁⲍⲧⲏ⸗ /xa-ḥtɛ/, /xa-ḥte'/ § 5.2f

ⲍⲁⲭⲛ̄-, ϧⲁⲭⲉⲛ-, ⲍⲁⲭⲱ⸗, ϧⲁⲭⲱ⸗ /xa-dn/, /xa-dɛn/, /ḥa-do'/ § 5.2f

ϧⲉⲙⲫⲟⲟⲩ /xɛm-pʰɔu'/ today, § 5.4f

ϧⲉⲛⲟⲩⲙⲏⲓ /xɛn-u-me'-i/ truly, § 5.4f

ⲍⲏⲧ⸗ /ḥet/ § 5.1

ⲍⲓ /ḥi/ tally

ϧⲙⲉⲛⲉ /xmɛn'-ɛ/ eighty, § 4.2

ⲍⲙⲧ, ⲍⲙⲧⲉ- /xmt/, /xm-tɛ/ three, § 4.2

ϧⲙ̄ⲧⲟⲩⲱⲧ /xmt-duot'/ sixty, § 4.2

ⲍⲛ̄-, ϧⲉⲛ- /xn/, /xɛn/ § 5.1

ⲍⲛⲟⲩⲙⲓⲉ /xn-u-mi'-ɛ/ truly, § 5.4f

ⲍⲟ /xɔ/ one thousand, § 4.2

ⲍⲟⲟⲡ /xɔ:p/ exist (stative of ⲍⲱⲡⲉ)

ϧⲟⲧϧⲉⲧ /xɔt'-xɛt/ learn by examination

ⲍⲟⲩⲛ, ϧⲟⲩⲛ /xun/ interior, inside, § 5.3

ⲍⲣⲏⲓ /xrei/ down, § 5.3

ⲍ̄ⲣⲡ- /xrp/ first, § 4.3

ⲍⲧⲁⲣⲧⲣⲉ /xtar'-trɛ/ trouble

ⲍⲱⲡϣ̄ /xo'-pš/ arm

ⲍⲱⲡⲉ /xo'-pɛ/ happen (ⲁ- for)

ⲍⲱⲧⲃⲉ/ϧⲱⲧⲉⲃ /xot'-bɛ/, /xo'-tɛb/ kill

ⲍⲟ̄ⲙϭⲁⲙ /xkm-kam'/ be able, § 9.7

ϫⲁⲁ⸗ /ḏa:/ say

ϫⲁⲁⲣ /ḏa:r/ strong

ϫⲁⲉⲓⲥ, ⲭ̄ⲥ̄ /ḏais/ lord

ϫⲁⲛϫⲓⲁ, ϫⲉⲛϫⲉ /ḏan'-ḏi-a/, /ḏɛn'-ḏɛ/ § 1.4

ϫⲁⲩ, ϫⲉⲩ, ϫⲟⲟⲩ /ḏau/, /ḏɛu/, /ḏɔu/ send, § 7.2

ϫⲁⲭⲣⲓⲙ /ḏad-rim'/ cliff

-ϫⲉ /ḏɛ/ so, again, § 4.6

ϫⲉ- /ḏɛ/ § 5.1

ϫⲉ- /ḏɛ/ or, that, § 4.5, 12.3, 12.5, 12.7

ϫⲉ-, ϫⲉ⸗ /ḏɛ/ say

ϫⲉⲕⲁⲥ, ϫⲉⲕⲁⲁⲥ, ϫⲉⲭⲁⲥ, ϫⲉⲕⲁⲥⲉ, ϫⲉⲕⲉⲥ, ϫⲉⲕⲉⲉⲥ /ḏɛ-ka(:)s'/, /ḏɛ-kʰas'/, /ḏɛ-kɛ(:)s'/ so that, § 4.5, 12.3

ϫⲉⲙⲙⲟϥ /ḏɛm-mɔf'/ for ϫⲉⲙϥ find him

ϫⲉⲛⲉⲡⲟⲣ /ḏɛ-nɛ-pɔr'/ roof

ϫⲉⲥ- /ḏɛs/ half § 4.4

ϫⲓ- /ḏi/ § 5.1

ϫⲓ /ḏi/ receive, take, accept

ϫⲓⲏⲡⲉ /ḏi-e'-pɛ/ count

ϫⲓⲙ̄ⲡⲕⲃⲁ /ḏi-m-pkba'/ take vengeance

ϫⲓⲛ- /ḏin/ § 2.6, 5.1

ϫⲓⲛⲕⲓⲙ /ḏin-kim'/ § 1.4

ϫⲓⲥⲉ /ḏi'-sɛ/ high

ϫⲓⲧ⸗ /ḏit/ take

ϫⲓϣⲁⲭⲛⲓ /ḏi-šaḏ'-ni/ advisor (ϫⲓ take plus ϣⲁⲭⲛⲓ counsel)

ϫⲓⲭⲣⲟⲡ /ḏi-drɔp'/ stumble (ϫⲓ- take ⲭⲣⲟⲡ obstacle)

ϫⲗⲟϫ /ḏlɔḏ/ bed

ϫⲛ̄- /ḏn/ § 12.6

ϫⲛ̄ /ḏn/ or, § 4.5

ϫⲛⲉ⸗ /ḏnɛ/ send

ϫⲛⲟⲩ /ḏnu/ question, § 7.2k

ϫⲟⲉⲓⲥ, ⲭ̄ⲥ̄ /ḏɔis/ lord

ⲭⲟⲥ /d̲ɔs/ half § 4.4

ⲭⲟⲟ⸗ /d̲ɔ:/ say

ⲭⲟⲅ-, ⲭⲟⲅⲧ- /d̲u/, /d̲ut/ twenty, § 4.2

ⲭⲟⲅⲱⲧ, ⲭⲟⲅⲟⲧ, ⲭⲟⲅⲱⲧⲉ /d̲uot/, /d̲ɔut/, /d̲uo'-
tɛ/ twenty, § 4.2

ⲭⲡⲟ, ⲭⲡⲁ⸗ /d̲pɔ'/ create, give birth to

ⲭⲱ /d̲o/ say

ⲭⲱⲕ /d̲ok/ complete, be fulfilled

ⲭⲱⲕⲉⲙ /d̲o'-kɛm/ wash

ⲭⲱⲛ̄ⲧ /d̲o'-nt/ wrath

ⲭⲱⲱⲙⲉ /d̲o:'-mɛ/ scroll

ⲭⲭⲉⲣⲁ /d̲dɛ-ra'/ light (a fire)

ⲭⲭⲣⲁ /d̲dra'/ diligent

ϭⲁⲗⲉⲅ /k̲a-leu'/ cripples

ϭⲁⲥ- /k̲as/ half, § 4.4

ϭⲃⲁⲓ /k̲bai/ arm

-ϭⲉ /k̲ɛ/ so, again § 4.6

ϭⲉⲡⲏ /k̲e-pe'/ hasten, quickly, 5.3

ϭⲉⲥ- /k̲es/ half, § 4.4

-ϭⲏ /k̲e/ so, again § 4.6

ϭⲏⲛ- /k̲en/ § 5.1

ϭⲓⲙⲁ /k̲i'-ma/ § 1.4

ϭⲓⲛⲉ /k̲i'-nɛ/ find

ϭⲓⲛ- /k̲in/ § 2.6

ϭⲓⲥ- /k̲is/ half, § 4.4

ϭⲓⲥⲧⲃⲁ, ϭⲓⲥⲧⲃⲉ /k̲is-tba'/, /k̲is tbɛ'/ five hundred, § 4.2

ϭⲗⲟⲭ /t̲lɔd̲/ bed

ϭⲛⲟⲅ /t̲nu'/ question, § 7.2k

ϭⲛ̄ⲧ⸗ /k̲nt/ find

ϭⲛ̄ϭⲁⲙ /k̲n-k̲am'/ prevail (cf. § 9.7)

ⲟ̄ⲥ (for ϭⲱⲓⲥ) /t̲ois/ lord

ϭⲟⲥ- /k̲ʲɔs/ half, § 4.4

ϭⲱ /k̲o/ stay

ϭⲱⲗ̄ⲡ /k̲o'-lp/ be revealed

ϭⲱⲛⲧ /t̲o'-nd/ wrath

ϭⲱⲡⲉ /k̲o'-pɛ/ seize

ϭⲱⲡⲧ /k̲o'-pt/ be defeated

GREEK

ἀγαθός ⲁⲅⲁⲑⲟⲥ good (person)

ἄγγελος ⲁⲅⲅⲉⲗⲟⲥ/ messenger, § 12.6

ἀγορά ⲁⲅⲟⲣⲁ market

ἀδικία ⲁⲇⲓⲕⲓⲁ injustice

αἴσθησις ⲁⲓⲥⲑⲏⲥⲓⲥ perception

αἰτεῖν ⲁⲓⲧⲓ ask, § 10.5

ἀλέκτωρ ⲁⲗⲉⲕⲧⲱⲣ rooster, § 12.6

ἀλλά ⲁⲗⲗⲁ but, § 4.5

ἀπαρνήσασθαι ⲁⲡⲁⲣⲛⲓ deny, § 12.6

ἄρα ⲁⲣⲁ then, so, § 4.5

ἀρνήσασθαι ⲉⲗⲁⲣⲛⲓⲥⲑⲉ deny

ἁρπάζειν ϩⲁⲣⲡⲁⲍⲉ abduction

ἀρχιερεύς ⲁⲣⲭⲓⲉⲣⲉⲅⲥ high priest

ἀρχή ⲁⲣⲭⲏ first

βαπτίζειν ⲃⲁⲡⲧⲓⲍⲉ baptize, § 12.8

βοήθεια ⲃⲟⲏⲑⲓⲁ help

γάρ ⲅⲁⲣ for, § 4.6

γραμματεύς ⲅⲣⲁⲙⲙⲁⲧⲉⲅⲥ record-keeper

γραφή ⲅⲣⲁⲫⲏ writing, scripture

δὲ -ⲇⲉ and, but, so, § 1.10, 4.6

δίκαιος ⲇⲓⲕⲁⲓⲟⲥ righteous, § 1.10

δικαιοσύνη ⲇⲓⲕⲁⲓⲟⲥⲅⲛⲏ righteousness

διώκειν ⲭⲟⲭⲓ pursue

δοκεῖν ⲇⲟϭⲓ think, § 12.7

δῶρον ⲇⲱⲣⲟⲛ gift

ἔθνος ⲉⲑⲛⲟⲥ, ϩⲉⲑⲛⲟⲥ nation, native

εἴδωλον ⲉⲓⲇⲱⲗⲟⲛ idol

εἰμὴ τί ⲉⲓⲙⲏⲧⲓ- § 5.1

εἰρήνη (ⲉ)ⲓⲣⲏⲛⲓ, (ⲉ)ⲓⲣⲏⲛⲏ peace

ἐλάχιστος ⲉⲗⲁⲭⲓⲥⲧⲟⲥ least

ἐντολή ⲉⲛⲧⲟⲗⲏ advice, commandment

ἐπειδή ⲉⲡⲉⲓⲇⲏ after, since § 12.6/8

ἐπιθυμέιν ⲉⲡⲓⲑⲩⲙⲉⲓ long

ἐπροφήτευσεν ⲉⲣⲡⲣⲟⲫⲏⲧⲉⲅⲓⲛ, ⲣ̄ⲡⲣⲟⲫⲏⲧⲉⲅⲉ,
ⲡⲣⲟⲫⲏⲧⲉⲅⲉ prophesy, § 7.3l

ἐφ' ὅσον ⲉⲡϩⲟⲥⲟⲛ, ⲉⲫⲟⲥⲟⲛ while, § 12.6

ἕως ϩⲉⲱⲥ as long as

ἤ ⲏ and, or; § 1.4, 4.5

ἡγεμών ϩⲏⲅⲉⲙⲁⲛ ruler

ἡγούμενος ϩⲏⲅⲟⲩⲙⲉⲛⲟⲥ leader

θάλασσα ⲑⲁⲗⲁⲥⲥⲁ the sea

θεραπεύειν ⲑⲉⲣⲁⲡⲉⲅⲓⲛ heal, § 10.4

Ἰησοῦς ⲓⲏⲥⲟⲩⲥ, ⲓ̅ⲥ̅ Jesus

ἵνα ϩⲓⲛⲁ so that, § 4.5

ἴσος ϩⲓⲥⲟⲥ equal

κάδος ⲋⲁⲧⲟⲩⲥ jar

καί τοι ⲕⲁⲓⲧⲟⲓ although, § 12.8

καλῶς ⲕⲁⲗⲱⲥ well, § 5.3

κἄν ⲕⲁⲛ, § 12.9

κατά ⲕⲁⲧⲁ- § 5.1

κατοιγορεῖν ⲕⲁⲧⲟⲓⲅⲟⲣⲉⲓ accuse

καταπατεῖν ⲕⲁⲧⲁⲡⲁⲧⲓ trample, § 12.3

κελεύειν ⲡ̅ⲕⲉⲗⲉⲅⲉ command, § 7.2l–3

κῆτος ⲕⲏⲧⲟⲥwhale

κοινή § 1.4

κολυμβήθρα ⲕⲟⲗⲩⲙⲃⲏⲑⲣⲁ, ⲕⲟⲗⲩⲃⲏⲑⲣⲁ bathing pool

κόσμος ⲕⲟⲥⲙⲟⲥ world

κρίνειν ⲕⲣⲓⲛⲉ judge, § 11.5, 12.3

λαός ⲗⲁⲟⲥ people

λίβανος ⲗⲓⲃⲁⲛⲟⲥ incense

λυχνία ⲗⲩⲭⲛⲓⲁ lampstand

μαθητής ⲙⲁⲑⲏⲧⲏⲥ disciple

μαργαρίτης ⲙⲁⲣⲅⲁⲣⲓⲧⲏⲥ pearl, § 12.3

μέν ... δέ ⲙⲉⲛ ... ⲇⲉ on the one hand ... on the other, § 6.3 n. 1

μετανοεῖν ⲙⲉⲧⲁⲛⲟⲓ repent, § 12.10

μή ⲙⲏ is it not the case that?, § 4.5

μήποτε ⲙⲏⲡⲟⲧⲉ lest, § 12.3

μήπως ⲙⲏⲡⲱⲥ lest, § 12.3

μήτι ⲙⲏⲧⲓ hasn't, § 11.4

μητρόπολις ⲙⲏⲧⲣⲟⲡⲟⲗⲓⲥ city

μόδιος ⲙⲟⲇⲓⲟⲛ bushel (about 2 gallons)

οἰκονόμος ⲟⲓⲕⲟⲛⲟⲙⲟⲥ steward, § 10.7

ὁμολογεῖν ⲉⲝⲟⲙⲟⲗⲟⲅⲓⲛ confess

νοεῖν ⲛⲟⲓ̈ understand

νόμος ⲛⲟⲙⲟⲥ law

ὀργή ⲟⲣⲅⲏ intensity

ὅσον ϩⲟⲥ, ϩⲟⲥⲟⲛ while, § 12.6

ὅταν ϩⲟⲧⲁⲛ when, § 12.6

ὅτε ϩⲟⲧⲉ when, while, § 12.6

οὐδέ ⲟⲩⲇⲉ nor

οὖν ⲟⲩⲛ therefore, § 12.6–7

παρά ⲙ̅ⲡⲁⲣⲁ-, ⲡⲁⲣⲁ- § 5.1

παράγειν ⲡⲁⲣⲁⲅⲉ pass by, § 12.7

πειράζειν ⲡ̅ⲡⲓⲣⲁⲍⲉ test, § 12.2

πιστεύειν ⲡ̅ⲡⲓⲥⲧⲉⲅⲉ believe, § 1.10

πλάνειν ⲡⲗⲁⲛⲏ go astray

πλάνος ⲡⲗⲁⲛⲟⲥ deceiver, § 12.6

πληγή ⲡⲗⲁⲅⲏ blow

πνεῦμα ⲡⲛⲉⲅⲙⲁ, ⲡ̅ⲛ̅ⲁ̅ breath, spirit

πόλεμος ⲡⲟⲗⲉⲙⲟⲥ war

πονηρός ⲡⲟⲛⲏⲣⲟⲥ evil, § 1.10

πρεσβύτερος ⲡⲣⲉⲥⲃⲩⲧⲉⲣⲟⲥ elder

προβατική ⲡⲣⲟⲃⲁⲧⲓⲕⲏ sheep-gate

προφήτης ⲡⲣⲟⲫⲏⲧⲏⲥ prophet

πύλη ⲡⲩⲗⲏ gate

σαγήνη ⲥⲁⲅⲏⲛⲏ dragnet, § 10.7

σάρξ ⲥⲁⲣⲝ flesh

σοφία ⲥⲟⲫⲓⲁ wisdom

σκύλλειν ⲥⲕⲩⲗⲗⲉ be troubled

στάδιον ⲥⲧⲁⲇⲓⲟⲛ stade (202¼ yards, 185m)

στατήρ ⲥⲁⲑⲉⲣⲓ, ⲥⲧⲁⲧⲉⲉⲣⲉ stater (a coin)

στοά ⲥⲧⲟⲁ colonnade

τόπος ⲧⲟⲡⲟⲥ place

τόλμα ⲧⲟⲗⲙⲁⲛ courage, § 9.7

τότε ⲧⲟⲧⲉ then, § 4.5

χαρακτήρ ⳉⲁⲣⲁⲕⲧⲏⲣ mark, sign, § 1.10

χόρτος **ⲭⲟⲣⲧⲟⲥ** pasture
χρῆμα **ⲭⲣⲏⲙⲁ** property
χρόνος **ⲭⲣⲟⲛⲟⲥ** time
χώρα **ⲭⲱⲣⲁ** place, country
χωρίς **ⲭⲱⲣⲓⲥ-** § 5.1

ψυχή **ⲯⲩⲭⲏ** life, spirit; § 2.3

ὡς **ϩⲱⲥ** as long as, § 5.1, 12.6
ὥστε **ϩⲱⲥⲧⲉ** § 12.4

Bibliography

Chassinat, Émile. 1902. "Fragments de manuscrits coptes en dialecte fayoumique." *Bulletin de l'Institut Français d'Archéologie Orientale* 2:171–206.

Crum, Walter Ewing. 1939. *A Coptic Dictionary*. Oxford.

Funk, Wolf-Peter. 1988. "Dialects Wanting Homes: A Numerical Approach to the Early Varieties of Coptic." Pages 139–92 in *Historical Dialectology, Regional and Social*. Edited by Jacob Fisiak. Trends in Linguistics: Studies and Monographs 37. Berlin.

Girgis, W. A. 1963–64. "Greek Loan Words in Coptic." *Bulletin de la Société d'Archéologie Copte* 17:63–73

———. 1965–66. "Greek Loan Words in Coptic." *Bulletin de la Société d'Archéologie Copt* 18:71–96

———. 1967–68. "Greek Loan Words in Coptic." *Bulletin de la Société d'Archéologie Copt* 19:57–87

———. 1969–70. "Greek Loan Words in Coptic." *Bulletin de la Société d'Archéologie Copt* 20:53–67

Grossman, Eitan, and Tonio Sebastian Richter. 2017. "Dialect Variation and Language Change: The Case of Greek Loan-Verb Integration Strategies in Coptic." Pages 207–36 in *Greek Influence on Egyptian-Coptic: Contact-Induced Change in an Ancient African Language*. Edited by E. Grossman et al. Hamburg.

Kasser, Rodolphe. 1964. *Compléments au Dictionnaire Copte de Crum*. Publications de l'Institut Français d'Archéologie Orientale; Bibliothèque d'études coptes 7. Cairo.

———. 1966. "Compléments morphologiques au dictionnaire de Crum." *Bulletin de l'Institut Français d'Archéologie Orientale* 64:19–66.

Lambdin, Thomas O. 1983. *Introduction to Sahidic Coptic*. Macon.

Layton, Bentley. 2007. *Coptic in 20 Lessons: Introduction to Sahidic Coptic, with Exercises and Vocabularies*. Leuven.

———. 2011. *A Coptic Grammar with Chrestomathy and Glossary: Sahidic Dialect*. 3rd, rev. ed. Porta linguarum orientalium, Neue Serie 20. Wiesbaden.

Mallon, Alexis. 1956. *Grammaire copte*, 4th ed. Beirut.

Müller, Matthias. 2015. "Relative Clauses in Later Egyptian." *Lingua Aegyptia* 23:107–73.

Plisch, Uwe-Karsten. 1999. *Einführung in die koptische Sprache: Sahidischer Dialekt*. Sprachen und Kulturen des christlichen Orients 5. Wiesbaden.

Polotsky, Hans Jakob. 1944. *Études de syntaxe copte*. Cairo.

Reintges, Chris H. 2004. *Coptic Egyptian (Sahidic Dialect): A Learner's Grammar*. Afrikawissenschaftliche Lehrbücher 15. Cologne.

Schenke, Hans-Martin. 1981. *Das Matthäus-Evangelium im mittelägyptischen Dialekt des Koptischen (Codex Scheide)*. Texte und Untersuchungen zur Geschichte der altchristlichen Literatur 127. Berlin.

Sharp, Daniel B. 2016. *Papyrus Bodmer III*. Berlin.

Shisha-Halevy, Ariel. 2007. *Topics in Coptic Syntax: Structural Studies in the Bohairic Dialect*. Orientalia Lovaniensia Analecta 160. Leuven.

Steindorff, Georg. 1899. *Die Apokalypse des Elias*. Leipzig.

———. 1951. *Lehrbuch der koptischen Grammatik*. Chicago.

Thompson, Herbert. 1924. *The Gospel of St. John According to the Earliest Coptic Manuscript*. British School of Archaeology in Egypt and Egyptian Reseach Account 29; London.

Till, Walter C. 1927. "Die Stellung des Achmimischen." *Aegyptus* 8:249–57.

———. 1928. "Achmisiches." *Zeitschrift für ägyptische Sprache und Altertumskunde* 63:144–49.

———. 1931. *Koptische Dialektgrammatik, mit Lesestücken und Wörterbuch*. Munich.

Westendorf, Wolfhart. 2008. *Koptisches Handwörterbuch*. 2nd ed. Heidelberg.

Worrell, William H. 1931. *The Proverbs of Solomon in Sahidic Coptic According to the Chicago Manuscript*. Chicago.

Yelenskaya, A. E. 1969. *Коптские Рукописи Государственной Публичной Библиотеки имени М.Е. Салтыкова-Шедрина*. Палестинский Сборник 20. Leningrad.

Abbreviations and References

1Clem.	biblical First Epistle of Clement
1Cor.	biblical First Epistle to the Corinthians
1Thess.	biblical First Epistle to the Thessalonians
2Cor.	biblical Second Epistle to the Corinthians
2Pet.	biblical Second Epistle of Peter
A	Akhmimic
Acts	biblical Book of Acts of the Apostles
AE	Steindorff, *Die Apokalypse des Elias* (see the Bibliography)
B	Bohairic
Col.	biblical Epistle to the Colossians
Crum	see the Bibliography
Eph.	biblical Epistle to the Ephesians
F	Fayumic
G	Dialect G
Gal.	biblical Epistle to the Galatians
Gen.	biblical Book of Genesis
Hebr.	biblical Epistle to the Hebrews
Is.	biblical Book of Isaiah
James	biblical Epistle of James
Job	biblical Book of Job
John	biblical Gospel of John
Jonah	biblical Book of Jonah
L	Lycopolitan
Luke	biblical Gospel of Luke
M	Oxyrhynchite
Mal.	biblical Book of Malachi
Mark	biblical Gospel of Mark
Matt.	biblical Gospel of Matthew
Num.	biblical Book of Numbers
OC	Old Coptic
P	Dialect P
Phil.	biblical Epistle to the Philippians
Prov.	biblical Book of Proverbs
Ps.	biblical Book of Psalms
PS	Worrell, *Proverbs of Solomon* (see the Bibliography)
Rev.	biblical Book of Revelations (Apocalypse)
Rom.	biblical Epistle to the Romans
S	Saidic

Texts Cited

1Clem. 16:3 — Ex. 11.6		2 Pet. 2:10 — 5.3	
1Cor. 1:11 — 8.2		Acts 1:13 — 10.2	
1Cor. 4:20 — 11.3		Acts 3:1 — Ex. 8.4	
1Cor. 6:6 — 8.3		Acts 3:10 — Ex. 6.6	
1Cor. 8:4 — 5.4c		Acts 5:38 — Ex. 12.4	
1Cor. 8:5 — 10.9		Acts 8:27 — 9.5	
1Cor. 11:3 — 6.4		Acts 8:35 — 10.2	
1Cor. 11:7 — 6.3		Acts 9:38 — 8.2	
1Cor. 14:23 — 11.4		Acts 10:28 — Ex. 6.4	
1Thess. 2:8 — 6.5		Acts 13:17 — 5.3	
1Thess. 5:6 — 9.4		Acts 16:1 — Ex. 6.3/5	
2Cor. 7:7 — 7.3		Acts 16:20 — Ex. 6.9	

Luke 23:34 — 7.7

Luke 24:19 — 3.2

Luke 24:23 — 12.7

Luke 24:39 — 8.8

Mal. 1:6 — 12.9

Mark 1:5 — 5.4c

Mark 1:7 — 4.5

Mark 1:10 — Ex. 10.2

Mark 1:16 — Ex. 12.7

Mark 2:4 — 3.1

Mark 3:7 — Ex. 2.4

Mark 3:34 — 5.4f

Mark 4:15 — 10.9

Mark 4:37 — 12.4

Mark 5:39 — 11.4

Mark 6:23 — 4.4

Mark 6:30 – 5.3

Mark 6:38 — Ex. 4.3

Mark 7:2 — 8.3

Mark 7:31 — Ex. 5.9

Mark 8:19 — 4.5

Mark 9:25 — 10.4

Mark 9:33 — 11.3

Mark 9:50 — 6.5

Mark 10:2 — 4.5

Mark 11:3 — 3.3

Matt. 12:6 — Ex. 8.10

Mark 12:7 — Ex. 9.10

Mark 12:34 — 9.7

Mark 12:28 — 4.3

Mark 12:31 — 4.3

Mark 14:3 — 5.4c

Mark 14:13 — 10.7

Mark 14:30 — 10.2

Mark 14:36 — 6.5

Mark 15:21 — 5.3

Mark 15:24 — 5.4a

Mark 15:36 — 8.6

Mark 15:44 — 12.5

Mark 16:4 — 12.7

Mark 16:6 — 8.7

Mark 16:9 — 12.5

Matt. 1:11 — 5.3

Matt. 1:12 — 5.4b

Matt. 1:16 — 3.3, 10.9

Matt. 1:18 — 9.2, Ex. 5.1

Matt. 1:20 — 12.5, Ex. 7.1

Matt. 1:21 — Ex. 8.3

Matt. 1:22 — 10.8, 12.2–3

Matt. 2:1 — 5.3

Matt. 2:1–15 — Chrestomathy M

Matt. 2:4 — 9.6

Matt. 2:5 — 5.4e, 9.2

Matt. 2:6 — 10.8

Matt. 2:8 — 10.4, Ex. 7.2; 12.9

Matt. 2:9 — 10.8

Matt. 2:11 — Ex. 5.2

Matt. 2:12 — 7.8, 9.4, 12.5

Matt. 2:15 — Ex. 10.4

Matt. 2:16 — 4.2, 5.3, 10.8, Ex. 2.3, Ex. 10.9

Matt. 2:18 — 6.6

Matt. 2:22 — 7.6

Matt. 3:1 — 4.5, Ex. 5.10

Matt. 3:2 — Ex. 2.1

Matt. 3:3 — 4.5

Matt. 3:7 — Ex. 10.7

Matt. 3:9 — 8.8

Matt. 3:11 — Ex. 9.7

Matt. 4:3 — 12.9, Ex. 2.2

Matt. 4:4 — 4.6, 11.5

Matt. 4:6 — 5.4a, 8.6, 12.3, Ex. 12.2

Matt. 4:8 — 5.4a

Matt. 4:9 — 3.3

Matt. 4:16 — 5.3

Matt. 4:18 — 4.2, 5.4f, 8.5

Matt. 4:19 — Ex. 7.10

Matt. 5:1 — 10.3

Matt. 5:15 — 2.7, 5.3, 10.4, Ex. 11.5

Matt. 5:16 — 4.5

Matt. 5:17 — Ex. 7.3–4

Matt. 5:18 — 8.3, 10.3

Matt. 5:19 — 4.2

Matt. 5:24 — 5.4c

Matt. 5:25 — 12.5

Matt. 5:26 — 10.3

Matt. 5:28 — 9.2

Matt. 5:29 — 3.7

Matt. 5:30 — Ex. 7.5

Matt. 5:34 — 5.3, 7.8

Matt. 5:35 — 6.3

Matt. 5:36 — 4.2

Matt. 5:38 — 5.3

Matt. 5:41 — 5.3

Matt. 5:43 — 5.4e

Matt. 5:45 — 5.3

Matt. 5:47 — 4.6, 10.8

Matt. 6:1 — 5.4c, Ex. 8.1

Matt. 6:3 — 7.6, 10.10

Matt. 6:9–13 — Ex. 1

Matt. 6:19 — Ex. 5.4

Matt. 6:21 — 5.3

Matt. 6:23 — 3.1, Ex. 5.5

Matt. 6:24— 3.7

Matt. 6:28 — 11.3

Matt. 7:1 — 12.3

Matt. 7:6 — 12.3

Matt. 7:15 — 6.3

Matt. 7:16 — 9.4

Matt. 7:25 — 8.5

Matt. 8:1 — 5.3

Matt. 8:7 — 3.5, 6.2

Matt. 8:9 — 5.4f, 6.2

Matt. 8:22 — 9.4

Matt. 8:24 — 12.4

Matt. 8:25 — Ex. 7.8

Matt. 8:28 — 5.3

Matt. 8:29 — Ex. 11.10

Matt. 8:32 — Ex. 5.3

Matt. 8:33 — 2.7

Matt. 8:34 — 8.5

Matt. 9:5 — 4.5

Matt. 9:15 — 12.5

Matt. 9:20 — Ex. 4.5

Matt. 9:24 — 2.7

Matt. 9:36 — 5.4f, Ex. 12.12

Matt. 9:37 — 6.3

Matt. 10:2 — 6.3

Matt. 10:10 — 4.2

Matt. 10:11— 3.2

Matt. 10:19 — 3.2

Matt. 10:35 — 5.3

Matt. 10:36 — 3.3

Matt. 11:3 — 6.2, 10.5

Matt. 11:8 — 10.2/7

Matt. 11:14 — 6.4

Matt. 11:15 — 8.8

Matt. 11:17 — 9.2

Matt. 11:21 — 12.10

Matt. 11:27 — 8.8

Matt. 11:29 — Ex. 2.6, Ex. 6.2

Matt. 12:2 — 8.3

Matt. 12:6 — 5.3

Matt. 12:7 — Ex. 2.8

Matt. 12:10 — 10.7

Matt. 12:13 — 3.7

Matt. 12:19 — 9.4

Matt. 12:22 — 10.4

Matt. 12:40 — Ex. 4.2

Matt. 12:48 — 3.2, 6.4

Matt. 12:50 — 6.4

Matt. 13:5 — 3.7

Matt. 13:6 — 12.5

Matt. 13:12 — 5.4c

Matt. 13:14 — 10.8

Matt. 13:24 — 10.7

Matt. 13:30 — 5.3, 8.6

Matt. 13:38 — Ex. 6.7

Matt. 13:44 — 2.7

Matt. 13:45 — 2.7

Matt. 13:47 — 10.7

Matt. 13:53 — 10.3

Matt. 13:54 — 11.3

Matt. 14:5 — 12.5

Matt. 14:25 — Ex. 4.8

Rev. 8:11 — 4.4

Rev. 10:4 — Ex. 10.5

Rev. 16:18 — 12.5

Rev. 17:1 — 10.8

Rev. 22:18 — 5.4a

Rom. 3:3 — 11.3

Rom. 8:23 — Ex. 2.10

Rom. 10:15 — 4.5

INDEX

This index lists subjects discussed. References are to section numbers rather than pages; Ch. and Ex. are abbreviations for Chapter and Exercise.